W9-CEB-135

BY YUVAL NOAH HARARI

Sapiens: A Brief History of Humankind

Homo Deus: A Brief History of Tomorrow

21 Lessons

for the

21st Century

21 Lessons

for the

21ˢᵗ Century

·····················

Yuval Noah Harari

SIGNAL
McCLELLAND
& STEWART

Copyright © 2018 by Yuval Noah Harari

Hardcover edition published 2018

Signal and colophon are registered trademarks of
Penguin Random House Canada Limited.

All rights reserved. The use of any part of this publication reproduced,
transmitted in any form or by any means, electronic, mechanical, photocopying,
recording, or otherwise, or stored in a retrieval system, without the prior written
consent of the publisher—or, in case of photocopying or other reprographic
copying, a licence from the Canadian Copyright Licensing Agency—is an
infringement of the copyright law.

Published simultaneously in the United States of America by Spiegel & Grau,
an imprint of Random House, a division of Penguin Random House LLC,
New York and in Great Britain by Jonathan Cape, an imprint of Vintage
Publishing, a division of the Penguin Random House group,
a Penguin Random House Company

Library and Archives Canada Cataloguing in Publication

Harari, Yuval N., author
21 lessons for the 21st century / Yuval Noah Harari.

Issued in print and electronic formats.
ISBN 978-0-7710-4885-2 (hardcover).—ISBN 978-0-7710-4886-9 (EPUB)

1. Civilization, Modern—21st century. 2. World politics. I. Title.
II. Title: Twenty-one lessons for the twenty first century.

CB428.H35 2018   909.82   C2018-902491-7
                                        C2018-902492-5

Text design by Caroline Cunningham
Printed and bound in the United States of America

Published by Signal,
an imprint of McClelland & Stewart,
a division of Penguin Random House Canada Limited,
a Penguin Random House Company
www.penguinrandomhouse.ca

2   3   4   5   22   21   20   19   18

Penguin
Random House
Canada

To my husband, Itzik, to my mother, Pnina,

and to my grandmother Fanny,

for their love and support throughout many years

CONTENTS

....

PART III: DESPAIR AND HOPE

PART IV: TRUTH

PART V: RESILIENCE

INTRODUCTION

. . . .

In a world deluged by irrelevant information, clarity is power. In theory, anybody can join the debate about the future of humanity, but it is so hard to maintain a clear vision. We might not even notice that a debate is going on, or what the key questions are. Most of us can't afford the luxury of investigating, because we have more pressing things to do: we have to go to work, take care of the kids, or look after elderly parents. Unfortunately, history does not give discounts. If the future of humanity is decided in your absence, because you are too busy feeding and clothing your kids, you and they will not be exempt from the consequences. This is unfair; but who said history was fair?

As a historian, I cannot give people food or clothes—but I can try to offer some clarity, thereby helping to level the global playing field. If this empowers even a handful of additional people to join the debate about the future of our species, I have done my job.

My first book, *Sapiens,* surveyed the human past, examining how an insignificant ape became the ruler of planet Earth.

Homo Deus, my second book, explored the long-term future of life, contemplating how humans might eventually become gods, and what the ultimate destiny of intelligence and consciousness might be.

In this book I want to zoom in on the here and now. My focus is on current affairs and on the immediate future of human societies. What is happening right now? What are today's greatest challenges and most important choices? What should we pay attention to? What should we teach our kids?

Of course, seven billion people have seven billion agendas, and as already noted, thinking about the big picture is a relatively rare luxury. A single mother struggling to raise two children in a Mumbai slum is focused on where she will find their next meal; refugees in a boat in the middle of the Mediterranean scan the horizon for any sign of land; a dying man in an overcrowded London hospital gathers all his remaining strength to take in one more breath. They all have far more urgent problems than global warming or the crisis of liberal democracy. No book can do justice to all of that, and I don't have lessons to teach people in such situations. I can only hope to learn from them.

My agenda here is global. I look at the major forces that shape societies all over the world and that are likely to influence the future of our planet as a whole. Climate change may be far beyond the concerns of people in the midst of a life-and-death emergency, but it might eventually make the Mumbai slums uninhabitable, send enormous new waves of refugees across the Mediterranean, and lead to a worldwide crisis in healthcare.

Reality is composed of many threads, and this book tries to cover different aspects of our global predicament without claiming to be exhaustive. Unlike *Sapiens* and *Homo Deus,* this book is intended not as a historical narrative but rather as a selection of lessons. These lessons do not conclude with simple answers. They aim to stimulate further thinking and help readers participate in some of the major conversations of our time.

The book was written in conversation with the public. Many of the chapters were composed in response to questions I was asked by readers, journalists, and colleagues. Earlier versions of some sections have already been published in different form, which gave me the opportunity to receive feedback and hone my arguments. Some sections focus on technology, some on politics, some on religion, and some on art. There are chapters that celebrate human wisdom, and others that highlight the crucial role of human stupidity. But the overarching question remains the same: what is happening in the world today, and what is the deep meaning of these events?

What does the rise of Donald Trump signify? What can we do about the epidemic of fake news? Why is liberal democracy in crisis? Is God back? Is a new world war coming? Which civilization dominates the world—the West, China, Islam? Should Europe keep its doors open to immigrants? Can nationalism solve the problems of inequality and climate change? What should we do about terrorism?

Though this book takes a global perspective, I do not neglect the personal level. On the contrary, I want to emphasize the connections between the great revolutions of our era and the internal lives of individuals. For example, terrorism is both a global political problem and an internal psychological mechanism. Terrorism works by pressing the fear button deep in our minds and hijacking the private imaginations of millions of individuals. Similarly, the crisis of liberal democracy is played out not just in parliaments and polling stations but also in neurons and synapses. It is a cliché to note that the personal is the political, but in an era when scientists, corporations, and governments are learning to hack the human brain, this truism is more sinister than ever. Accordingly, this book offers observations about the conduct of individuals as well as entire societies.

A global world puts unprecedented pressure on our personal conduct and morality. Each of us is ensnared within numerous all-encompassing spiderwebs, which on the one hand restrict our movements but on the other transmit our tiniest jiggle to faraway destinations. Our daily routines influence the lives of people and animals halfway across the world, and some personal gestures can unexpectedly set the entire world ablaze, as happened with the self-immolation of Mohamed Bouazizi in Tunisia, which ignited the Arab Spring, and with the women who shared their stories of sexual harassment and sparked the #MeToo movement.

This global dimension of our personal lives means that it is more important than ever to uncover our religious and political biases, our racial and gender privileges, and our unwitting complicity in institutional oppression. But is that a realistic enterprise? How can I find a firm ethical ground in a world that extends far beyond my horizons, that spins completely out of human control, and that holds all gods and ideologies suspect?

This book begins by surveying our current political and technological predicament. At the close of the twentieth century it appeared that the great ideological battles between fascism, communism, and liberalism had resulted in the overwhelming victory of liberalism. Democratic politics, human rights, and free-market capitalism seemed destined to conquer the entire world. But as usual, history took an unexpected turn, and after fascism and communism collapsed, now liberalism is in trouble. So where are we heading?

This question is particularly poignant because liberalism is losing credibility exactly when the twin revolutions in information technology and biotechnology confront us with the biggest challenges our species has ever encountered. The merger of infotech and biotech might soon push billions of humans out of the job market and undermine both liberty and equality. Big Data algorithms might create digital dictatorships in which all power is concentrated in the hands of a tiny elite while most people suffer not from exploitation but from something far worse—irrelevance.

I discussed the merger of infotech and biotech at length in my previous book *Homo Deus*. But whereas that book focused on the long-term prospects—taking the perspective of centuries and even millennia—this book concentrates on the more immediate social, economic, and political crises. My interest here is less in the eventual creation of inorganic life and more in the threat to the welfare state and to particular institutions such as the European Union.

The book does not attempt to cover all the impacts of the new technologies. In particular, though technology holds many wonderful promises, my intention here is to highlight mainly its threats and dangers. Since the corporations and entrepreneurs who lead the technological revolution naturally tend to sing the praises of their creations, it falls to sociologists, philosophers, and historians such as myself to sound the alarm and explain all the ways things can go terribly wrong.

After sketching out the challenges we face, in the second part of the book we examine a wide range of potential responses. Could Facebook engineers use AI to create a global community that will safeguard human liberty and equality? Perhaps the answer is to reverse the process of globalization and reempower the nation-state? Maybe we need to go back even further and draw hope and wisdom from the wellsprings of ancient religious traditions?

In the third part of the book we see that though the technological challenges are unprecedented and the political disagreements intense, humankind can rise to the occasion if we keep our fears under control and be a bit more humble about our views. This part investigates what can be done about the menace of terrorism, about the danger of global war, and about the biases and hatreds that spark such conflicts.

The fourth part engages with the notion of post-truth and asks to what extent we can still understand global developments and distinguish wrongdoing from justice. Is *Homo sapiens* capable of making sense of the world it has created? Is there still a clear border separating reality from fiction?

In the fifth and final part I gather together the different threads and take a more general look at life in an age of bewilderment, when the old stories have collapsed and no new story has emerged so far to replace them. Who are we? What should we do in life? What kinds of skills do we need? Given everything we know and don't know about science, about God, about politics, and about religion, what can we say about the meaning of life today?

This may sound overambitious, but *Homo sapiens* cannot wait. Philosophy, religion, and science are all running out of time. People have debated the meaning of life for thousands of years. We cannot continue this debate indefinitely. The looming ecological crisis, the growing threat of weapons of mass destruction, and the rise of new disruptive technologies will not allow it. Perhaps most important, artificial intelligence and biotechnology are giving humanity the power to reshape and reengineer life. Very soon somebody will have to decide how to use this power—based on some implicit or explicit story about the meaning of life. Philosophers are very patient people, but engineers are far less so, and investors are the least patient of all. If you don't know what to do with the power to engineer life, market forces will not wait a thousand years for you to come up with an answer. The invisible hand of the market will force upon you its own blind reply. Unless you are happy to entrust the future of life to the mercy of quarterly revenue reports, you need a clear idea what life is all about.

In the final chapter I indulge in a few personal remarks, talking as one *Homo sapiens* to another, just before the curtain goes down on our species and a completely different drama begins.

Before embarking on this intellectual journey, I would like to highlight one crucial point. In much of this book I discuss the shortcomings of the liberal worldview and the democratic system. I do so not because I believe liberal democracy is uniquely problematic but rather because I think it is the most successful and most versatile political model humans have so far developed for dealing with the challenges of the modern world. While it might not be appropriate for every society in every stage of development, it has proven its worth in more societies and in more situations than any of its alternatives. So when we are examining the new challenges that lie ahead of us, it is necessary to understand the limitations of liberal democracy and to explore how we can adapt and improve its current institutions.

Unfortunately, in the present political climate any critical thinking about liberalism and democracy might be hijacked by autocrats and various illiberal movements, whose sole interest is to discredit liberal democracy rather than to engage in an open discussion about the future of humanity. While they are more than happy to debate the problems of liberal democracy, they have almost no tolerance of any criticism directed at them.

As an author, I was therefore required to make a difficult choice. Should I speak my mind openly and risk that my words might be taken out of context and used to justify burgeoning autocracies? Or should I censor myself? It is a mark of illiberal regimes that they make free speech more difficult even outside their borders. Due to the spread of such regimes, it is becoming increasingly dangerous to think critically about the future of our species.

After some soul-searching, I chose free discussion over self-censorship. Without criticizing the liberal model, we cannot repair its faults or move beyond it. But please note that this book could have been written only when people are still relatively free to think what they like and to express themselves as they wish. If you value this book, you should also value the freedom of expression.

....

PART I

The Technological Challenge

Humankind is losing faith in the liberal story that dominated global politics in recent decades, exactly when the merger of biotech and infotech confronts us with the biggest challenges humankind has ever encountered.

1

....

Disillusionment

The End of History Has Been Postponed

Humans think in stories rather than in facts, numbers, or equations, and the simpler the story, the better. Every person, group, and nation has its own tales and myths. But during the twentieth century the global elites in New York, London, Berlin, and Moscow formulated three grand stories that claimed to explain the whole past and to predict the future of the entire world: the fascist story, the communist story, and the liberal story. The Second World War knocked out the fascist story, and from the late 1940s to the late 1980s the world became a battleground between just two stories: communism and liberalism. Then the communist story collapsed, and the liberal story remained the dominant guide to the human past and the indispensable manual for the future of the world—or so it seemed to the global elite.

The liberal story celebrates the value and power of liberty. It says that for thousands of years humankind lived under oppressive regimes that allowed people few political rights, economic opportunities, or personal liberties, and which heavily restricted the movements of individuals, ideas, and goods. But people fought for their freedom, and step by step, liberty gained ground. Democratic regimes took the place of brutal dictatorships. Free enterprise overcame economic restrictions. People learned to think for themselves and follow their hearts instead of blindly obeying bigoted priests and hidebound traditions. Open roads, wide bridges, and bustling airports replaced walls, moats, and barbed-wire fences.

The liberal story acknowledges that not all is well in the world and that there are still many hurdles to overcome. Much of our planet is dominated by tyrants, and even in the most liberal countries many citizens suffer from poverty, violence, and oppression. But at least we know what we need to do in order to overcome these problems: give people more liberty. We need to protect human rights, grant everybody the vote, establish free markets, and let individuals, ideas, and goods move throughout the world as easily as possible. According to this liberal panacea—accepted, in slight variations, by George W. Bush and Barack Obama alike—if we just continue to liberalize and globalize our political and economic systems, we will produce peace and prosperity for all.[1]

Countries that join this unstoppable march of progress will be rewarded with peace and prosperity sooner. Countries that try to resist the inevitable will suffer the consequences until they too see the light, open their borders, and liberalize their societies, their politics, and their markets. It may take time, but eventually even North Korea, Iraq, and El Salvador will look like Denmark or Iowa.

In the 1990s and 2000s this story became a global mantra. Many governments from Brazil to India adopted liberal recipes in an attempt to join the inexorable march of history. Those failing to do so seemed like fossils from a bygone era. In 1997 U.S. president Bill Clinton confidently rebuked the Chinese government, stating that its refusal to liberalize Chinese politics put it "on the wrong side of history."[2]

However, since the global financial crisis of 2008 people all over the world have become increasingly disillusioned with the liberal story. Walls and firewalls are back in vogue. Resistance to immigration and to trade agreements is mounting. Ostensibly democratic governments undermine the independence of the judiciary system, restrict the freedom of the press, and portray any opposition as treason. Strongmen in countries such as Turkey and Russia experiment with new types of illiberal democracies and outright dictatorships. Today, few would confidently declare that the Chinese Communist Party is on the wrong side of history.

The year 2016—marked by the Brexit vote in Britain and the rise of Donald Trump in the United States—signified the moment when this tidal wave of disillusionment reached the core liberal states of Western Europe and North America. Whereas a few years ago Americans and Europeans were still trying to liberalize Iraq and Libya at gunpoint, many people in Kentucky and Yorkshire now have come to see the liberal vision as either undesirable or unattainable. Some discovered a liking for the old hierarchical world, and they just don't want to give up their racial, national, or gendered privileges. Others have concluded (rightly or wrongly) that liberalization and globalization are a huge racket empowering a tiny elite at the expense of the masses.

In 1938 humans were offered three global stories to choose from, in 1968 just two, and in 1998 a single story seemed to prevail. In 2018 we are down to zero. No wonder that the liberal elites, who dominated much of the world in recent decades, are in a state of shock and disorientation. To have one story is the most reassuring situation of all. Everything is perfectly clear. To be suddenly left without any story is terrifying. Nothing makes any sense. A bit like the Soviet elite in the 1980s, liberals don't understand how history deviated from its preordained course, and they lack an alternative prism through which to interpret reality. Disorientation causes them to think in apocalyptic terms, as if the failure of history to come to its envisioned happy ending can only mean that it is hurtling toward Armageddon. Unable to conduct a reality check, the mind latches onto catastrophic scenarios. Like a person imagining that a bad headache signifies a terminal brain tumor, many liberals fear that Brexit and the rise of Donald Trump portend the end of human civilization.

FROM KILLING MOSQUITOES TO KILLING THOUGHTS

Our sense of disorientation and impending doom is exacerbated by the accelerating pace of technological disruption. The liberal political system was shaped during the industrial era to manage a world of steam engines, oil refineries, and television sets. It has difficulty dealing with the ongoing revolutions in information technology and biotechnology.

Both politicians and voters are barely able to comprehend the new technologies, let alone regulate their explosive potential. Since the 1990s the internet has changed the world probably more than any other factor, yet the internet revolution was directed by engineers more than by political parties. Did you ever vote about the internet? The democratic system is still struggling to understand what hit it, and it is unequipped to deal with the next shocks, such as the rise of AI and the blockchain revolution.

Already today, computers have made the financial system so complicated that few humans can understand it. As AI improves, we might soon reach a point when no human can make sense of finance anymore. What will that do to the political process? Can you imagine a government that waits humbly for an algorithm to approve its budget or its new tax reform? Meanwhile, peer-to-peer blockchain networks and cryptocurrencies such as Bitcoin might completely revamp the monetary system, making radical tax reforms inevitable. For example, it might become impossible or irrelevant to calculate and tax incomes in dollars, because most transactions will not involve a clear-cut exchange of national currency, or any currency at all. Governments might therefore need to invent entirely new taxes—perhaps a tax on information (which will be both the most important asset in the economy and the only thing exchanged in numerous transactions). Will the political system manage to deal with the crisis before it runs out of money?

Even more important, the twin revolutions in infotech and biotech could restructure not just economies and societies but our very bodies and minds. In the past, we humans learned to control the world outside us, but we had very little control over the world inside us. We knew how to build a dam and stop a river from flowing, but we did not know how to stop the body from aging. We knew how to design an irrigation system, but we had no idea how to design a brain. If a mosquito buzzed in our ear and disturbed our sleep, we knew how to kill the mosquito, but if a thought buzzed in our mind and kept us awake at night, most of us did not know how to kill the thought.

The revolutions in biotech and infotech will give us control of the world inside us and will enable us to engineer and manufacture life. We will learn how to design brains, extend lives, and kill thoughts at our discretion. Nobody knows what the consequences will be. Humans were always far better at inventing tools than using them wisely. It is easier to manipulate a river by building a dam than it is to predict all the complex consequences this will have for the wider ecological system. Similarly, it will be easier to redirect the flow of our minds than to divine what that will do to our personal psychology or to our social systems.

In the past, we gained the power to manipulate the world around us and reshape the entire planet, but because we didn't understand the complexity of the global ecology, the changes we made inadvertently disrupted the entire ecological system, and now we face an ecological collapse. In the coming century biotech and infotech will give us the power to manipulate the world inside us and reshape ourselves, but because we don't understand the complexity of our own minds, the changes we will make might upset our mental system to such an extent that it too might break down.

The revolutions in biotech and infotech are currently being started by engineers, entrepreneurs, and scientists who are hardly aware of the political implications of their decisions, and who certainly don't represent anyone. Can parliaments and political parties take matters into their own hands? At present it does not seem so. Technological disruption is not even a leading item on the political agenda. During the 2016 U.S. presidential race, the main reference to disruptive technology concerned Hillary Clinton's email debacle, and despite all the talk about job loss, neither candidate addressed the potential impact of automation.[3] Donald Trump warned voters that the Mexicans and Chinese would take their jobs, and that they should therefore build a wall on the Mexican border.[4] He never warned voters that algorithms would take their jobs, nor did he suggest building a firewall on the border with California.

This might be one of the reasons (though not the only one) voters even in the heartlands of the liberal West are losing faith in the liberal story and in the democratic process. Ordinary people may not understand artificial intelligence and biotechnology, but they can sense that the future is passing them by. In 1938 the condition of the common person in the USSR, Germany, or the United States may have been grim, but he was constantly told that he was the most important thing in the world, and that he was the future (provided, of course, that he was an "ordinary person" rather than a Jew or an African). He looked at the propaganda posters—which typically depicted coal miners, steelworkers, and housewives in heroic poses—and saw himself there: "I am in that poster! I am the hero of the future!"[5]

In 2018 the common person feels increasingly irrelevant. Lots of mysterious words are bandied around excitedly in TED Talks, government think tanks, and high-tech conferences—globalization, blockchain, genetic engineering, artificial intelligence, machine learning—and common people may well suspect that none of these words are about them. The liberal story was the story of ordinary people. How can it remain relevant to a world of cyborgs and networked algorithms?

In the twentieth century, the masses revolted against exploitation and sought to translate their vital role in the economy into political power. Now the masses fear irrelevance, and they are frantic to use their remaining political power before it is too late. Brexit and the rise of Trump might therefore demonstrate a trajectory opposite to that of traditional socialist revolutions. The Russian, Chinese, and Cuban revolutions were made by people who were vital to the economy but who lacked political power; in 2016, Trump and Brexit were supported by many people who still enjoyed political power but who feared that they were losing their economic worth. Perhaps in the twenty-first century populist revolts will be staged not against an economic elite that exploits people but against an economic elite that does not need them anymore.[6] This may well be a losing battle. It is much harder to struggle against irrelevance than against exploitation.

THE LIBERAL PHOENIX

This is not the first time the liberal story has faced a crisis of confidence. Ever since this story gained global influence, in the second half of the nineteenth century, it has endured periodic crises. The first era of globalization and liberalization ended in the bloodbath of the First World War, when imperial power politics cut short the global march of progress. In the days following the murder of Archduke Franz Ferdinand in Sarajevo it turned out that the great powers believed in imperialism far more than in liberalism, and instead of uniting the world through free and peaceful commerce they focused on conquering a bigger slice of the globe by brute force. Yet liberalism survived the Franz Ferdinand moment and emerged from the maelstrom stronger than before, promising that this had been "the war to end all wars." It seemed that the unprecedented butchery had taught humankind the terrible price of imperialism, and now humanity was finally ready to create a new world order based on the principles of freedom and peace.

Then came the Hitler moment, when, in the 1930s and early 1940s, fascism seemed irresistible for a while. Victory over this threat merely ushered in the next. During the Che Guevara moment, between the 1950s and the 1970s, it again seemed that liberalism was on its last legs and that the future belonged to communism. In the end it was communism that collapsed. The supermarket proved to be far stronger than the gulag. More important, the liberal story proved to be far more supple and dynamic than any of its opponents. It triumphed over imperialism, over fascism, and over communism by adopting some of their best ideas and practices. In particular, the liberal story learned from communism to expand the circle of empathy and to value equality alongside liberty.

In the beginning, the liberal story cared mainly about the liberties and privileges of middle-class European men and seemed blind to the plight of working-class people, women, minorities, and non-Westerners. When in 1918 victorious Britain and France talked excitedly about liberty, they were not thinking about the subjects of their worldwide empires. For example, Indian demands for self-determination were answered by the Amritsar massacre of 1919, in which the British army slaughtered hundreds of unarmed demonstrators.

Even in the wake of the Second World War, Western liberals still had a very hard time applying their supposedly universal values to non-Western people. Thus when the Dutch emerged in 1945 from five years of brutal Nazi occupation, almost the first thing they did was raise an army and send it halfway across the world to reoccupy their former colony of Indonesia. Whereas in 1940 the Dutch gave up their own independence after little more than four days of fighting, they fought for more than four long and bitter years to suppress Indonesian independence. No wonder that many national liberation movements throughout the world placed their hopes on communist Moscow and Beijing rather than on the self-proclaimed champions of liberty in the West.

Gradually, however, the liberal story expanded its horizons, and at least in theory came to value the liberties and rights of all human beings without exception. As the circle of liberty expanded, the liberal story also came to recognize the importance of communist-style welfare programs. Liberty is not worth much unless it is coupled with some kind of social safety net. Social-democratic welfare states combined democracy and human rights with state-sponsored education and healthcare. Even the ultracapitalist United States has realized that the protection of liberty requires at least some government welfare services. Starving children have no liberties.

By the early 1990s, thinkers and politicians alike hailed "the End of History," confidently asserting that all the big political and economic questions of the past had been settled and that the refurbished liberal package of democracy, human rights, free markets, and government welfare services remained the only game in town. This package seemed destined to spread around the whole world, overcome all obstacles, erase all national borders, and turn humankind into one free global community.[7]

But history has not ended, and following the Franz Ferdinand moment, the Hitler moment, and the Che Guevara moment, we now find ourselves in the Trump moment. This time, however, the liberal story is not faced by a coherent ideological opponent like imperialism, fascism, or communism. The Trump moment is far more nihilistic.

Whereas the major movements of the twentieth century all had a vision for the entire human species—be it global domination, revolution, or liberation—Donald Trump offers no such thing. Just the opposite. His main message is that it's not America's job to formulate and promote any global vision. Similarly, the British Brexiteers barely have a plan for the future of the Disunited Kingdom—the future of Europe and of the world is far beyond their horizon. Most people who voted for Trump and Brexit didn't reject the liberal package in its entirety—they lost faith mainly in its globalizing part. They still believe in democracy, free markets, human rights, and social responsibility, but they think these fine ideas can stop at the border. Indeed, they believe that in order to preserve liberty and prosperity in Yorkshire or Kentucky, it is best to build a wall on the border and adopt illiberal policies toward foreigners.

The rising Chinese superpower presents an almost mirror image of this scenario. It is wary of liberalizing its domestic politics, but it has adopted a far more liberal approach to the rest of the world. In fact, when it comes to free trade and international cooperation, Xi Jinping looks like Obama's real successor. Having put Marxism-Leninism on the back burner, China seems rather happy with the liberal international order.

Resurgent Russia sees itself as a far more forceful rival of the global liberal order, but though it has reconstituted its military might, it is ideologically bankrupt. Vladimir Putin is certainly popular both in Russia and among various right-wing movements across the world, yet he has no global worldview that might attract unemployed Spaniards, disgruntled Brazilians, or starry-eyed students in Cambridge.

Russia does offer an alternative model to liberal democracy, but this model is not a coherent political ideology. Rather, it is a political practice in which a number of oligarchs monopolize most of a country's wealth and power and then use their control of the media to hide their activities and cement their rule. Democracy is based on Abraham Lincoln's principle that "you can fool all the people some of the time, and some people all of the time, but you cannot fool all the people all the time." If a government is corrupt and fails to improve people's lives, enough citizens will eventually realize this and replace the government. But government control of the media undermines Lincoln's logic, because it prevents citizens from realizing the truth. Through its monopoly over the media, the ruling oligarchy can repeatedly blame all its failures on others and divert attention to external threats, either real or imaginary.

When you live under such an oligarchy, there is always some crisis or other that takes priority over boring stuff like healthcare and pollution. If the nation is facing external invasion or diabolical subversion, who has time to worry about overcrowded hospitals and polluted rivers? By manufacturing a never-ending stream of crises, a corrupt oligarchy can prolong its rule indefinitely.[8]

Yet though enduring in practice, this oligarchic model appeals to no one. Unlike other ideologies that proudly expound their vision, ruling oligarchies are not proud of their practices, and they tend to use other ideologies as a smoke screen. Thus Russia pretends to be a democracy, and its leadership proclaims allegiance to the values of Russian nationalism and Orthodox Christianity rather than to oligarchy. Right-wing extremists in France and Britain may well rely on Russian help and express admiration for Putin, but their voters would not actually like to live in a country that copies the Russian model—a country with endemic corruption, malfunctioning services, no rule of law, and staggering inequality. According to some measures, Russia is one of the most unequal countries in the world, with 87 percent of wealth concentrated in the hands of the richest 10 percent of people.[9] How many working-class supporters of the National Front want to copy this wealth distribution pattern in France?

Humans vote with their feet. In my travels around the world I have met numerous people in many countries who wish to immigrate to the United States, Germany, Canada, or Australia. I have met a few who want to move to China or Japan. But I have yet to meet a single person who dreams of immigrating to Russia.

As for "global Islam," it attracts mainly those who were born in its lap. While it may appeal to some people in Syria and Iraq, and even to alienated Muslim youth in Germany and Britain, it is hard to see Greece or South Africa—not to mention Canada or South Korea—joining a global caliphate as the remedy to their problems. In this case too, people vote with their feet. For every Muslim youth from Germany who traveled to the Middle East to live under a Muslim theocracy, probably a hundred Middle Eastern youths would have liked to make the opposite journey and start a new life for themselves in liberal Germany.

This might imply that the present crisis of faith is less severe than its predecessors. Any liberal who is driven to despair by the events of the last few years can recollect how much worse things looked in 1918, 1938, or 1968. At the end of the day, humankind won't abandon the liberal story, he might think, because it doesn't have any alternative. People might give the system an angry kick in the stomach but, having nowhere else to go, they will eventually return to it.

Alternatively, people might completely give up on having a global story of any kind and instead seek shelter in local nationalist and religious tales. In the twentieth century, nationalist movements were an extremely important political player, but they lacked a coherent vision for the future of the world other than supporting the division of the globe into independent nation-states. Indonesian nationalists fought against Dutch domination, and Vietnamese nationalists wanted a free Vietnam, but there was no Indonesian or Vietnamese story for humanity as a whole. When it came time to explain how Indonesia, Vietnam, and all the other free nations should relate to one another, and how humans should deal with global problems such as the threat of nuclear war, nationalists invariably turned to either liberal or communist ideas.

But if both liberalism and communism are now discredited, maybe humans should abandon the very idea of a single global story. After all, weren't all these global stories—even communism—the product of Western imperialism? Why should Vietnamese villagers put their faith in the brainchild of a German from Trier and a Manchester industrialist? Maybe each country should adopt a different idiosyncratic path, defined by its own ancient traditions. Perhaps even Westerners should take a break from trying to run the world, and focus on their own affairs for a change.

This is arguably what is happening all over the globe, as the vacuum left by the breakdown of liberalism is tentatively filled by nostalgic fantasies about some local golden past. Donald Trump coupled his calls for American isolationism with a promise to "Make America Great Again"—as if the United States of the 1980s or 1950s was a perfect society that Americans should somehow recreate in the twenty-first century. The Brexiteers dream of making Britain an independent power, as if they were still living in the days of Queen Victoria and as if "splendid isolation" were a viable policy for the era of the internet and global warming. Chinese elites have rediscovered their native imperial and Confucian legacies as a supplement to or even substitute for the doubtful Marxist ideology they imported from the West. In Russia, Putin's official vision is not to build a corrupt oligarchy but rather to resurrect the old tsarist empire. A century after the Bolshevik Revolution, Putin promises a return to ancient tsarist glories with an autocratic government buoyed by Russian nationalism and Orthodox piety spreading its might from the Baltic to the Caucasus.

Similar nostalgic dreams that mix nationalist attachment with religious traditions underpin regimes in India, Poland, Turkey, and numerous other countries. Nowhere are these fantasies more extreme than in the Middle East, where Islamists want to copy the system established by the Prophet Muhammad in the city of Medina 1,400 years ago, while fundamentalist Jews in Israel outdo even the Islamists and dream of going back 2,500 years to biblical times. Members of Israel's ruling coalition government talk openly about their hope of expanding modern Israel's borders to match more closely those of biblical Israel, of reinstating biblical law, and even of rebuilding the ancient Temple of Yahweh in Jerusalem in place of the Al-Aqsa mosque.[10]

Liberal elites look in horror at these developments and hope that humanity will return to the liberal path in time to avert disaster. In his final speech to the United Nations in September 2016, President Obama warned his listeners against retreating "into a world sharply divided, and ultimately in conflict, along age-old lines of nation and tribe and race and religion." Instead, he said, "the principles of open markets and accountable governance, of democracy and human rights and international law . . . remain the firmest foundation for human progress in this century."[11]

Obama has rightly pointed out that despite the numerous shortcomings of the liberal package, it has a much better record than any of its alternatives. Most humans never enjoyed greater peace or prosperity than they did under the aegis of the liberal order of the early twenty-first century. For the first time in history, infectious diseases kill fewer people than old age, famine kills fewer people than obesity, and violence kills fewer people than accidents.

But liberalism has no obvious answers to the biggest problems we face: ecological collapse and technological disruption. Liberalism traditionally relied on economic growth to magically solve difficult social and political conflicts. Liberalism reconciled the proletariat with the bourgeoisie, the faithful with atheists, natives with immigrants, and Europeans with Asians by promising everybody a larger slice of the pie. With a constantly growing pie, that was possible. However, economic growth will not save the global ecosystem; just the opposite, in fact, for economic growth is the cause of the ecological crisis. And economic growth will not solve technological disruption, for it is predicated on the invention of more and more disruptive technologies.

The liberal story and the logic of free-market capitalism encourage people to have grand expectations. During the latter part of the twentieth century, each generation—whether in Houston, Shanghai, Istanbul, or São Paulo—enjoyed better education, superior healthcare and larger incomes than the one that came before it. In coming decades, however, owing to a combination of technological disruption and ecological meltdown, the younger generation might be lucky to simply stay in place.

We are consequently left with the task of creating an updated story for the world. Just as the upheavals of the Industrial Revolution gave birth to the novel ideologies of the twentieth century, so the coming revolutions in biotechnology and information technology are likely to require fresh visions. The next decades might therefore be characterized by intense soul-searching and by the formulation of new social and political models. Can liberalism reinvent itself yet again, just as it did in the wake of the 1930s and 1960s crises, emerging as more attractive than ever before? Can traditional religion and nationalism provide the answers that escape the liberals, and might they use ancient wisdom to fashion an up-to-date worldview? Or perhaps the time has come to make a clean break with the past and craft a completely new story that goes beyond not just the old gods and nations but even the core modern values of liberty and equality.

At present, humankind is far from reaching any consensus on these questions. We are still in the nihilist moment of disillusionment and anger, after people have lost faith in the old stories but before they have embraced a new one. So what next? The first step is to tone down the prophecies of doom and switch from panic mode to bewilderment. Panic is a form of hubris. It comes from the smug feeling that one knows exactly where the world is heading: down. Bewilderment is more humble and therefore more clearsighted. Do you feel like running down the street crying "The apocalypse is upon us"? Try telling yourself, "No, it's not that. Truth is, I just don't understand what's going on in the world."

The following chapters will try to clarify some of the bewildering new possibilities we face, and how we might proceed from here. But before exploring potential solutions to humanity's predicaments we need a better grasp of the challenge technology poses. The revolutions in information technology and biotechnology are still in their infancy, and it is debatable to what extent they are really responsible for the current crisis of liberalism. Most people in Birmingham, Istanbul, St. Petersburg, and Mumbai are only dimly aware, if at all, of the rise of artificial intelligence and its potential impact on their lives. It is undoubtable, however, that the technological revolutions will gather momentum in the next few decades and will confront humankind with the hardest trials we have ever encountered. Any story that seeks to gain humanity's allegiance will be tested above all in its ability to deal with the twin revolutions in infotech and biotech. If liberalism, nationalism, Islam, or some novel creed wishes to shape the world of the year 2050, it will need not only to make sense of artificial intelligence, Big Data algorithms, and bioengineering but also to incorporate them into a new and meaningful narrative.

To understand the nature of this technological challenge, perhaps it would be best to start with the job market. Since 2015 I have been traveling around the world talking with government officials, businesspeople, social activists, and schoolkids about the human predicament. Whenever they become impatient or bored by all the talk of artificial intelligence, Big Data algorithms, and bioengineering, I usually need to mention just one magic word to snap them back to attention: jobs. The technological revolution might soon push billions of humans out of the job market and create a massive new "useless class," leading to social and political upheavals that no existing ideology knows how to handle. All the talk about technology and ideology might sound very abstract and remote, but the very real prospect of mass unemployment—or personal unemployment—leaves nobody indifferent.

2

....

Work

When You Grow Up, You Might Not Have a Job

We have no idea what the job market will look like in 2050. It is generally agreed that machine learning and robotics will change almost every line of work, from producing yogurt to teaching yoga. However, there are conflicting views about the nature of the change and its imminence. Some believe that within a mere decade or two, billions of people will become economically redundant. Others maintain that even in the long run automation will keep generating new jobs and greater prosperity for all.

So are we on the verge of a terrifying upheaval, or are such forecasts yet another example of ill-founded Luddite hysteria? It is hard to say. Fears that automation will create massive unemployment go back to the nineteenth century, and so far they have never materialized. Since the beginning of the Industrial Revolution, for every job lost to a machine at least one new job was created, and the average standard of living has increased dramatically.[1] Yet there are good reasons to think that this time it is different and that machine learning will be a real game changer.

Humans have two types of abilities—physical and cognitive. In the past, machines competed with humans mainly in raw physical abilities, while humans retained an immense edge over machines in cognition. Therefore, as manual jobs in agriculture and industry were automated, new service jobs emerged that required the kind of cognitive skills only humans possessed: learning, analyzing, communicating, and above all understanding human emotions. However, AI is now beginning to outperform humans in more and more of these skills, including in the understanding of human emotions.[2] We don't know of any third field of activity—beyond the physical and the cognitive—where humans will always retain a secure edge.

It is crucial to realize that the AI revolution is not just about computers getting faster and smarter. It is fueled by breakthroughs in the life sciences and the social sciences as well. The better we understand the biochemical mechanisms that underpin human emotions, desires, and choices, the better computers can become in analyzing human behavior, predicting human decisions, and replacing human drivers, bankers, and lawyers.

In the last few decades research in areas such as neuroscience and behavioral economics allowed scientists to hack humans, and in particular to gain a much better understanding of how humans make decisions. It turns out that our choices of everything from food to mates result not from some mysterious free will but rather from billions of neurons calculating probabilities within a split second. Vaunted "human intuition" is in reality "pattern recognition."[3] Good drivers, bankers, and lawyers don't have magical intuitions about traffic, investment, or negotiation; rather, by recognizing recurring patterns, they spot and try to avoid careless pedestrians, inept borrowers, and sly crooks. It also turns out that the biochemical algorithms of the human brain are far from perfect. They rely on heuristics, shortcuts, and outdated circuits adapted to the African savannah rather than to the urban jungle. No wonder that even good drivers, bankers, and lawyers sometimes make stupid mistakes.

This means that AI can outperform humans even in tasks that

supposedly demand "intuition." If you think AI needs to compete against the human soul in terms of mystical hunches, the task sounds impossible. But if AI really needs to compete against neural networks in calculating probabilities and recognizing patterns, that sounds far less daunting.

In particular, AI can be better at jobs that demand intuitions *about other people*. Many lines of work—such as driving a vehicle in a street full of pedestrians, lending money to strangers, and negotiating a business deal—require the ability to correctly assess the emotions and desires of others. Is that kid about to run into the road? Does the man in the suit intend to take my money and disappear? Will that lawyer act upon his threats or is he just bluffing? As long as it was thought that such emotions and desires were generated by an immaterial spirit, it seemed obvious that computers would never be able to replace human drivers, bankers, and lawyers. For how could a computer understand the divinely created human spirit? Yet if these emotions and desires are in fact no more than biochemical algorithms, there is no reason computers cannot decipher these algorithms—and do so far better than any *Homo sapiens*.

A driver predicting the intentions of a pedestrian, a banker assessing the credibility of a potential borrower, and a lawyer gauging the mood at the negotiating table don't rely on witchcraft. Rather, unbeknownst to them, their brains are recognizing biochemical patterns by analyzing facial expressions, tones of voice, hand movements, and even body odors. An AI equipped with the right sensors could do all that far more accurately and reliably than a human.

For this reason the threat of job loss does not result merely from the rise of infotech. It results from the confluence of infotech with biotech. The way from the fMRI scanner to the labor market is long and tortuous, but it can still be covered within a few decades. What brain scientists are learning today about the amygdala and the cerebellum might make it possible for computers to outperform human psychiatrists and bodyguards in 2050.

Not only does AI stand poised to hack humans and outperform

them in what were hitherto uniquely human skills, but it also enjoys uniquely nonhuman abilities, which make the difference between AI and a human worker one of kind rather than merely of degree. Two particularly important nonhuman abilities that AI possesses are connectivity and updatability.

Since humans are individuals, it is difficult to connect them to one another and to make sure that they are all up to date. In contrast, computers aren't individuals, and it is easy to integrate them into a single flexible network. What we are facing is not the replacement of millions of individual human workers by millions of individual robots and computers; rather, individual humans are likely to be replaced by an integrated network. When considering automation, therefore, it is wrong to compare the abilities of a single human driver to that of a single self-driving car, or of a single human doctor to that of a single AI doctor. Rather, we should compare the abilities of a collection of human individuals to the abilities of an integrated network.

For example, many drivers are unfamiliar with all the changing traffic regulations, and they often violate them. In addition, since every vehicle is an autonomous entity, when two vehicles approach the same intersection at the same time, the drivers might miscommunicate their intentions and collide. Self-driving cars, in contrast, can all be connected to one another. When two such vehicles approach the same junction, they are not really two separate entities—they are part of a single algorithm. The chances that they might miscommunicate and collide are therefore far smaller. And if the transportation department decides to change some traffic regulation, all self-driving vehicles can be easily updated at exactly the same moment, and barring some bug in the program, they will all follow the new regulation to the letter.[4]

Similarly, if the World Health Organization identifies a new disease, or if a laboratory produces a new medicine, it is almost impossible to update all the human doctors in the world about these developments. In contrast, even if you have ten billion AI doctors in the world—each monitoring the health of a single human being— you can still update all of them within a split second, and they can all communicate to each other their feedback on the new disease or medicine. These potential advantages of connectivity and updatability are so huge that at least in some lines of work it might make sense to replace *all* humans with computers, even if individually some humans still do a better job than the machines.

You might object that by switching from individual humans to a computer network we will lose the advantages of individuality. For example, if one human doctor makes a wrong judgment, he does not kill all the patients in the world, and he does not block the development of all new medications. In contrast, if all doctors are really just a single system, and that system makes a mistake, the results might be catastrophic. In truth, however, an integrated computer system can maximize the advantages of connectivity without losing the benefits of individuality. You can run many alternative algorithms on the same network, so a patient in a remote jungle village can access through her smartphone not just a single authoritative doctor but actually a hundred different AI doctors, whose relative performance is constantly being compared. You don't like what the IBM doctor told you? No problem. Even if you are stranded somewhere on the slopes of Kilimanjaro, you can easily contact the Baidu doctor for a second opinion.

The benefits for human society are likely to be immense. AI doctors could provide far better and cheaper healthcare for billions of people, particularly for those who currently receive no healthcare at all. Thanks to learning algorithms and biometric sensors, a poor villager in an underdeveloped country might come to enjoy far better healthcare via her smartphone than the richest person in the world gets today from the most advanced urban hospital.[5]

Similarly, self-driving vehicles could provide people with much better transportation services, and in particular reduce mortality from traffic accidents. Today close to 1.25 million people are killed annually in traffic accidents (twice the number killed by war, crime, and terrorism combined).[6] More than 90 percent of these accidents are caused by very human errors: somebody drinking alcohol and driving, somebody texting a message while driving, somebody falling asleep at the wheel, somebody daydreaming instead of paying attention to the road. The National Highway Traffic Safety Administration estimated in 2012 that 31 percent of fatal crashes in the United States involved alcohol abuse, 30 percent involved speeding, and 21 percent involved distracted drivers.[7] Self-driving vehicles will never do any of these things. Though they suffer from their own problems and limitations, and though some accidents are inevitable, replacing all human drivers by computers is expected to reduce deaths and injuries on the road by about 90 percent.[8] In other words, switching to autonomous vehicles is likely to save the lives of one million people every year.

It would therefore be madness to block automation in fields such as transport and healthcare just in order to protect human jobs. After all, what we ultimately ought to protect is humans—not jobs. Displaced drivers and doctors will just have to find something else to do.

THE MOZART IN THE MACHINE

At least in the short term, AI and robotics are unlikely to completely eliminate entire industries. Jobs that require specialization in a narrow range of routinized activities will be automated. But it will be much more difficult to replace humans with machines in less routine jobs that demand the simultaneous use of a wide range of skills and involve dealing with unforeseen scenarios. Take healthcare, for example. Many doctors focus almost exclusively on processing information: they absorb medical data, analyze it, and produce a diagnosis. Nurses, in contrast, need good motor and emotional skills in order to give a painful injection, replace a bandage, or restrain a violent patient. Therefore we will probably have an AI family doctor on our smartphone decades before we have a reliable nurse robot.[9] The human care industry—which takes care of the sick, the young, and the elderly—is likely to remain a human bastion for a long time. Indeed, as people live longer and have fewer children, care of the elderly will probably be one of the fastest-growing sectors in the human labor market.

Alongside care, creativity too poses particularly difficult hurdles for automation. We don't need humans to sell us music any-more—we can download it directly from the iTunes store—but the composers, musicians, singers, and DJs are still flesh and blood. We rely on their creativity not just to produce completely new music but also to choose among a mind-boggling range of available possibilities.

Nevertheless, in the long run no job will remain absolutely safe from automation. Even artists should be put on notice. In the modern world art is usually associated with human emotions. We tend to think that artists are channeling internal psychological forces, and that the whole purpose of art is to connect us with our emotions or to inspire in us some new feeling. Consequently, when we come to evaluate art, we tend to judge it by its emotional impact on the audience. Yet if art is defined by human emotions, what might happen once external algorithms are able to understand and manipulate human emotions better than Shakespeare, Frida Kahlo, or Beyoncé?

After all, emotions are not some mystical phenomenon—they are the result of a biochemical process. Therefore, in the not too distant future a machine-learning algorithm could analyze the biometric data streaming from sensors on and inside your body, determine your personality type and your changing moods, and calculate the emotional impact that a particular song—even a particular musical key—is likely to have on you.[10]

Of all forms of art, music is probably the most susceptible to Big Data analysis, because both inputs and outputs lend themselves to precise mathematical depiction. The inputs are the mathematical patterns of sound waves, and the outputs are the electrochemical patterns of neural storms. Within a few decades, an algorithm that goes over millions of musical experiences might learn to predict how particular inputs result in particular outputs.[11]

Suppose you just had a nasty fight with your boyfriend. The algorithm in charge of your sound system will immediately discern your inner emotional turmoil, and based on what it knows about you personally and about human psychology in general, it will play songs tailored to resonate with your gloom and echo your distress. These particular songs might not work well with other people, but they are just perfect for your personality type. After helping you get in touch with the depths of your sadness, the algorithm would then play the one song in the world that is likely to cheer you up— perhaps because your subconscious connects it with a happy childhood memory that even you are not aware of. No human DJ could ever hope to match the skills of such an AI.

You might object that the AI would thereby kill serendipity and lock us inside a narrow musical cocoon, woven by our previous likes and dislikes. What about exploring new musical tastes and styles? No problem. You could easily adjust the algorithm to make 5 percent of its choices completely at random, unexpectedly throwing at you a recording of an Indonesian gamelan ensemble, a Rossini opera, or the latest K-pop hit. Over time, by monitoring your reactions, the AI could even determine the ideal level of randomness that will optimize exploration while avoiding annoyance, perhaps lowering its serendipity level to 3 percent or raising it to 8 percent.

Another possible objection is that it is unclear how the algorithm could establish its emotional goal. If you just fought with your boyfriend, should the algorithm aim to make you sad or joyful? Would it blindly adhere to a rigid set of "good" and "bad" emotions? Maybe there are times in life when it's good to feel sad. The same question, of course, could be directed at human musicians and DJs. Yet with an algorithm, there are many interesting solutions to this puzzle.

One option is to just leave it to the customer. You can evaluate your emotions whichever way you like, and the algorithm will follow your dictates. Whether you want to wallow in self-pity or jump for joy, the algorithm will slavishly follow your lead. Indeed, the algorithm may learn to recognize your wishes even without your being explicitly aware of them.

Alternatively, if you don't trust yourself, you might instruct the algorithm to follow the recommendation of whichever eminent psychologist you do trust. If your boyfriend eventually dumps you, the algorithm may walk you through the official five stages of grief, first helping you deny what happened by playing Bobby McFerrin's "Don't Worry, Be Happy," then whipping up your anger with Alanis Morissette's "You Oughta Know," encouraging you to bargain with Jacques Brel's "Ne Me Quitte Pas" and Paul Young's "Come Back and Stay," dropping you into the pit of depression with Adele's "Someone Like You" and "Hello," and finally helping you accept the situation with Gloria Gaynor's "I Will Survive."

The next step might be for the algorithm to start tinkering with the songs and melodies themselves, changing them ever so slightly to fit your quirks. Perhaps you dislike a particular bit in an otherwise excellent song. The algorithm knows it because your heart skips a beat and your oxytocin levels drop slightly whenever you hear that annoying part. The algorithm could rewrite or edit out the offending notes.

In the long run, algorithms may learn how to compose entire tunes, playing on human emotions as if they were a piano keyboard. Using your biometric data, the algorithms could even produce personalized melodies, which you alone in the entire universe would appreciate.

It is often said that people connect with art because they find themselves in it. This may lead to surprising and somewhat sinister results if and when, say, Facebook begins creating personalized art based on everything it knows about you. If your boyfriend leaves you, Facebook will treat you to an individualized song about that particular bastard rather than about the unknown person who broke the heart of Adele or Alanis Morissette. The song will even remind you of real incidents from your relationship that nobody else in the world knows about.

Of course, personalized art might never catch on, because people will continue to prefer common hits that everybody likes. How can you dance or sing together to a song nobody besides you knows? But algorithms could prove even more adept at producing global hits than personalized rarities. By using massive biometric databases garnered from millions of people, the algorithm could know which biochemical buttons to press in order to produce a global hit that would get everybody swinging like crazy on the dance floors. If art is really about inspiring (or manipulating) human emotions, few if any human musicians will be able to compete with such an algorithm, because they cannot match it in understanding the chief instrument they are playing on: the human biochemical system.

Will all this result in great art? That depends on the definition of art. If beauty is indeed in the ears of the listener, and if the customer is always right, then biometric algorithms stand a chance of producing the best art in history. If art is about something deeper than human emotions and should express a truth beyond our biochemical vibrations, biometric algorithms might not make very good artists. But neither do most humans. In order to enter the art market and displace many human composers and performers, algorithms won't have to begin by surpassing Tchaikovsky. It would be enough if they outperform Britney Spears.

NEW JOBS?

The loss of many traditional jobs in everything from art to healthcare will partly be offset by the creation of new human jobs. Primary care doctors who focus on diagnosing known diseases and administering familiar treatments will probably be replaced by AI doctors. But precisely because of that, there will be much more money to pay human doctors and lab assistants to do groundbreaking research and develop new medicines or surgical procedures.[12]

AI might help create new human jobs in another way. Instead of humans competing with AI, they could focus on servicing and leveraging AI. For example, the replacement of human pilots by drones has eliminated some jobs but created many new opportunities in maintenance, remote control, data analysis, and cybersecurity. The U.S. armed forces need thirty people to operate every unmanned Predator or Reaper drone flying over Syria, while analyzing the resulting harvest of information occupies at least eighty people more. In 2015 the U.S. Air Force lacked sufficient trained humans to fill all these positions, and therefore faced an ironic crisis in manning its unmanned aircraft.[13]

If so, the job market of 2050 might well be characterized by human-AI cooperation rather than competition. In fields ranging from policing to banking, teams of humans-plus-AIs could outperform both humans and computers. After IBM's chess program Deep Blue beat Garry Kasparov in 1997, humans did not stop playing chess. Rather, thanks to AI trainers, human chess masters became better than ever, and at least for a while human-AI teams known as "centaurs" outperformed both humans and computers in chess. AI might similarly help groom the best detectives, bankers, and soldiers in history.[14]

The problem with all such new jobs, however, is that they will probably demand high levels of expertise, and will therefore not solve the problems of unemployed unskilled laborers. Creating new human jobs might prove easier than retraining humans to actually fill these jobs. During previous waves of automation, people could usually switch from one routine low-skill job to another. In 1920 a farm worker laid off due to the mechanization of agriculture could find a new job in a factory producing tractors. In 1980 an unemployed factory worker could start working as a cashier in a supermarket. Such occupational changes were feasible, because the move from farm to factory and from factory to supermarket required only limited retraining.

But in 2050, a cashier or textile worker losing her job to a robot will not be able to start working as a cancer researcher, as a drone operator, or as part of a human-AI banking team. She won't have the necessary skills. In the First World War it made sense to send millions of raw conscripts to charge machine guns and die in the thousands. Their individual skills mattered little. Today, despite the shortage of drone operators and data analysts, the U.S. Air Force is unwilling to fill the gaps with Walmart dropouts. You wouldn't want an inexperienced recruit to mistake an Afghan wedding party for a high-level Taliban conference.

Consequently, despite the appearance of many new human jobs, we might nevertheless witness the rise of a new useless class. We might actually get the worst of both worlds, suffering simultaneously from high unemployment and a shortage of skilled labor. Many people might share the fate not of nineteenth-century wagon drivers, who switched to driving taxis, but of nineteenth-century horses, who were increasingly pushed out of the job market altogether.[15]

In addition, no remaining human job will ever be safe from the threat of future automation, because machine learning and robotics will continue to improve. A forty-year-old unemployed Walmart cashier who through superhuman effort manages to reinvent herself as a drone pilot might have to reinvent herself again ten years later, because by then the flying of drones may also have been automated. This volatility will also make it more difficult to organize unions or secure labor rights. Already today, many new jobs in advanced economies involve unprotected temporary work, freelancing, and one-time gigs.[16] How do you unionize a profession that mushrooms and disappears within a decade?

Similarly, human-computer centaur teams are likely to be characterized by a constant tug-of-war between the humans and the computers, instead of settling down to a lifelong partnership. Teams made exclusively of humans—such as Sherlock Holmes and Dr. Watson—usually develop permanent hierarchies and routines that last decades. But a human detective who teams up with IBM's Watson computer system (which became famous after winning the TV quiz show *Jeopardy!* in 2011) will find that every routine is an invitation for disruption, every hierarchy an invitation for revolution. Yesterday's sidekick might morph into tomorrow's superintendent, and all protocols and manuals will have to be rewritten each year.[17]

A closer look at the world of chess might indicate where things are heading in the long run. It is true that for several years after Deep Blue defeated Kasparov, human-computer cooperation flourished in chess. Yet in recent years computers have become so good at playing chess that their human collaborators have lost their value and might soon become utterly irrelevant.

On December 7, 2017, a critical milestone was reached, not when a computer defeated a human at chess—that's old news—but when Google's AlphaZero program defeated the Stockfish 8 program. Stockfish 8 was the world's computer chess champion for 2016. It had access to centuries of accumulated human experience in chess, as well as decades of computer experience. It was able to calculate seventy million chess positions per second. In contrast, AlphaZero performed only eighty thousand such calculations per second, and its human creators had not taught it any chess strategies—not even standard openings. Rather, AlphaZero used the latest machine-learning principles to self-learn chess by playing against itself. Nevertheless, out of a hundred games the novice AlphaZero played against Stockfish, AlphaZero won twenty-eight and tied seventy-two. It didn't lose even once. Since AlphaZero had learned nothing from any human, many of its winning moves and strategies seemed unconventional to the human eye. They may well be considered creative, if not downright genius.

Can you guess how long it took AlphaZero to learn chess from scratch, prepare for the match against Stockfish, and develop its genius instincts? Four hours. That's not a typo. For centuries, chess was considered one of the crowning glories of human intelligence. AlphaZero went from utter ignorance to creative mastery in four hours, without the help of any human guide.[18]

AlphaZero is not the only imaginative software out there. Many programs now routinely outperform human chess players not just in brute calculation but even in "creativity." In human-only chess tournaments, judges are constantly on the lookout for players who try to cheat by secretly getting help from computers. One of the ways to catch cheaters is to monitor the level of originality players display. If they play an exceptionally creative move, the judges will often suspect that it cannot possibly be a human move—it must be a computer move. At least in chess, creativity is already considered to be the trademark of computers rather than humans! So if chess is our canary in the coal mine, we are duly warned that the canary is dying. What is happening today to human-AI chess teams might happen down the road to human-AI teams in policing, medicine, and banking too.[19]

Consequently, creating new jobs and retraining people to fill them will not be a one-time effort. The AI revolution won't be a single watershed event after which the job market will just settle into a new equilibrium. Rather, it will be a cascade of ever-bigger disruptions. Already today few employees expect to work in the same job for their entire life.[20] By 2050, not only the idea of a job for life but even that of a profession for life might seem antediluvian.

Even if we could constantly invent new jobs and retrain the workforce, we might wonder whether the average human would have the emotional stamina necessary for a life of such endless upheavals. Change is always stressful, and the hectic world of the early twenty-first century has produced a global epidemic of stress.[21] As the volatility of the job market and of individual careers increases, will people be able to cope? We will probably need far more effective stress-reduction techniques—ranging from drugs to neurofeedback to meditation—to prevent the human mind from snapping. By

2050 a useless class might emerge due not merely to an absolute lack of jobs or a lack of relevant education but also to insufficient mental stamina.

Obviously, most of this is just speculation. At the time of writing—early 2018—automation has disrupted many industries, but it has not resulted in massive unemployment. In fact, in many countries, such as the United States, unemployment is at a historical low. Nobody can know for sure what sort of impact machine learning and automation will have on different professions in the future, and it is extremely difficult to estimate the timetable of relevant developments, especially because they depend on political decisions and cultural traditions as much as on purely technological breakthroughs. Thus even after self-driving vehicles prove themselves safer and cheaper than human drivers, politicians and consumers might nevertheless block the change for years, perhaps decades.

However, we cannot allow ourselves to be complacent. It is dangerous to just assume that enough new jobs will appear to compensate for any losses. The fact that this has happened during previous waves of automation is absolutely no guarantee that it will happen again under the very different conditions of the twenty-first century. The potential social and political disruptions are so alarming that even if the probability of systemic mass unemployment is low, we should take it very seriously.

In the nineteenth century the Industrial Revolution created new conditions and problems that none of the existing social, economic, and political models could cope with. Feudalism, monarchism, and traditional religions were not adapted to managing industrial metropolises, millions of uprooted workers, or the constantly changing nature of the modern economy. Consequently, humankind had to develop completely new models—liberal democracies, communist dictatorships, and fascist regimes—and it took more than a century of terrible wars and revolutions to experiment with these models, separate the wheat from the chaff, and implement the best solutions. Child labor in Dickensian coal mines, the First World

War, and the Great Ukrainian Famine of 1932–33 constituted just a small part of the tuition fees humankind had to pay.

The challenge posed to humankind in the twenty-first century by infotech and biotech is arguably much bigger than the challenge posed in the previous era by steam engines, railroads, and electricity. And given the immense destructive power of our civilization, we just cannot afford more failed models, world wars, and bloody revolutions. This time around, the failed models might result in nuclear wars, genetically engineered monstrosities, and a complete breakdown of the biosphere. We have to do better than we did in confronting the Industrial Revolution.

FROM EXPLOITATION TO IRRELEVANCE

Potential solutions fall into three main categories: what to do in order to prevent jobs from being lost; what to do in order to create enough new jobs; and what to do if, despite our best efforts, job losses significantly outstrip job creation.

Preventing job losses altogether is an unattractive and probably untenable strategy, because it means giving up the immense positive potential of AI and robotics. Nevertheless, governments might decide to deliberately slow down the pace of automation, in order to lessen the resulting shocks and allow time for readjustments. Technology is never deterministic, and the fact that something can be done does not mean it must be done. Government regulation can successfully block new technologies even if they are commercially viable and economically lucrative. For example, for many decades we have had the technology to create a marketplace for human organs, complete with human "body farms" in underdeveloped countries and an almost insatiable demand from desperate affluent buyers. Such body farms could well be worth hundreds of billions of dollars. Yet regulations have prevented free trade in human body parts, and though there is a black market in organs, it is far smaller and more circumscribed than what one might have expected.[22]

Slowing down the pace of change may give us time to create enough new jobs to replace most of the losses. Yet as noted earlier, economic entrepreneurship will have to be accompanied by a revolution in education and psychology. Assuming that the new jobs won't be just government sinecures, they will probably demand high levels of expertise, and as AI continues to improve, human employees will need to repeatedly learn new skills and change their profession. Governments will have to step in, both by subsidizing a lifelong education sector and by providing a safety net for the inevitable periods of transition. If a forty-year-old former drone pilot takes three years to reinvent herself as a designer of virtual worlds, she may well need a lot of government help to sustain herself and her family during that time. (This kind of scheme is currently being pioneered in Scandinavia, where governments follow the motto "Protect workers, not jobs.")

Yet even if enough government help were forthcoming, it is far from clear that billions of people would be able to repeatedly reinvent themselves without losing their mental balance. For this reason, if despite all our efforts a significant percentage of humankind is pushed out of the job market, we would have to explore new models for post-work societies, post-work economies, and post-work politics. The first step is to honestly acknowledge that the social, economic, and political models we have inherited from the past are inadequate for dealing with such a challenge.

Take, for example, communism. As automation threatens to shake the capitalist system to its foundation, one might suppose that communism would make a comeback. But communism was not built to exploit that kind of crisis. Twentieth-century communism assumed that the working class was vital for the economy, and communist thinkers tried to teach the proletariat how to translate its immense economic power into political clout. The communist political plan called for a working-class revolution. How relevant will these teachings be if the masses lose their economic value and therefore need to struggle against irrelevance rather than against exploitation? How do you start a working-class revolution without a working class?

Some might argue that humans could never become economically irrelevant, because even if they cannot compete with AI in the workplace, they will always be needed as consumers. However, it is far from certain that the future economy will need us even as consumers. Machines and computers could do that too. Theoretically, you can have an economy in which a mining corporation produces and sells iron to a robotics corporation, and the robotics corporation produces and sells robots to the mining corporation, which mines more iron, which is used to produce more robots, and so on. These corporations can grow and expand to the far reaches of the galaxy, and all they need are robots and computers—they don't even need humans to buy their products.

In fact, today computers and algorithms are already beginning to function as clients in addition to being producers. In the stock exchange, for example, algorithms are becoming the most important buyers of bonds, shares, and commodities. Similarly in the advertising business, the most important customer of all is an algorithm: the Google search algorithm. When people design web pages, they often cater to the taste of the Google search algorithm rather than to the taste of any human being.

Algorithms obviously have no consciousness, so unlike human consumers, they cannot enjoy what they buy, and their decisions are not shaped by sensations and emotions. The Google search algorithm cannot taste ice cream. However, algorithms select things based on their internal calculations and built-in preferences, and these preferences increasingly shape our world. The Google search algorithm has a very sophisticated taste when it comes to ranking the web pages of ice cream vendors, and the most successful ice cream vendors in the world are those that the Google algorithm ranks first—not those that produce the tastiest ice cream.

I know this from personal experience. When I publish a book, my publishers ask me to write a short description that they use for publicity online. But they have a special expert who adapts what I write to the taste of the Google algorithm. The expert goes over my text and says, "Don't use this word—use that word instead. Then we will get more attention from the Google algorithm." We know that if we can just catch the eye of the algorithm, we can take the humans for granted.

So if humans are needed neither as producers nor as consumers, what will safeguard their physical survival and their psychological well-being? We cannot wait for the crisis to erupt in full force before we start looking for answers. By then it will be too late. In order to cope with the unprecedented technological and economic disruptions of the twenty-first century, we need to develop new social and economic models as soon as possible. These models should be guided by the principle of protecting humans rather than jobs. Many jobs are uninspiring drudgery and are not worth saving. Nobody's life's dream is to be a cashier. We should focus instead on providing for people's basic needs and protecting their social status and self-worth.

One new model gaining increasing attention is universal basic income. UBI proposes that governments tax the billionaires and corporations controlling the algorithms and robots, and use that money to provide every person with a generous stipend covering his or her basic needs. This will cushion the poor against job loss and economic dislocation, while protecting the rich from populist rage.[23] A related idea proposes to widen the range of human activities that are considered to be "jobs." At present, billions of parents take care of children, neighbors look after one another, and citizens organize communities, without any of these valuable activities being recognized as jobs. Maybe we need to flip a switch in our minds and realize that taking care of a child is arguably the most important and challenging job in the world. If so, there won't be a shortage of work even if computers and robots replace all the drivers, bankers, and lawyers. The question, of course, is who would evaluate and pay for these newly recognized jobs? Assuming that six-month-old babies will not pay a salary to their mothers, the government will probably have to take this expense upon itself. Assuming too that we would want these salaries to cover all of a family's basic needs, the end result will be something that is not very different from universal basic income.

Alternatively, governments could subsidize universal basic *services* rather than income. Instead of giving money to people, who then shop around for whatever they want, the government might subsidize free education, free healthcare, free transportation, and so forth. This is in fact the utopian vision of communism. Though the communist plan to start a working-class revolution might well become outdated, perhaps we should still aim to realize the communist goal by other means.

It is debatable whether it is better to provide people with universal basic income (the capitalist paradise) or universal basic services (the communist paradise). Both options have advantages and drawbacks. But no matter which paradise you choose, the real problem is in defining what "universal" and "basic" actually mean.

WHAT IS UNIVERSAL?

When people speak about universal basic support—whether in the shape of income or services—they usually mean *national* basic support. Until now, all UBI initiatives have been strictly national or municipal. In January 2017, Finland began a two-year experiment, providing two thousand unemployed Finns with 560 euros a month, irrespective of whether they found work or not. Similar experiments are under way in the Canadian province of Ontario, in the Italian city of Livorno, and in several Dutch cities.[24] (In 2016 Switzerland held a referendum on instituting a national basic income scheme, but voters rejected the idea.)[25]

The problem with such national and municipal schemes, however, is that the main victims of automation may not live in Finland, Ontario, Livorno, or Amsterdam. Globalization has made people in one country utterly dependent on markets in other countries, but automation might unravel large parts of this global trade network with disastrous consequences for the weakest links. In the twentieth century, developing countries lacking natural resources made economic progress mainly by selling the cheap labor of their unskilled workers. Today millions of Bangladeshis make a living by producing shirts and selling them to customers in the United States, while people in Bangalore earn their keep in call centers dealing with the complaints of American customers.[26]

Yet with the rise of AI, robots, and 3-D printers, cheap unskilled labor will become far less important. Instead of manufacturing a shirt in Dhaka and shipping it all the way to the United States, you could buy the shirt's code online from Amazon and print it in New York. The Zara and Prada stores on Fifth Avenue could be replaced by 3-D printing centers in Brooklyn, and some people might even have a printer at home. Simultaneously, instead of calling customer service in Bangalore to complain about your printer, you could talk with an AI representative in the Google cloud (whose accent and tone of voice would be tailored to your preferences). The newly unemployed workers and call center operators in Dhaka and Bangalore don't have the education necessary to switch to designing fashionable shirts or writing computer code—so how will they survive?

If AI and 3-D printers indeed take over from the Bangladeshis and Bangalorians, the revenues that previously flowed to South Asia will now fill the coffers of a few tech giants in California. Instead of economic growth improving conditions all over the world, we might see immense new wealth created in high-tech hubs such as Silicon Valley, while many developing countries collapse.

Of course, some emerging economies—including India and Bangladesh—might advance fast enough to join the winning team. The children or grandchildren of textile workers and call center operators might well become the engineers and entrepreneurs who build and own the computers and 3-D printers. But the time to make such a transition is running out. In the past, cheap unskilled labor served as a secure bridge across the global economic divide, and even if a country advanced slowly, it could expect to reach safety eventually. Taking the right steps was more important than making speedy progress. Yet now the bridge is shaking, and soon it might collapse. Those who have already crossed it—graduating from cheap labor to high-skill industries—will probably be okay. But those lagging behind might find themselves stuck on the wrong side of the chasm without any means of crossing over. What do you do when nobody needs your cheap unskilled laborers and you don't have the resources to build a good education system and teach them new skills?[27]

What then will be the fate of the stragglers? American voters might conceivably agree that taxes paid by Amazon and Google for their U.S. business could be used to give stipends or free services to unemployed miners in Pennsylvania and jobless taxi drivers in New York. But would American voters also agree that these taxes should be sent to support unemployed people in places defined by President Trump as "shithole countries"?[28] If you believe that, you might just as well believe that Santa Claus and the Easter Bunny will solve the problem.

WHAT IS BASIC?

Universal basic support is meant to take care of basic human needs, but there is no accepted definition for that. From a purely biological perspective, a human being needs just 1,500–2,500 calories per day in order to survive. Anything more is a luxury. Yet over and above this biological poverty line, every culture in history has defined additional needs as "basic." In medieval Europe, access to church services was seen as even more important than food, because religion took care of your eternal soul rather than your ephemeral body. In today's Europe, decent education and healthcare services are considered basic human needs, and some argue that even access to the internet is now essential for every man, woman, and child. If in 2050 the United World Government agrees to tax Google, Amazon, Baidu, and Tencent in order to provide basic support for every human being on earth—in Dhaka as well as in Detroit—how will it define "basic"?

For example, what does basic education include: just reading and writing, or also composing computer code and playing the violin? Just six years of elementary school, or everything up to a PhD? And what about healthcare? If by 2050 medical advances make it possible to slow down the aging process and significantly extend human lifespans, will the new treatments be available to all ten billion humans on the planet, or just to a few billionaires? If biotechnology enables parents to upgrade their children, would this be considered a basic human need, or would we see humankind splitting into different biological castes, with rich superhumans enjoying abilities that far surpass those of poor *Homo sapiens*?

Whichever way you choose to define "basic human needs," once you provide them to everyone free of charge, they will be taken for granted, and then fierce social competitions and political struggles will focus on luxuries—be they fancy self-driving cars, access to virtual-reality parks, or enhanced bioengineered bodies. Yet if the unemployed masses command no economic assets, it is hard to see how they could ever hope to obtain such luxuries. Consequently, the gap between the rich (Tencent managers and Google shareholders) and the poor (those dependent on universal basic income) might become not merely bigger but actually unbridgeable.

For this reason, even if some universal support scheme provides poor people in 2050 with much better healthcare and education than they receive today, they might still be extremely angry about global inequality and the lack of social mobility. People will feel that the system is rigged against them, that the government serves only the superrich, and that the future will be even worse for them and their children.[29]

Homo sapiens is just not built for satisfaction. Human happiness depends less on objective conditions and more on our own expectations. Expectations, however, tend to adapt to conditions, including the conditions of *other people*. When things improve, expectations balloon, and so even dramatic improvements in conditions might leave us as dissatisfied as before. If universal basic support is aimed at improving the objective conditions of the average person in 2050, it has a fair chance of succeeding. But if it is aimed at making people subjectively more satisfied with their lot and preventing social discontent, it is likely to fail.

To really achieve its goals, universal basic support will have to be supplemented with some meaningful pursuits, ranging from sports to religion. Perhaps the most successful experiment so far in how to live a contented life in a post-work world has been conducted in Israel. There, about 50 percent of ultra-Orthodox Jewish men never work. They dedicate their lives to studying holy scriptures and performing religious rituals. They and their families don't starve partly because the wives often work and partly because the government provides them with generous subsidies and free services, making sure that they don't lack the basic necessities of life. That's universal basic support *avant la lettre*.[30]

Although they are poor and unemployed, in survey after survey these ultra-Orthodox Jewish men report higher levels of life satisfaction than any other section of Israeli society. This is due to the strength of their community bonds, as well as to the deep meaning they find in studying scripture and performing rituals. A small room full of Jewish men discussing the Talmud might well generate more joy, engagement, and insight than a huge textile sweatshop full of hardworking factory hands. In global surveys of life satisfaction, Israel is usually somewhere near the top, thanks in part to the contribution of these jobless poor people.[31]

Secular Israelis often complain bitterly that the ultra-Orthodox don't contribute enough to society and live off other people's hard work. Secular Israelis also tend to argue that the ultra-Orthodox way of life is unsustainable, especially as ultra-Orthodox families have seven children on average.[32] Sooner or later, the state will not be able to support so many unemployed people, and the ultra-Orthodox will have to go to work. Yet it might be just the reverse. As robots and AI push humans out of the job market, the ultra-Orthodox Jews may come to be seen as the model for the future rather than as a fossil from the past. Not that everyone will become Orthodox Jews and go to yeshivas to study the Talmud. But in the lives of all people, the quest for meaning and community might eclipse the quest for a job.

If we manage to combine a universal economic safety net with strong communities and meaningful pursuits, losing our jobs to algorithms might actually turn out to be a blessing. Losing control over our lives, however, is a much scarier scenario. Notwithstanding the danger of mass unemployment, what we should worry about even more is the shift in authority from humans to algorithms, which might destroy any remaining faith in the liberal story and open the way to the rise of digital dictatorships.

3

....

Liberty

Big Data Is Watching You

The liberal story cherishes human liberty as its number one value. It argues that all authority ultimately stems from the free will of individual humans, as expressed in their feelings, desires, and choices. In politics, liberalism believes that the voter knows best. It therefore upholds democratic elections. In economics, liberalism maintains that the customer is always right. It therefore hails free-market principles. In personal matters, liberalism encourages people to listen to themselves, be true to themselves, and follow their hearts—as long as they do not infringe on the liberties of others. This personal freedom is enshrined in human rights.

In Western political discourse the term "liberal" is sometimes used today in a much narrower partisan sense, to denote those who support specific causes such as gay marriage, gun control, and abortion rights. Yet most so-called conservatives also embrace the broad liberal worldview. In the United States, for example, both Republicans and Democrats should occasionally take a break from their heated quarrels to remind themselves that they all agree on fundamentals, such as free elections, an independent judiciary, and human rights.

In particular, it is vital to remember that right-wing heroes such as Ronald Reagan and Margaret Thatcher were great champions not only of economic freedoms but also of individual liberties. In a famous interview in 1987, Thatcher said, "There is no such thing as society. There is [a] living tapestry of men and women . . . and the quality of our lives will depend upon how much each of us is prepared to take responsibility for ourselves."[1]

Thatcher's heirs in the Conservative Party fully agree with the Labour Party that political authority comes from the feelings, choices, and free will of individual voters. When Britain needed to decide whether it should leave the European Union, Prime Minister David Cameron didn't ask Queen Elizabeth II, the Archbishop of Canterbury, or the Oxford and Cambridge dons to resolve the issue. He didn't even ask the members of Parliament. Rather, he held a referendum in which each and every Brit was asked: "What do you *feel* about it?"

You might counter that people were asked "What do you think?" rather than "What do you feel?," but this is a common misperception. Referendums and elections are always about human *feelings*, not about human rationality. If democracy were a matter of rational decision-making, there would be absolutely no reason to give all people equal voting rights—or perhaps any voting rights at all. There is ample evidence that some people are far more knowledgeable and rational than others, certainly when it comes to specific economic and political questions.[2] In the wake of the Brexit vote, eminent biologist Richard Dawkins protested that the vast majority of the British public—including himself—should never have been asked to vote in the referendum, because they lacked the necessary background in economics and political science. "You might as well call a nationwide plebiscite to decide whether Einstein got his algebra right, or let passengers vote on which runway the pilot should land."[3]

However, for better or worse, elections and referendums are not about what we think. They are about what we feel. And when it comes to feelings, Einstein and Dawkins are no better than anyone else. Democracy assumes that human feelings reflect a mysterious and profound "free will," that this "free will" is the ultimate source of authority, and that while some people are more intelligent than others, all humans are equally free. Like Einstein and Dawkins, an illiterate maid also has free will, and therefore on election day her feelings—represented by her vote—count just as much as anybody else's.

Feelings guide not just voters but their leaders as well. In the 2016 Brexit referendum the Leave campaign was headed by Boris Johnson and Michael Gove. After David Cameron resigned, Gove initially supported Johnson for the premiership, but at the very last minute Gove declared Johnson unfit for the position and announced his own intention to run for it. Gove's action, which destroyed Johnson's chances, was described as a Machiavellian political assassination.[4] But Gove defended his conduct by appealing to his feelings, explaining, "In every step in my political life I have asked myself one question: 'What is the right thing to do? What does your heart tell you?'"[5] That's why, according to Gove, he fought so hard for Brexit, and that's why he felt compelled to backstab his erstwhile ally Boris Johnson and make a bid for the alpha-dog position himself—because his heart told him to do it.

This reliance on the heart might prove to be the Achilles' heel of liberal democracy. For once somebody (whether in Beijing or in San Francisco) gains the technological ability to hack and manipulate the human heart, democratic politics will mutate into an emotional puppet show.

LISTEN TO THE ALGORITHM

The liberal belief in the feelings and free choices of individuals is neither natural nor very ancient. For thousands of years people believed that authority came from divine laws rather than from the human heart, and that we should therefore sanctify the word of God rather than human liberty. Only in the last few centuries did the source of authority shift from celestial deities to flesh-and-blood humans.

Soon authority might shift again—from humans to algorithms. Just as divine authority was legitimized by religious mythologies, and human authority was justified by the liberal story, so the coming technological revolution might establish the authority of Big Data algorithms, while undermining the very idea of individual freedom.

As mentioned in the previous chapter, scientific insights into the way our brains and bodies work suggest that our feelings are not some uniquely human spiritual quality, and they do not reflect any kind of "free will." Rather, feelings are biochemical mechanisms that all mammals and birds use in order to quickly calculate probabilities of survival and reproduction. Feelings aren't based on intuition, inspiration, or freedom—they are based on calculation.

When a monkey, mouse, or human sees a snake, fear arises because millions of neurons in the brain swiftly calculate the relevant data and conclude that the probability of death is high. Feelings of sexual attraction arise when other biochemical algorithms calculate that a nearby individual offers a high probability of successful mating, social bonding, or some other coveted goal. Moral feelings such as outrage, guilt, or forgiveness derive from neural mechanisms that evolved to enable group cooperation. All these biochemical algorithms were honed through millions of years of evolution. If the feelings of some ancient ancestor were wrong and as a result that person made a fatal mistake, the genes shaping these feelings did not pass on to the next generation. Feelings are therefore not the opposite of rationality—they embody evolutionary rationality.

We usually fail to realize that feelings are in fact calculations, because the rapid process of calculation occurs far below our threshold of awareness. We don't feel the millions of neurons in the brain computing probabilities of survival and reproduction, so we erroneously believe that our fear of snakes, our choice of sexual mates, or our opinions about the European Union are the result of some mysterious "free will."

Though liberalism is wrong to think that our feelings reflect free will, up until today relying on feelings still made good practical sense. For although there was nothing magical or free about our feelings, they were the best method in the universe for deciding what to study, whom to marry, and which party to vote for. And no outside system could hope to understand my feelings better than me. Even if the Spanish Inquisition or the Soviet KGB spied on me every minute of every day, they lacked the biological knowledge and the computing power necessary to hack the biochemical processes shaping my desires and choices. For all practical purposes, it was reasonable to argue that I have free will, because my will was shaped mainly by the interplay of inner forces, which nobody outside me could see. I could enjoy the illusion that I controlled my secret inner arena, while outsiders could never really understand what was happening inside me and how I make decisions.

Accordingly, liberalism was correct in counseling people to follow their hearts rather than the dictates of some priest or party apparatchik. However, soon computer algorithms might be able to give you better counsel than human feelings. As the Spanish Inquisition and the KGB give way to Google and Baidu, "free will" likely will be exposed as a myth, and liberalism might lose its practical advantages.

For we are now at the confluence of two immense revolutions. Biologists are deciphering the mysteries of the human body, and in particular of the brain and human feelings. At the same time computer scientists are giving us unprecedented data-processing power. When the biotech revolution merges with the infotech revolution, it will produce Big Data algorithms that can monitor and understand my feelings much better than I can, and then authority will probably shift from humans to computers. My illusion of free will is likely to disintegrate as I daily encounter institutions, corporations, and government agencies that understand and manipulate what was until now my inaccessible inner realm.

This is already happening in the field of medicine. The most important medical decisions in our lives rely not on our feelings of illness or wellness, or even on the informed predictions of our doctor, but on the calculations of computers that understand our bodies much better than we do. Within a few decades, Big Data algorithms informed by a constant stream of biometric data could monitor our health 24/7. They might be able to detect the very beginning of influenza, cancer, or Alzheimer's disease, long before we feel anything is wrong with us. They could then recommend appropriate treatments, diets, and daily regimens, custom-built for our unique physique, DNA, and personality.

People will enjoy the best healthcare in history, but for precisely this reason they will probably be sick all the time. There is always something wrong somewhere in the body. There is always something that can be improved. In the past, you felt perfectly healthy as long as you didn't sense pain and you didn't manifest an apparent disability by, say, limping. But by 2050, thanks to biometric sensors and Big Data algorithms, diseases may be diagnosed and treated long before they lead to pain or disability. As a result, you will always find yourself suffering from some "medical condition" and following this or that algorithmic recommendation. If you refuse, perhaps your medical insurance will become invalid, or your boss will fire you—why should they pay the price of your obstinacy?

It is one thing to continue smoking despite general statistics that connect smoking with lung cancer. It is a very different thing to continue smoking despite a concrete warning from a biometric sensor that has just detected seventeen cancerous cells in your upper left lung. And if you are willing to defy the sensor, what will you do when the sensor forwards the warning to your insurance agency, your manager, and your mother?

Who will have the time and energy to deal with all these illnesses? In all likelihood, we could just instruct our health algorithm to deal with most of these problems as it sees fit. At most, it will send periodic updates to our smartphones, telling us that "seventeen cancerous cells were detected and destroyed." Hypochondriacs might dutifully read these updates, but most of us will ignore them, just as we ignore those annoying antivirus notices on our computers.

THE DRAMA OF DECISION-MAKING

What is already beginning to happen in medicine is likely to occur in more and more fields. The key invention is the biometric sensor, which people can wear on or inside their bodies, and which converts biological processes into electronic information that computers can store and analyze. Given enough biometric data and enough computing power, external data-processing systems can hack all your desires, decisions, and opinions. They can know exactly who you are.

Most people don't know themselves very well. When I was twenty-one, I finally realized that I was gay, after several years of living in denial. That's hardly exceptional. Many gay men spend their entire teenage years unsure about their sexuality. Now imagine the situation in 2050, when an algorithm can tell any teenager exactly where he is on the gay/straight spectrum (and even how malleable that position is). Perhaps the algorithm will show you pictures or videos of attractive men and women, track your eye movements, blood pressure, and brain activity, and within five minutes display a number on the Kinsey scale.[6] Such an invention could have saved me years of frustration. Perhaps you personally wouldn't want to take such a test, but then maybe you'll find yourself with a group of friends at Michelle's boring birthday party, and somebody suggests that you all take turns checking yourself on this cool new algorithm (with everybody standing around to watch the results—and comment on them). Would you just walk away?

Even if you do, and even if you keep hiding from yourself and your classmates, you won't be able to hide from Amazon, Alibaba, or the secret police. As you surf the web, watch YouTube, or read your social media feed, the algorithms will discreetly monitor you, analyze you, and tell Coca-Cola that if it wants to sell you some fizzy drink, it had better use the advertisement with the shirtless guy rather than the shirtless girl. You won't even know. But they will know, and such information will be worth billions.

Then again, maybe people will share their information willingly in order to get better recommendations—and eventually in order to get the algorithm to make decisions for them. It starts with simple things, like sitting down with friends to spend a cozy evening in front of the TV. Fifty years ago you had very little choice about what you could watch, but today, with the rise of view-on-demand services, there are thousands of titles available. Reaching an agreement can be quite difficult, because while you like science-fiction thrillers, Jack prefers romantic comedies, and Jill votes for artsy French films. You may well end up compromising on some mediocre B-movie that disappoints all of you.

An algorithm might help. You can tell it which previous movies each of you really liked, and based on its massive statistical database, the algorithm can then find the perfect match for the group. Unfortunately, such a crude algorithm is easily misled, particularly because self-reporting is a notoriously unreliable gauge for people's true preferences. It often happens that when we hear lots of people praise some movie as a masterpiece, we feel compelled to watch it, and even though we might fall asleep midway through, we don't want to look like philistines, so we tell everyone it was an amazing experience.[7]

Such problems, however, can be solved if we just allow the algorithm to collect real-time data on us as we actually watch movies, instead of relying on our own dubious self-reports. For starters, the algorithm can monitor which movies we completed, and which we stopped watching halfway through. Even if we tell the whole world that *Gone with the Wind* is the best movie ever made, the algorithm will know that we never made it past the first half-hour and never saw Atlanta burning.

Yet the algorithm can go much deeper than that. Engineers are currently developing software that can detect human emotions based on the movements of our eyes and facial muscles.[8] Add a good camera to the television, and such software will know which scenes made us laugh, which scenes made us sad, and which scenes bored us. Next, connect the algorithm to biometric sensors, and the algorithm will know how each frame influenced our heart rate, our blood pressure, and our brain activity. As we watch, say, Tarantino's *Pulp Fiction*, the algorithm might note that the rape scene caused us an almost imperceptible tinge of sexual arousal, that when Vincent accidentally shot Marvin in the face it made us laugh guiltily, and that we didn't get the joke about the Big Kahuna Burger but we laughed anyway so that we wouldn't look stupid. When you force yourself to laugh, you use different brain circuits and muscles than when you laugh because something is really funny. Humans cannot usually detect the difference. But a biometric sensor could.[9]

The word "television" comes from Greek *tele*, which means "far," and Latin *visio*, "sight." It was originally conceived as a device that would allow us to see from afar. But soon it might allow us also to *be seen* from afar. As George Orwell envisioned in *1984*, the television might watch us while we are watching it. After we've finished watching Tarantino's entire filmography, we may have forgotten most of it. But Netflix, or Amazon, or whoever owns the TV algorithm will know our personality type and how to press our emotional buttons. Such data could enable Netflix and Amazon to choose movies for us with uncanny precision, but it could also enable them to make the most important decisions in life for us—such as what to study, where to work, and whom to marry.

Of course, Amazon won't be correct all the time. That's impossible. Algorithms will repeatedly make mistakes due to insufficient data, faulty programming, muddled goal definitions, and the chaotic nature of life.[10] But Amazon won't have to be perfect. It will just need to be better on average than us humans. And that is not so difficult, because most people don't know themselves very well, and most people often make terrible mistakes in the most important decisions of their lives. Even more than algorithms, humans suffer from insufficient data, from faulty programming (genetic and cultural), from muddled definitions, and from the chaos of life.

You may well list the many problems that beset algorithms, and conclude that people will never trust them. But this is a bit like cataloguing all the drawbacks of democracy and concluding that no sane person would ever choose to support such a system. Winston Churchill famously said that democracy is the worst political system in the world, except for all the others. Rightly or wrongly, people might reach the same conclusions about Big Data algorithms: they have lots of glitches, but we have no better alternative.

As scientists gain a deeper understanding of the way humans make decisions, the temptation to rely on algorithms is likely to increase. Hacking human decision-making not only will make Big Data algorithms more reliable but also will simultaneously make human feelings *less* reliable. As governments and corporations succeed in hacking the human operating system, we will be exposed to a barrage of precision-guided manipulation, advertisements, and propaganda. It might become so easy to manipulate our opinions and emotions that we will be forced to rely on algorithms in the same way that a pilot suffering an attack of vertigo must ignore what his own senses are telling him and put all his trust in the machinery.

In some countries and in some situations, people might not be given any choice, and they will be forced to obey the decisions of

Big Data algorithms. Yet even in allegedly free societies, algorithms might gain authority because we will learn from experience to trust them on more and more issues, and we will gradually lose our ability to make decisions for ourselves. Just think of the way that within a mere two decades, billions of people have come to entrust the Google search algorithm with one of the most important tasks of all: searching for relevant and trustworthy information. We no longer search for information. Instead, we google. And as we increasingly rely on Google for answers, so our ability to search for information by ourselves diminishes. Already today, "truth" is defined by the top results of the Google search.[11]

This has also been happening with physical abilities, such as navigating space. People ask Google to guide them around. When they reach an intersection, their gut feeling might tell them "turn left," but Google Maps says "turn right." At first they listen to their gut feeling, turn left, get stuck in a traffic jam, and miss an important meeting. Next time they listen to Google, turn right, and make it on time. They learn from experience to trust Google. Within a year or two, they blindly rely on whatever Google Maps tells them, and if their smartphone fails, they are completely clueless. In March 2012 three Japanese tourists in Australia decided to take a day trip to a small offshore island, and drove their car straight into the Pacific Ocean. The driver, twenty-one-year-old Yuzu Nuda, later said that she just followed the instructions of the GPS and "it told us we could drive down there. It kept saying it would navigate us to a road. We got stuck."[12] In several similar incidents people drove into a lake or fell off a demolished bridge by following GPS instructions.[13] The ability to navigate is like a muscle—use it or lose it.[14] The same is true for the ability to choose spouses or professions.

Every year millions of youngsters need to decide what to study in college. This is a very important and difficult decision. You are under pressure from your parents, your friends, and your teachers, who have different interests and opinions. You also have your own fears and fantasies to deal with. Your judgment is clouded and manipulated by Hollywood blockbusters, trashy novels, and sophisticated advertising campaigns. It is particularly difficult to make a wise decision because you do not really know what it takes to succeed in different professions, and you don't necessarily have a realistic image of your own strengths and weaknesses. What does it take to succeed as a lawyer? How do I perform under pressure? Am I a good team worker?

One student might start law school because she has an inaccurate understanding of her own skills and an even more distorted view of what being a lawyer actually involves (you don't get to give dramatic speeches and shout "Objection, Your Honor!" all day). Meanwhile, her friend decides to fulfill a childhood dream and study professional ballet, even though she doesn't have the necessary bone structure or discipline. Years later, both deeply regret their choices. In the future we will be able to rely on Google to make such decisions for us. Google could tell me that I would be wasting my time in law or ballet school but that I might make an excellent (and very happy) psychologist or plumber.[15]

Once AI makes better decisions than we do about careers and perhaps even relationships, our concept of humanity and of life will have to change. Humans are used to thinking about life as a drama of decision-making. Liberal democracy and free-market capitalism see the individual as an autonomous agent constantly making choices about the world. Works of art—be they Shakespeare plays, Jane Austen novels, or tacky Hollywood comedies—usually revolve around the hero having to make some particularly crucial decision. To be or not to be? To listen to my wife and kill King Duncan, or listen to my conscience and spare him? To marry Mr. Collins or Mr. Darcy? Christian and Muslim theology similarly focus on the drama of decision-making, arguing that everlasting salvation depends on making the right choice.

What will happen to this view of life as we increasingly rely on AI to make decisions for us? At present we trust Netflix to recommend movies, and Google Maps to choose whether we turn right or left.

But once we begin to count on AI to decide what to study, where to work, and whom to marry, human life will cease to be a drama of decision-making. Democratic elections and free markets will make little sense. So would most religions and works of art. Imagine Anna Karenina taking out her smartphone and asking the Facebook algorithm whether she should stay married to Karenin or elope with the dashing Count Vronsky. Or imagine your favorite Shakespeare play with all the crucial decisions made by the Google algorithm. Hamlet and Macbeth will have much more comfortable lives, but what kind of lives will those be? Do we have models for making sense of such lives?

As authority shifts from humans to algorithms, we may no longer view the world as the playground of autonomous individuals struggling to make the right choices. Instead, we might perceive the entire universe as a flow of data, see organisms as little more than biochemical algorithms, and believe that humanity's cosmic vocation is to create an all-encompassing data-processing system—and then merge into it. Already today we are becoming tiny chips inside a giant data-processing system that nobody really understands. Every day I absorb countless data bits through emails, tweets, and articles, process the data, and transmit back new bits through more emails, tweets, and articles. I don't really know where I fit into the great scheme of things, or how my bits of data connect with the bits produced by billions of other humans and computers. I don't have time to find out, because I am too busy answering all these emails.

THE PHILOSOPHICAL CAR

People might argue that algorithms will never make important decisions for us, because important decisions usually involve an ethical dimension, and algorithms don't understand ethics. Yet there is no reason to assume that algorithms won't be able to outperform the average human even in ethics. Today, as devices such as smartphones and autonomous vehicles undertake decisions that used to be a human monopoly, their creators are already starting to grapple with the same kinds of ethical problems that have bedeviled humans for millennia.

For example, suppose two kids chasing a ball jump right in front of a self-driving car. Based on its lightning calculations, the algorithm driving the car concludes that the only way to avoid hitting the two kids is to swerve into the opposite lane and risk colliding with an oncoming truck. The algorithm calculates that in such a case there is a 70 percent chance that the owner of the car—who is fast asleep in the backseat—will be killed. What should the algorithm do?[16]

Philosophers have been arguing about such "trolley problems" for millennia (they are so called because the textbook examples in modern philosophical debates refer to a runaway trolley car racing down a track, rather than to a self-driving car).[17] Up till now, these arguments have had embarrassingly little impact on actual behavior, because in times of crisis humans all too often forget about their philosophical views and follow their emotions and gut instincts instead.

One of the nastiest experiments in the history of the social sciences was conducted in December 1970 on a group of students at the Princeton Theological Seminary, who were training to become ministers in the Presbyterian Church. Each student was asked to hurry to a distant lecture hall to give a talk on the Good Samaritan parable, which tells how a Jew traveling from Jerusalem to Jericho was robbed and beaten by criminals, who then left him to die by the side of the road. After some time a priest and a Levite walk by, but both ignore the man. In contrast, a Samaritan—a member of a sect much despised by the Jews—stops when he sees the victim, takes care of him, and saves his life. The moral of the parable is that people's merit should be judged by their actual behavior rather than by their religious affiliation and philosophical views.

The eager young seminarians rushed to the lecture hall, contemplating on the way how best to explain the moral of the parable. But the experimenters planted in their path a shabbily dressed person who was sitting slumped in a doorway with his head down and his eyes closed. As each unsuspecting seminarian hurried past, the "victim" coughed and groaned pitifully. Most seminarians did not even stop to inquire what was wrong with the man, let alone offer any help. The emotional stress created by the need to hurry to the lecture hall trumped their moral obligation to help strangers in distress.[18]

Human emotions trump philosophical theories in countless other situations. This makes the ethical and philosophical history of the world a rather depressing tale of wonderful ideals and less-than-ideal behavior. How many Christians actually turn the other cheek, how many Buddhists actually rise above egoistic obsessions, and how many Jews actually love their neighbors as themselves? That's just the way natural selection has shaped Homo sapiens. Like all mammals, Homo sapiens uses emotions to quickly make life-and-death decisions. We have inherited our anger, our fear, and our lust from millions of ancestors, all of whom passed the most rigorous quality control tests of natural selection.

Unfortunately, what was good for survival and reproduction in the African savannah a million years ago does not necessarily make for responsible behavior on twenty-first-century motorways. Distracted, angry, and anxious human drivers kill more than a million people in traffic accidents every year. We can send all our philosophers, prophets, and priests to preach ethics to these drivers, but on the road, mammalian emotions and savannah instincts will still take over. Consequently, seminarians in a rush will ignore people in distress, and drivers in a crisis will run over hapless pedestrians.

This disjunction between the seminary and the road is one of the biggest practical problems in ethics. Immanuel Kant, John Stuart Mill, and John Rawls can sit in some cozy university hall and discuss theoretical ethical problems for days—but would their conclusions actually be implemented by stressed-out drivers caught in a split-second emergency? Perhaps Michael Schumacher—the Formula One champion who is sometimes hailed as the best driver in history—had the ability to think about philosophy while racing a car, but most of us aren't Schumacher.

Computer algorithms, however, have not been shaped by natural selection, and they have neither emotions nor gut instincts. Therefore in moments of crisis they could follow ethical guidelines much better than humans—provided we find a way to code ethics in precise numbers and statistics. If we could teach Kant, Mill, and Rawls to write code, they would be able to program the self-driving car in their cozy laboratory and be certain that the car would follow their commandments on the highway. In effect, every car would be driven by Michael Schumacher and Immanuel Kant rolled into one.

If you program a self-driving car to stop and help strangers in distress, it will do so come hell or high water (unless, of course, you insert an exception clause for infernal or high-water scenarios). Similarly, if your self-driving car is programmed to swerve into the opposite lane in order to save the two kids in its path, you can bet your life this is exactly what it will do. Which means that when designing their self-driving car, Toyota or Tesla will be transforming a theoretical problem in the philosophy of ethics into a practical problem of engineering.

Granted, the philosophical algorithms will never be perfect. Mistakes will still happen, resulting in injuries, deaths, and extremely complicated lawsuits. (For the first time in history, you might be able to sue a philosopher for the unfortunate results of his or her theories, because for the first time in history you might be able to prove a direct causal link between philosophical ideas and real-life events.) However, in order to take over from human drivers, the algorithms won't have to be perfect. They will just have to be better than the humans. Given that human drivers kill more than a million people each year, that isn't such a tall order. When all is said and done, would you rather the car next to you was being driven by a drunk teenager or by the Schumacher-Kant team?[19]

The same logic is true not just of driving but of many other situations as well. Take, for example, job applications. In the twenty-first century, the decision whether to hire somebody for a job will increasingly be made by algorithms. We cannot rely on the machine to set the relevant ethical standards; humans will still need to do that. But once we decide on an ethical standard in the job market—that it is wrong to discriminate against blacks or against women, for example—we can rely on machines to implement and maintain this standard better than humans.[20]

A human manager may know and even agree that it is unethical to discriminate against blacks and women, but then when a black woman applies for a job, the manager subconsciously discriminates against her and decides not to hire her. If we allow a computer to evaluate job applications and program the computer to completely ignore race and gender, we can be certain that the computer will indeed ignore these factors, because computers don't have a subconscious. Of course, it won't be easy to write code for evaluating job applications, and there is always a danger that the engineers will somehow program their own subconscious biases into the software.[21] Yet once we discover such mistakes, it would probably be far easier to debug the software than to rid humans of their racist and misogynist biases.

We saw that the rise of artificial intelligence might push most humans out of the job market—including drivers and traffic police (since when rowdy humans are replaced by obedient algorithms, traffic police will be redundant). However, there might be some new openings for philosophers, because their skills—until now devoid of much market value—will suddenly be in very high demand. So if you want to study something that will guarantee a good job in the future, maybe philosophy is not such a bad gamble.

Of course, philosophers seldom agree on the right course of action. Few trolley problems have been solved to the satisfaction of all philosophers, and consequentialist thinkers such as John Stuart Mill (who judge actions by consequences) hold quite different opinions from deontologists such as Immanuel Kant (who judge actions by absolute rules). Would Tesla have to actually take a stance on such knotty matters in order to produce a car?

Well, maybe Tesla will just leave it to the market. Tesla could produce two models of the self-driving car: the Tesla Altruist and the Tesla Egoist. In an emergency, the Altruist sacrifices its owner to the greater good, whereas the Egoist does everything in its power to save its owner, even if it means killing the two kids. Customers will then be able to buy the car that best fits their favorite philosophical view. If more people buy the Tesla Egoist, you won't be able to blame Tesla for that. After all, the customer is always right.

This is not a joke. In a pioneering 2015 study people were presented with a hypothetical scenario of a self-driving car about to run over several pedestrians. Most said that in such a case the car should save the pedestrians even at the price of killing its owner. When they were then asked whether they personally would buy a car programmed to sacrifice its owner for the greater good, most said no. For themselves, they would prefer the Tesla Egoist.[22]

Imagine this situation: you have bought a new car, but before you can start using it, you must open the settings menu and check one of several boxes. In case of an accident, do you want the car to sacrifice your life or to kill the family in the other vehicle? Is this a choice you even want to make? Just think of the arguments you are going to have with your husband about which box to check.

So maybe the state should intervene to regulate the market and lay down an ethical code binding all self-driving cars. Some lawmakers will doubtless be thrilled by the opportunity to finally make laws that are *always* followed to the letter. Others may be alarmed by such unprecedented and totalitarian responsibility. After all, throughout history the limitations of actually enforcing laws provided a welcome check on the biases, mistakes, and excesses of lawmakers. It was an extremely lucky thing that laws against homosexuality and blasphemy were only partially enforced. Do we really want a system in which the decisions of fallible politicians become as inexorable as gravity?

DIGITAL DICTATORSHIPS

AI often frightens people because they don't trust the AI to remain obedient. We have seen too many science-fiction movies about robots rebelling against their human masters, running amok in the streets, and slaughtering everyone. Yet the real problem with robots is exactly the opposite. We should fear them because they will probably always obey their masters and never rebel.

There is nothing wrong with blind obedience, of course, as long as the robots happen to serve benign masters. Even in warfare, reliance on killer robots could ensure that for the first time in history, the laws of war would actually be obeyed on the battlefield. Human soldiers are sometimes driven by their emotions to murder, pillage, and rape in violation of the laws of war. We usually associate emotions with compassion, love, and empathy, but in wartime, the emotions that take control are all too often fear, hatred, and cruelty. Since robots have no emotions, they could be trusted to always adhere to the dry letter of the military code and never be swayed by personal fears and hatreds.[23]

On March 16, 1968, a company of American soldiers went berserk in the South Vietnamese village of My Lai and massacred about four hundred civilians. This war crime resulted from the local initiative of men who had been involved in jungle guerrilla warfare for several months. It did not serve any strategic purpose and contravened both U.S. legal code and military policy. It was the fault of human emotions.[24] If the United States had deployed killer robots in Vietnam, the massacre at My Lai never would have occurred.

Nevertheless, before we rush to develop and deploy killer robots, we need to remind ourselves that the robots always reflect and amplify the qualities of their code. If the code is restrained and benign, the robots will probably be a huge improvement over the average human soldier. Yet if the code is ruthless and cruel, the results will be catastrophic. The real problem with robots is not their own artificial intelligence but rather the natural stupidity and cruelty of their human masters.

In July 1995 Bosnian Serb troops massacred more than eight thousand Muslim Bosniaks around the town of Srebrenica. Unlike the haphazard My Lai massacre, the Srebrenica killings were a protracted and well-organized operation that reflected Bosnian Serb policy to "ethnically cleanse" Bosnia of Muslims.[25] If the Bosnian Serbs had had killer robots in 1995, it would likely have made the atrocity worse rather than better. Not one robot would have had a moment's hesitation carrying out whatever orders it received, and none would have spared the life of a single Muslim child due to feelings of compassion, disgust, or mere lethargy.

A ruthless dictator armed with such killer robots will never have to fear that his soldiers will turn against him, no matter how heartless or crazy his orders. A robot army would probably have strangled the French Revolution in its cradle in 1789, and if in 2011 Hosni Mubarak had had a contingent of killer robots he could have unleashed them on the populace without fear of defection. Similarly, an imperialist government relying on a robot army could wage unpopular wars without any concern that its robots might lose their motivation, or that their families might stage protests. If the United States had had killer robots in the Vietnam War, the My Lai massacre might have been prevented, but the war itself could have dragged on for many more years, because the American government would have had fewer worries about demoralized soldiers, massive antiwar demonstrations, or a movement of "veteran robots against the war." (Some American citizens might still have objected to the war, but without the fear of being drafted themselves, the memory of personally committing atrocities, or the painful loss of a dear relative, the protesters probably would have been both less numerous and less committed.)[26]

These kinds of problems are far less relevant to autonomous civilian vehicles, since no car manufacturer would maliciously program its vehicles to target and kill people. Yet autonomous weapon systems are a catastrophe waiting to happen, because too many governments tend to be ethically corrupt, if not downright evil.

The danger is not restricted to killing machines. Surveillance systems could be equally risky. In the hands of a benign government, powerful surveillance algorithms could be the best thing that ever happened to humankind. Yet the same Big Data algorithms might also empower a future Big Brother, so we might end up with an Orwellian surveillance regime in which all individuals are monitored all the time.[27]

In fact, we might end up with something that even Orwell could barely imagine: a total surveillance regime that follows not just all our external activities and utterances but can even go under our skin to observe our inner experiences. Consider, for example, what the Kim regime in North Korea might do with the new technology. In the future, each North Korean citizen might be required to wear a biometric bracelet that monitors everything that person does and says, as well as their blood pressure and brain activity. By using our growing understanding of the human brain and drawing on the immense powers of machine learning, the North Korean regime might be able for the first time in history to gauge what each and every citizen is thinking at each and every moment. If a North Korean looks at a picture of Kim Jong-un and the biometric sensors pick up the telltale signs of anger (higher blood pressure, increased activity in the amygdala), that person will be in the gulag tomorrow morning.

Granted, due to its isolation the North Korean regime might have difficulty developing the required technology by itself. However, the technology might be pioneered in more tech-savvy nations and copied or bought by the North Koreans and other backward dictatorships. Both China and Russia are constantly improving their surveillance tools, as are a number of democratic countries, ranging from the United States to my home country, Israel. Nicknamed "the start-up nation," Israel has an extremely vibrant high-tech sector and a cutting-edge cybersecurity industry. At the same time it is also locked in a deadly conflict with the Palestinians, and at least some of its leaders, generals, and citizens might well be happy to create a total surveillance regime in the West Bank as soon as they have the necessary technology.

Already today whenever Palestinians make a phone call, post something on Facebook, or travel from one city to another, they are likely to be monitored by Israeli microphones, cameras, drones, or spy software. The gathered data is then analyzed with the aid of Big Data algorithms. This helps the Israeli security forces to pinpoint and neutralize potential threats without having to place too many boots on the ground. The Palestinians may administer some towns and villages in the West Bank, but the Israelis control the sky, the airwaves, and cyberspace. It therefore takes surprisingly few Israeli soldiers to effectively control about 2.5 million Palestinians in the West Bank.[28]

In one tragicomic incident in October 2017, a Palestinian laborer posted to his private Facebook account a picture of himself in his workplace, alongside a bulldozer. Adjacent to the image he wrote "Good morning!" An automatic algorithm made a small error when transliterating the Arabic letters. Instead of *ysabechhum* (which means "good morning"), the algorithm identified the letters as *ydbachhum* (which means "kill them"). Suspecting that the man might be a terrorist intending to use a bulldozer to run people over, Israeli security forces swiftly arrested him. He was released after they realized that the algorithm made a mistake. But the offending Facebook post was nevertheless taken down. You can never be too careful.[29] What Palestinians are experiencing today in the West Bank might be just a primitive preview of what billions will eventually experience all over the planet.

In the late twentieth century democracies usually outperformed dictatorships because democracies were better at data processing. A democracy diffuses the power to process information and make decisions among many people and institutions, whereas a dictatorship concentrates information and power in one place. Given twentieth-century technology, it was inefficient to concentrate too much information and power in one place. Nobody had the ability to process all the information fast enough and make the right decisions. This is part of the reason the Soviet Union made far worse decisions than the United States, and why the Soviet economy lagged far behind the American economy.

However, soon AI might swing the pendulum in the opposite direction. AI makes it possible to process enormous amounts of information centrally. In fact, AI might make centralized systems far more efficient than diffused systems, because machine learning works better the more information it can analyze. If you disregard all privacy concerns and concentrate all the information relating to a billion people in one database, you can train much better algorithms than if you respect individual privacy and have in your database only partial information on a million people. For example, if an authoritarian government orders all its citizens to have their DNA scanned and to share all their medical data with some central authority, it would gain an immense advantage in genetics and medical research over societies in which medical data is strictly private. The main handicap of authoritarian regimes in the twentieth century—the attempt to concentrate all information in one place—might become their decisive advantage in the twenty-first century.

As algorithms come to know us so well, authoritarian governments could gain absolute control over their citizens, even more so than in Nazi Germany, and resistance to such regimes might be utterly impossible. Not only will the regime know exactly how you feel, but it could make you feel whatever it wants. The dictator might not be able to provide citizens with healthcare or equality, but he could make them love him and hate his opponents. Democracy in its present form cannot survive the merger of biotech and infotech. Either democracy will successfully reinvent itself in a radically new form or humans will come to live in "digital dictatorships."

This will not be a return to the days of Hitler and Stalin. Digital dictatorships will be as different from Nazi Germany as Nazi Germany was different from ancien régime France. Louis XIV was a centralizing autocrat, but he did not have the technology to build a modern totalitarian state. He suffered no opposition to his rule, yet in the absence of radios, telephones, and trains, he had little control over the day-to-day lives of peasants in remote Breton villages, or even of townspeople in the heart of Paris. He had neither the will nor the ability to establish a mass party, a countrywide youth movement, or a national education system.[30] It was the new technologies of the twentieth century that gave Hitler both the motivation and the power to do such things. We cannot predict the motivations and powers of digital dictatorships in 2084, but it is very unlikely that they will just copy Hitler and Stalin. Those gearing themselves up to refight the battles of the 1930s might be caught off guard by an attack from a totally different direction.

Even if democracy manages to adapt and survive, people might become the victims of new kinds of oppression and discrimination. Today more and more banks, corporations, and institutions are already using algorithms to analyze data and make decisions about us. For example, when you apply to your bank for a loan, it is likely that your application will be processed by an algorithm rather than by a human being. The algorithm analyzes lots of data about you and statistics about millions of other people and decides whether you are reliable enough to receive a loan. Often the algorithm does a better job than a human banker. But the problem is that if the algorithm discriminates against some people unjustly, it is difficult to know that. If the bank refuses to give you a loan, and you ask, "Why?," the bank replies, "The algorithm said no." You ask, "Why did the algorithm say no? What's wrong with me?," and the bank replies, "We don't know. No human understands this algorithm, because it is based on advanced machine learning. But we trust our algorithm, so we won't give you a loan."[31]

When discrimination is directed against entire groups, such as women or blacks, these groups can organize and protest against their collective discrimination. But now an algorithm might discriminate against you personally, and you will have no idea why. Maybe the algorithm will find something in your DNA, your personal history, or your Facebook account that it does not like. The algorithm discriminates against you not because you are a woman or an African American but because you are you. You don't know the exact reasons, and even if you knew, you would not be able to organize a protest with other people, because there are no other people suffering the exact same prejudice. Instead of just collective discrimination, in the twenty-first century we might face a growing problem of individual discrimination.[32]

At the highest levels of authority, we will probably retain human figureheads, who will give us the illusion that the algorithms are only advisers and that ultimate authority is still in human hands. We will not appoint an AI to be the chancellor of Germany or the CEO of Google. However, the decisions taken by the chancellor and the CEO will be shaped by AI. The chancellor could still choose between several different options, but all those options will be the outcome of Big Data analysis, and they will reflect the way AI views the world more than the way humans view it.

To take an analogous example, today politicians all over the world can choose between several different economic policies, but in almost all cases the various policies on offer reflect a capitalist outlook on economics. The politicians have an illusion of choice, but the really important decisions have already been made much earlier by the economists, bankers, and businesspeople who shaped the different options on the menu. Within a couple of decades, politicians might find themselves choosing from a menu written by AI.

ARTIFICIAL INTELLIGENCE AND NATURAL STUPIDITY

One piece of good news is that at least for the next few decades, we won't have to deal with the full-blown science-fiction nightmare of AI gaining consciousness and deciding to enslave or wipe out humanity. We will increasingly rely on algorithms to make decisions for us, but it is unlikely that the algorithms will start to consciously manipulate us. They won't have any consciousness.

Science fiction tends to confuse intelligence with consciousness and assume that in order to match or surpass human intelligence, computers will have to develop consciousness. The basic plot of almost all movies and novels about AI revolves around the magical moment when a computer or a robot gains consciousness. Once that happens, either the human hero falls in love with the robot or the robot tries to kill all the humans; sometimes both things happen simultaneously.

But in reality, there is no reason to assume that artificial intelligence will gain consciousness, because intelligence and consciousness are very different things. Intelligence is the ability to solve problems. Consciousness is the ability to feel things such as pain, joy, love, and anger. We tend to confuse the two because in humans and other mammals intelligence goes hand in hand with consciousness. Mammals solve most problems by feeling things. Computers, however, solve problems in a very different way.

There are several different paths leading to high intelligence, and only some of these paths involve gaining consciousness. Just as airplanes fly faster than birds without ever developing feathers, so computers may come to solve problems much better than mammals without ever developing feelings. True, AI will have to analyze human feelings accurately in order to treat human illnesses, identify human terrorists, recommend human mates, and navigate a street full of human pedestrians. But it could do so without having any feelings of its own. An algorithm does not need to feel joy, anger, or fear in order to recognize the different biochemical patterns of joyful, angry, or frightened apes.

Of course, it is not absolutely impossible that AI will develop feelings of its own. We still don't know enough about consciousness to be sure. In general, there are three possibilities we need to consider:

1. Consciousness is somehow linked to organic biochemistry in such a way that it will never be possible to create consciousness in nonorganic systems.

2. Consciousness is not linked to organic biochemistry, but it is linked to intelligence in such a way that computers could develop consciousness, and computers will *have to* develop consciousness if they are to pass a certain threshold of intelligence.

3. There are no essential links between consciousness and either organic biochemistry or high intelligence. Therefore computers might develop consciousness—but not necessarily. They could become superintelligent while still having zero consciousness.

With our present state of knowledge, we cannot rule out any of these options. Yet precisely because we know so little about consciousness, it seems unlikely that we could program conscious computers anytime soon. Therefore, despite the immense power of artificial intelligence, for the foreseeable future its usage will continue to depend to some extent on human consciousness.

The danger is that if we invest too much in developing AI and too little in developing human consciousness, the very sophisticated artificial intelligence of computers might only serve to empower the natural stupidity of humans. We are unlikely to face a robot rebellion in the coming decades, but we might have to deal with hordes of bots that know how to press our emotional buttons better than our mother does and that use this uncanny ability to try to sell us something—be it a car, a politician, or an entire ideology. The bots could identify our deepest fears, hatreds, and cravings and use these inner leverages against us. We have already been given a foretaste of this in recent elections and referendums across the world, when hackers learned how to manipulate individual voters by analyzing data about them and exploiting their existing prejudices.[33] While science fiction thrillers are drawn to dramatic apocalypses of fire and smoke, in reality we might be facing a banal apocalypse by clicking.

To avoid such outcomes, for every dollar and every minute we invest in improving artificial intelligence, it would be wise to invest a dollar and a minute in advancing human consciousness. Unfortunately, at present we are not doing much in the way of research into human consciousness and ways to develop it. We are researching and developing human abilities mainly according to the immediate needs of the economic and political system, rather than according to our own long-term needs as conscious beings. My boss wants me to answer emails as quickly as possible, but he has little interest in my ability to taste and appreciate the food I am eating. Consequently, I check my emails even during meals, which means I lose the ability to pay attention to my own sensations. The economic system pressures me to expand and diversify my investment portfolio, but it gives me zero incentive to expand and diversify my compassion. So I strive to understand the mysteries of the stock exchange while making far less effort to understand the deep causes of suffering.

In this, humans are similar to other domesticated animals. We have bred docile cows that produce enormous amounts of milk but are otherwise far inferior to their wild ancestors. They are less agile, less curious, and less resourceful.[34] We are now creating tame humans that produce enormous amounts of data and function as very efficient chips in a huge data-processing mechanism, but these data-cows hardly maximize the human potential. Indeed, we have no idea what our full human potential is, because we know so little about the human mind. And yet we don't invest much in exploring the human mind, instead focusing on increasing the speed of our internet connections and the efficiency of our Big Data algorithms. If we are not careful, we will end up with downgraded humans misusing upgraded computers to wreak havoc on themselves and on the world.

Digital dictatorships are not the only danger awaiting us. Alongside liberty, the liberal order has also set great store in the value of equality. Liberalism has always cherished political equality, and it gradually came to realize that economic equality is almost as important. For without a social safety net and a modicum of economic equality, liberty is meaningless. But just as Big Data algorithms might extinguish liberty, they might simultaneously create the most unequal societies that ever existed. All wealth and power might be concentrated in the hands of a tiny elite, while most people will suffer not from exploitation but from something far worse—irrelevance.

4

....

Equality

Those Who Own the Data Own the Future

For the last few decades, people all over the world were told that humankind is on the path to equality, and that globalization and new technologies will help us get there sooner. In reality, the twenty-first century might create the most unequal societies in history. Though globalization and the internet bridge the gap between countries, they threaten to enlarge the rift between classes. And just as humankind seems about to achieve global unification, the species itself might divide into different biological castes.

Inequality goes back to the Stone Age. Thirty thousand years ago, hunter-gatherer bands buried some members in sumptuous graves replete with thousands of ivory beads, bracelets, jewels, and art objects, while other members had to settle for a bare hole in the ground. Nevertheless, ancient hunter-gatherer bands were still more egalitarian than any subsequent human society, because they had very little property. Property is a prerequisite for long-term inequality.

Following the Agricultural Revolution, property multiplied and with it inequality. As humans gained ownership of land, animals, plants, and tools, rigid hierarchical societies emerged, in which small elites monopolized most wealth and power for generation after generation. Humans came to accept this arrangement as natural and even divinely ordained. Hierarchy was not just the norm but also the ideal. How could there be order without a clear hierarchy between aristocrats and commoners, between men and women, or between parents and children? Priests, philosophers, and poets all over the world patiently explained that just as in the human body not all members are equal—the feet must obey the head—so also in human society equality would bring nothing but chaos.

In the late modern era, however, equality became an ideal in almost all human societies. This was partly due to the rise of the new ideologies of communism and liberalism. But it was also due to the Industrial Revolution, which made the masses more important than ever before. Industrial economies relied on masses of common workers, while industrial armies relied on masses of common soldiers. Governments in both democracies and dictatorships invested heavily in the health, education, and welfare of the masses, because they needed millions of healthy laborers to operate the production lines and millions of loyal soldiers to fight in the trenches.

Consequently, the history of the twentieth century revolved to a large extent around the reduction of inequality between classes, races, and genders. Though the world of the year 2000 still had its share of hierarchies, it was nevertheless a far more equal place than the world of 1900. In the first years of the twenty-first century people expected that the egalitarian process would continue and even accelerate. In particular, they hoped that globalization would spread economic prosperity throughout the world, and that as a result people in India and Egypt would come to enjoy the same opportunities and privileges as people in Finland and Canada. An entire generation grew up on this promise.

Now it seems that this promise might not be fulfilled. Globalization has certainly benefited large segments of humanity, but there are signs of growing inequality both between and within societies. Some groups increasingly monopolize the fruits of globalization, while billions are left behind. Today, the richest 1 percent own half the world's wealth. Even more alarmingly, the richest one hundred people together own more than the poorest four billion.[1]

This situation could get far worse. As explained in earlier chapters, the rise of AI might eliminate the economic value and political power of most humans. At the same time, improvements in biotechnology might make it possible to translate economic inequality into biological inequality. The superrich will finally have something really worthwhile to do with their stupendous wealth. While up until now they have only been able to buy little more than status symbols, soon they might be able to buy life itself. If new treatments for extending life and upgrading physical and cognitive abilities prove to be expensive, humankind might split into biological castes.

Throughout history the rich and the aristocracy always imagined that they had skills superior to everybody else's, which is why they were in control. As far as we can tell, this wasn't true. The average duke wasn't more talented than the average peasant—he owed his superiority only to unjust legal and economic discrimination. However, by 2100 the rich might really be more talented, more creative, and more intelligent than the slum-dwellers. Once a real gap in ability opens between the rich and the poor, it will become almost impossible to close it. If the rich use their superior abilities to enrich themselves further, and if more money can buy them enhanced bodies and brains, with time the gap will only widen. By 2100, the richest 1 percent might own not merely most of the world's wealth but also most of the world's beauty, creativity, and health.

The two processes together—bioengineering coupled with the rise of AI—might therefore result in the separation of humankind into a small class of superhumans and a massive underclass of useless *Homo sapiens*. To make an already ominous situation even worse, as the masses lose their economic importance and political power, the state might lose at least some of the incentive to invest in their health, education, and welfare. It's very dangerous to be redundant. The future of the masses will then depend on the goodwill of a small elite. Maybe there is goodwill for a few decades. But in a time of crisis—like climate catastrophe—it would be very tempting and easy to toss the superfluous people overboard.

In countries such as France and New Zealand, with a long tradition of liberal beliefs and welfare-state practices, perhaps the elite will go on taking care of the masses even when it doesn't need them. In the more capitalist United States, however, the elite might use the first opportunity to dismantle what's left of the American welfare state. An even bigger problem looms in large developing countries such as India, China, South Africa, and Brazil. There, once common people lose their economic value, inequality might skyrocket.

Consequently, instead of globalization resulting in global unity, it might actually result in speciation: the divergence of humankind into different biological castes or even different species. Globalization will unite the world horizontally by erasing national borders, but it will simultaneously divide humanity vertically. Ruling oligarchies in countries as diverse as the United States and Russia might merge and make common cause against the mass of ordinary humans. From this perspective, current populist resentment of "the elites" is well founded. If we are not careful, the grandchildren of Silicon Valley tycoons and Moscow billionaires might become a separate species superior to the grandchildren of Appalachian hillbillies and Siberian villagers.

In the long run, such a scenario might even deglobalize the world, as the upper caste congregates inside a self-proclaimed "civilization" and builds walls and moats to separate it from the hordes of "barbarians" outside. In the twentieth century, industrial civilization depended on the "barbarians" for cheap labor, raw materials, and markets, and it often conquered and absorbed them. But in the twenty-first century, a post-industrial civilization relying on AI, bioengineering, and nanotechnology might be far more self-contained and self-sustaining. Not just entire classes but entire countries and continents might become irrelevant. Fortifications guarded by drones and robots might separate the self-proclaimed civilized zone, where cyborgs fight one another with logic bombs, from the barbarian lands where feral humans fight one another with machetes and Kalashnikovs.

Throughout this book, I often use the first person plural to speak about the future of humankind. I talk about what "we" need to do about "our" problems. But maybe there is no "we." Maybe one of our biggest problems is that different human groups have completely different futures. Maybe in some parts of the world you should teach your kids to write computer code, while in others you had better teach them to draw fast and shoot straight.

WHO OWNS THE DATA?

If we want to prevent the concentration of all wealth and power in the hands of a small elite, the key is to regulate the ownership of data. In ancient times land was the most important asset in the world, politics was a struggle to control land, and if too much land became concentrated in too few hands, society split into aristocrats and commoners. In the modern era machines and factories became more important than land, and political struggles focused on controlling these vital means of production. If too many of the machines became concentrated in too few hands, society split into capitalists and proletarians. In the twenty-first century, however, data will eclipse both land and machinery as the most important asset, and politics will be a struggle to control the flow of data. If data becomes concentrated in too few hands, humankind will split into different species.

The race to obtain the data is already on, headed by data giants such as Google, Facebook, Baidu, and Tencent. So far, many of these giants seem to have adopted the business model of "attention merchants."[2] They capture our attention by providing us with free information, services, and entertainment, and they then resell our attention to advertisers. Yet the data giants probably aim far higher than any previous attention merchant. Their true business isn't to sell advertisements at all. Rather, by capturing our attention they manage to accumulate immense amounts of data about us, which is worth more than any advertising revenue. We aren't their customers—we are their product.

In the medium term, this data hoard opens a path to a radically different business model whose first victim will be the advertising industry itself. The new model is based on transferring authority from humans to algorithms, including the authority to choose and buy things. Once algorithms choose and buy things for us, the traditional advertising industry will go bust. Consider Google. Google wants to reach a point where we can ask it *anything* and get the best answer in the world. What will happen once we can say to Google, "Hi, Google. Based on everything you know about cars, and based on everything you know about me (including my needs, my habits, my views on global warming, and even my opinions about Middle Eastern politics), what is the best car for me?" If Google can give us a good answer to that, and if we learn by experience to trust Google's wisdom instead of our own easily manipulated feelings, what could possibly be the use of car advertisements?[3]

In the longer term, by bringing together enough data and enough computing power, the data giants could hack the deepest secrets of life, and then use this knowledge not just to make choices for us or manipulate us but also to reengineer organic life and create inorganic life-forms. Selling advertisements may be necessary to sustain the giants in the short term, but tech companies often evaluate apps, products, and other companies according to the data they harvest rather than according to the money they generate. A popular app may lack a business model and may even lose money in the short term, but as long as it sucks data, it could be worth billions.[4]

Even if you don't know how to cash in on the data today, it is worth having it because it might hold the key to controlling and shaping life in the future. I don't know for certain that the data giants explicitly think about this in such terms, but their actions indicate that they value the accumulation of data in terms beyond those of mere dollars and cents.

Ordinary humans will find it very difficult to resist this process. At present, people are happy to give away their most valuable asset—their personal data—in exchange for free email services and funny cat videos. It's a bit like African and Native American tribes who unwittingly sold entire countries to European imperialists in exchange for colorful beads and cheap trinkets. If, later on, ordinary people decide to try to block the flow of data, they might find it increasingly difficult, especially as they might come to rely on the network for all their decisions, and even for their healthcare and physical survival.

Humans and machines might merge so completely that humans will not be able to survive at all if they are disconnected from the network. They will be connected starting in the womb, and if later in life you choose to disconnect, insurance agencies might refuse to insure you, employers might refuse to employ you, and healthcare services might refuse to take care of you. In the big battle between health and privacy, health is likely to win hands down.

As more and more data flows from your body and brain to smart machines via biometric sensors, it will become easy for corporations and government agencies to know you, manipulate you, and make decisions on your behalf. Even more important, they could be able to decipher the deep mechanisms of all bodies and brains, and thereby gain the power to engineer life. If we want to prevent a small elite from monopolizing such godlike powers, and if we want to prevent humankind from splitting into biological castes, the key question is: who owns the data? Does the data about my DNA, my brain, and my life belong to me, to the government, to a corporation, or to the human collective?

Mandating governments to nationalize the data will probably curb the power of big corporations, but it might also result in creepy digital dictatorships. Politicians are a bit like musicians, and the instrument they play on is the human emotional and biochemical system. They give a speech, and there is a wave of fear in the country. They tweet, and there is an explosion of hatred. I don't think we should give these musicians a more sophisticated instrument to play on. Once politicians can press our emotional buttons directly, generating anxiety, hatred, joy, and boredom at will, politics will become a mere emotional circus. As much as we should fear the power of big corporations, history suggests that we are not necessarily better off in the hands of overly mighty governments. As of March 2018, I would prefer to give my data to Mark Zuckerberg than to Vladimir Putin (though the Cambridge Analytica scandal revealed that perhaps there isn't much of a choice here, as any data entrusted to Zuckerberg may well find its way to Putin).

Private ownership of one's own data may sound more attractive than either of these options, but it is unclear what it actually means. We have had thousands of years of experience in regulating the ownership of land. We know how to build a fence around a field, place a guard at the gate, and control who can go in. Over the past two centuries we have become extremely sophisticated in regulating the ownership of industry; thus today I can own a piece of General Motors and a bit of Toyota by buying their shares. But we don't have much experience in regulating the ownership of data, which is inherently a far more difficult task, because unlike land and machines, data is everywhere and nowhere at the same time, it can move at the speed of light, and you can create as many copies of it as you want.

So we had better call upon our lawyers, politicians, philosophers, and even poets to turn their attention to this conundrum: how do you regulate the ownership of data? This may well be the most important political question of our era. If we cannot answer this question soon, our sociopolitical system might collapse. People are already sensing the coming cataclysm. Perhaps this is why citizens all over the world are losing faith in the liberal story, which just a decade ago seemed irresistible.

How, then, do we go forward from here, and how do we cope with the immense challenges of the biotech and infotech revolutions? Perhaps the very same scientists and entrepreneurs who disrupted the world in the first place can engineer some technological solution. For example, might networked algorithms form the scaffolding for a global human community that could collectively own all the data and oversee the future development of life? As global inequality rises and social tensions increase around the world, perhaps Mark Zuckerberg could call upon his two billion friends to join forces and do something together.

. . . .

PART II

The Political Challenge

The merger of infotech and biotech threatens the core modern values of liberty and equality. Any solution to the technological challenge has to involve global cooperation. But nationalism, religion, and culture divide humankind into hostile camps and make it very difficult to cooperate on a global level.

5

....

Community

Humans Have Bodies

California is used to earthquakes, but the political tremor of the 2016 U.S. elections still came as a rude shock to Silicon Valley. Realizing that they might be part of the problem, the computer wizards reacted by doing what engineers do best: they searched for a technical solution. Nowhere was the reaction more forceful than in Facebook's headquarters in Menlo Park. This is understandable. Since Facebook's business is social networking, it is most attuned to social disturbances.

After three months of soul-searching, on February 16, 2017, Mark Zuckerberg published an audacious manifesto on the need to build a global community, and on Facebook's role in that project.[1] In a follow-up speech at the inaugural Communities Summit on June 22, 2017, Zuckerberg explained that the sociopolitical upheavals of our time—from rampant drug addiction to murderous totalitarian regimes—result to a large extent from the disintegration of human communities. He lamented the fact that "for decades, membership in all kinds of groups has declined as much as one-quarter. That's a lot of people who now need to find a sense of purpose and support somewhere else."[2] He promised that Facebook would lead the charge to rebuild these communities and that his engineers would pick up the burden discarded by parish priests. "We're going to start rolling out some tools," he said, to "make it easier to build communities."

He further explained, "We started a project to see if we could get better at suggesting groups that will be meaningful to you. We started building artificial intelligence to do this. And it works. In the first six months, we helped 50% more people join meaningful communities." His ultimate goal is "to help 1 billion people join meaningful communities. . . . If we can do this, it will not only turn around the whole decline in community membership we've seen for decades, it will start to strengthen our social fabric and bring the world closer together." This is such an important goal that Zuckerberg vowed "to change Facebook's whole mission to take this on."[3]

Zuckerberg is certainly correct in lamenting the breakdown of human communities. Yet several months after Zuckerberg made this vow, and just as this book was going to print, the Cambridge Analytica scandal revealed that data entrusted to Facebook was harvested by third parties and used to manipulate elections around the world. This made a mockery of Zuckerberg's lofty promises, and shattered public trust in Facebook. One can only hope that before undertaking the building of new human communities, Facebook first commits itself to protecting the privacy and security of existing communities.

It is nevertheless worthwhile to consider Facebook's communal vision in depth and examine whether once security is beefed up, online social networks can help build a global human community. Though in the twenty-first century humans might be upgraded into gods, as of 2018 we are still Stone Age animals. In order to flourish we still need to ground ourselves in intimate communities. For millions of years, humans have been adapted to living in small bands of no more than a few dozen people. Even today most of us find it impossible to really know more than 150 individuals, irrespective of how many Facebook friends we boast.[4] And if we don't belong to any intimate community, we humans feel lonely and alienated.

Unfortunately, over the past two centuries intimate communities have been disintegrating. The attempt to replace small groups of people who actually know one another with the imagined communities of nations and political parties will never succeed in full. Your millions of brothers in the national family and your millions of comrades in the Communist Party cannot provide you with the warm intimacy that a single real sibling or friend can. Consequently, people live ever more lonely lives in an ever more connected planet. Many of the social and political disruptions of our time can be traced back to this malaise.[5]

Zuckerberg's vision of reconnecting humans to one another is therefore a timely and noble one. But words are cheaper than actions, and in order to implement this vision, Facebook might have to change its entire business model. You can hardly build a global community when you make your money from capturing people's attention and selling it to advertisers. Despite this, Zuckerberg's willingness to even formulate such a vision deserves praise. Most corporations believe that they should focus on making money, governments should do as little as possible, and humankind should trust market forces to make the really important decisions on our behalf.[6] So if Facebook intends to make a real ideological commitment to building human communities, those who fear its power should not push it back into the corporate cocoon with cries of "Big Brother!" Instead, we should urge other corporations, institutions, and governments to challenge Facebook by making their own ideological commitments.

Of course, there is no lack of organizations that lament the breakdown of human communities and strive to rebuild them. A wide variety of groups, from feminist activists to Islamic fundamentalists, are in the business of community-building, and we will examine some of these efforts in later chapters. What makes Facebook's gambit unique is its global scope, its corporate backing, and its deep faith in technology. Zuckerberg sounds convinced that the new Facebook AI can not only identify "meaningful communities" but also "strengthen our social fabric and bring the world closer together." That is far more ambitious than using AI to drive a car or diagnose cancer.

Facebook's community vision is perhaps the first explicit attempt to use AI for centrally planned social engineering on a global scale. It therefore constitutes a crucial test case. If it succeeds, we are likely to see many more such attempts, and algorithms will be acknowledged as the new masters of human social networks. If it fails, it will uncover the limitations of the new technologies—algorithms may be good for navigating vehicles and curing diseases, but when it comes to solving social problems, we should still rely on politicians and priests.

ONLINE VERSUS OFFLINE

In recent years Facebook has had astonishing success, and it currently has more than two billion active users. Yet in order to implement its new vision it will have to bridge the chasm between online and offline. A community may begin as an online gathering, but in order to truly flourish it will have to put down roots in the offline world too. If one day some dictator bars Facebook from his country or completely pulls the plug on the internet, will the communities evaporate, or will they regroup and fight back? Will they be able to organize a demonstration without online communication?

Zuckerberg explained in his February 2017 manifesto that online communities help foster offline ones. This is sometimes true. Yet in many cases online comes at the expense of offline, and there is a fundamental difference between the two. Physical communities have a depth that virtual communities cannot match, at least not in the near future. If I lie in bed sick at home in Israel, my online friends from California can talk to me, but they cannot bring me soup or a cup of tea.

Humans have bodies. During the last century technology has been distancing us from our bodies. We have been losing our ability to pay attention to what we smell and taste. Instead we are absorbed in our smartphones and computers. We are more interested in what is happening in cyberspace than in what is happening down the street. It is easier than ever to talk to my cousin in Switzerland, but it is harder to talk to my husband over breakfast, because he constantly looks at his smartphone instead of at me.[7]

In the past, humans could not afford such carelessness. Ancient foragers were always alert and attentive. Wandering in the forest in search of mushrooms, they watched the ground for any telltale bulge. They listened to the slightest movement in the grass to learn whether a snake might be lurking there. When they found an edible mushroom, they examined it with the utmost attention to distinguish it from its poisonous cousins. Members of today's affluent societies don't need such keen awareness. We can wander the supermarket aisles while texting messages, and we can buy any of a thousand dishes, all supervised by the health authorities. But whatever we choose, we might end up eating it in haste in front of a screen, checking emails or watching television, while hardly paying attention to the actual taste.

Zuckerberg says that Facebook is committed "to continue improving our tools to give you the power to share your experience" with others.[8] Yet what people might really need are the tools to connect to their own experiences. In the name of "sharing experiences," people are encouraged to understand what happens to them in terms of how others see it. If something exciting happens, the gut instinct of Facebook users is to pull out their smartphones, take a picture, post it online, and wait for the "likes." In the process they barely notice what they themselves feel. Indeed, what they feel is increasingly determined by the online reactions.

People estranged from their bodies, senses, and physical environment are likely to feel alienated and disoriented. Pundits often
blame such feelings of alienation on the decline of religious and
national bonds, but losing touch with your body is probably more
important. Humans lived for millions of years without religions
and without nations; they can probably live happily without them
in the twenty-first century too. Yet they cannot live happily if they
are disconnected from their bodies. If you don't feel at home in
your body, you will never feel at home in the world.

Up till now, Facebook's own business model encouraged people
to spend more and more time online even if that meant having less
time and energy to devote to offline activities. Can it adopt a new
model that encourages people to go online only when it is really
necessary, and to devote more attention to their physical environment and to their own bodies and senses? What would Facebook's
shareholders think about this model? (A blueprint of such an alternative model has been suggested recently by Tristan Harris, a tech
philosopher and former Google employee who came up with a new
metric of "time well spent.")[9]

The limitations of online relationships also undermine Zuckerberg's solution to social polarization. He rightly points out that just
connecting people and exposing them to different opinions will not
bridge social divides because "showing people an article from the
opposite perspective, actually deepens polarization by framing
other perspectives as foreign." Instead, Zuckerberg suggests that
"the best solutions for improving discourse may come from getting
to know each other as whole people instead of just opinions—
something Facebook may be uniquely suited to do. If we connect
with people about what we have in common—sports teams, TV
shows, interests—it is easier to have dialogue about what we dis-
agree on."[10]

Yet it is extremely difficult to know each other as "whole" people.
It takes a lot of time, and it demands direct physical interaction. As
noted earlier, the average *Homo sapiens* is probably incapable of inti-

mately knowing more than 150 individuals. Ideally, building communities should not be a zero-sum game. Humans can feel loyal to different groups at the same time. Unfortunately, intimate relations probably are a zero-sum game. Beyond a certain point, the time and energy you spend on getting to know your online friends from Iran or Nigeria will come at the expense of your ability to know your next-door neighbors.

Facebook's crucial test will come when an engineer invents a new tool that causes people to spend less time buying stuff online and more time in meaningful offline activities with friends. Will Facebook adopt or suppress such a tool? Will Facebook take a true leap of faith and privilege social concerns over financial interests? If it does so—and manages to avoid bankruptcy—that will be a momentous transformation.

Devoting more attention to the offline world than to its quarterly reports also has a bearing on Facebook's taxation policies. Like Amazon, Google, Apple, and several other tech giants, Facebook has been repeatedly accused of tax evasion.[11] The difficulties inherent in taxing online activities make it easier for these global corporations to engage in all sorts of creative accounting. If you think that people live mainly online and that you provide them with all the necessary tools for their online existence, you can view yourself as a beneficial social service even as you avoid paying taxes to offline governments. But once you remember that human beings have bodies and that they therefore still need roads, hospitals, and sewage systems, it becomes far more difficult to justify tax evasion. How can you extol the virtues of community while refusing to financially support the most important community services?

We can only hope that Facebook can change its business model, adopt a more offline-friendly tax policy, help unite the world—and still remain profitable. Yet we should not cultivate unrealistic expectations about Facebook's ability to realize its global community vision. Historically, corporations were not the ideal vehicle for leading social and political revolutions. A real revolution sooner or later demands sacrifices that corporations, their employees, and their share-holders are not willing to make. That's why revolutionaries establish churches, political parties, and armies. The so-called Facebook and Twitter revolutions in the Arab world started in hopeful online communities, but once they emerged into the messy offline world, they were commandeered by religious fanatics and military juntas. If Facebook now aims to instigate a global revolution, it will have to do a much better job in bridging the gap between online and off-line. It and the other online giants tend to view humans as audio-visual animals—a pair of eyes and a pair of ears connected to ten fingers, a screen, and a credit card. A crucial step toward uniting humankind is to appreciate that humans have bodies.

Of course, this appreciation too has its downside. Realizing the limitations of online algorithms might only prompt the tech giants to extend their reach further. Devices such as Google Glass and games such as Pokémon Go are designed to erase the distinction between online and offline, merging them into a single augmented reality. On an even deeper level, biometric sensors and direct brain-to-computer interfaces aim to erode the border between electronic machines and organic bodies and to literally get under our skin. Once the tech giants come to terms with the human body, they might end up manipulating our entire bodies in the same way they currently manipulate our eyes, fingers, and credit cards. We may come to miss the good old days when online was separated from offline.

6

....

Civilization

There Is Just One Civilization in the World

While Mark Zuckerberg dreams of uniting humankind online, recent events in the offline world seem to breathe fresh life into the "clash of civilizations" thesis. Many pundits, politicians, and ordinary citizens believe that the Syrian civil war, the rise of the Islamic State, the Brexit mayhem, and the instability of the European Union all result from a clash between "Western civilization" and "Islamic civilization." They believe that Western attempts to impose democracy and human rights on Muslim nations resulted in a violent Islamic backlash, and a wave of Muslim immigration coupled with Islamic terrorist attacks caused European voters to abandon multicultural dreams in favor of xenophobic local identities.

According to this thesis, humankind has always been divided into diverse civilizations whose members view the world in irreconcilable ways. These incompatible worldviews make conflicts between civilizations inevitable. Just as in nature different species fight for survival according to the remorseless laws of natural selection, so throughout history civilizations have repeatedly clashed and only the fittest have survived to tell the tale. Those who overlook this grim fact—be they liberal politicians or head-in-the-clouds engineers—do so at their peril.[1]

The "clash of civilizations" thesis has far-reaching political implications. Its supporters contend that any attempt to reconcile "the West" with "the Muslim world" is doomed to failure: Muslim countries will never adopt Western values, and Western countries will never successfully absorb Muslim minorities. Accordingly, the United States should not admit immigrants from Syria or Iraq, and the European Union should renounce its multicultural fallacy in favor of an unabashed Western identity. In the long run, only one civilization can survive the unforgiving tests of natural selection, and if the bureaucrats in Brussels refuse to save the West from the Islamic peril, then Britain, Denmark, or France had better go it alone.

Though widely held, this thesis is misleading. Islamic fundamentalism may indeed pose a radical challenge, but the "civilization" it challenges is a global civilization rather than a uniquely Western phenomenon. And even Islamic fundamentalists, for all their medieval fantasies, are grounded in contemporary global culture far more than in seventh-century Arabia. They are catering to the fears and hopes of alienated modern youth rather than to those of medieval peasants and merchants. As Pankaj Mishra and Christopher de Bellaigue have convincingly argued, radical Islamists have been influenced by Marx and Foucault as much as by Muhammad, and they have inherited the legacy of nineteenth-century European anarchists as much as of the Umayyad and Abbasid caliphs.[2] It is therefore more accurate to see even the Islamic State as an errant offshoot of the global culture we all share, rather than as a branch of some mysterious and alien tree.

More important, the analogy between history and biology that underpins the "clash of civilizations" thesis is false. Human groups—all the way from small tribes to huge civilizations—are fundamentally different from animal species, and historical conflicts differ greatly from natural selection processes. Animal species have objective identities that endure for thousands upon thousands of generations. Whether you are a chimpanzee or a gorilla depends on your genes rather than your beliefs, and different genes dictate distinct social behaviors. Chimpanzees live in mixed groups of males and females. They compete for power by building coalitions of supporters from among both sexes. Amid gorillas, in contrast, a single dominant male establishes a harem of females, and usually expels any adult male that might challenge his position. Chimpanzees cannot adopt gorilla-like social arrangements; gorillas cannot start organizing themselves like chimpanzees; and as far as we know, exactly the same social systems have characterized chimpanzees and gorillas not only in recent decades but for hundreds of thousands of years.

You find nothing like that among humans. Yes, human groups may have distinct social systems, but these are not genetically determined, and they seldom endure for more than a few centuries. Think of twentieth-century Germans, for example. In less than a hundred years the Germans organized themselves into six very different systems: the Hohenzollern Empire, the Weimar Republic, the Third Reich, the German Democratic Republic (aka communist East Germany), the Federal Republic of Germany (aka West Germany), and finally democratic reunited Germany. Of course the Germans kept their language and their love of beer and bratwurst. But is there some unique German essence that distinguishes them from all other nations and that has remained unchanged from Wilhelm II to Angela Merkel? And if you do come up with something, was it also there a thousand years ago, or five thousand years ago?

The (unratified) Preamble of the European Constitution begins by stating that it draws inspiration "from the cultural, religious and humanist inheritance of Europe, from which have developed the universal values of the inviolable and inalienable rights of the human person, democracy, equality, freedom and the rule of law."[3] This may easily give one the impression that European civilization is defined by the values of human rights, democracy, equality, and freedom. Countless speeches and documents draw a direct line from ancient Athenian democracy to the present-day European Union, celebrating twenty-five hundred years of European freedom and democracy. This is reminiscent of the proverbial blind man who takes hold of an elephant's tail and concludes that an elephant is a kind of brush. Yes, democratic ideas have been part of European culture for centuries, but they were never the whole. For all its glory and impact, Athenian democracy was a halfhearted experiment that survived for barely two hundred years in a small corner of the Balkans. If European civilization for the past twenty-five centuries has been defined by democracy and human rights, what are we to make of Sparta and Julius Caesar, of the Crusaders and the conquistadores, of the Inquisition and the slave trade, of Louis XIV and Napoleon, of Hitler and Stalin? Were they all intruders from some foreign civilization?

In truth, European civilization is anything Europeans make of it, just as Christianity is anything Christians make of it, Islam is anything Muslims make of it, and Judaism is anything Jews make out of it. And they have made of it remarkably different things over the centuries. Human groups are defined more by the changes they undergo than by any continuity, but they nevertheless manage to create for themselves ancient identities thanks to their storytelling skills. No matter what revolutions they experience, they can usually weave old and new into a single yarn.

Even an individual can knit revolutionary personal changes into a coherent and powerful life story: "I am that person who was once a socialist, but then became a capitalist; I was born in France, and now live in the United States; I was married, and then got divorced; I had cancer, and then got well again." Similarly, a human group such as the Germans may come to define itself by the very changes it underwent: "Once we were Nazis, but we have learned our lesson, and now we are peaceful democrats." You don't need to look for some unique German essence that manifested itself first in Wilhelm II, then in Hitler, and finally in Merkel. These radical transformations are precisely what define German identity. To be German in 2018 means to grapple with the difficult legacy of Nazism while upholding liberal and democratic values. Who knows what it will mean in 2050.

People often refuse to recognize these changes, especially when it comes to core political and religious values. We insist that our values are a precious legacy from ancient ancestors. Yet the only thing that allows us to say this is that our ancestors are long dead and cannot speak for themselves. Consider, for example, Jewish attitudes toward women. Nowadays ultra-Orthodox Jews ban images of women from the public sphere. Billboards and advertisements aimed at ultra-Orthodox Jews usually depict only men and boys—never women and girls.[4]

In 2011, a scandal erupted when the ultra-Orthodox Brooklyn paper *Di Tzeitung* published a photo of American officials watching the raid on Osama bin Laden's compound but digitally erased all women from the photo, including Secretary of State Hillary Clinton. The paper explained it was forced to do so by Jewish "laws of modesty." A similar scandal erupted when the paper *HaMevaser* expunged Angela Merkel from a photo of a demonstration against the *Charlie Hebdo* massacre, lest her image arouse any lustful thoughts in the minds of devout readers. The publisher of a third ultra-Orthodox newspaper, *Hamodia*, defended this policy by explaining, "We are backed by thousands of years of Jewish tradition."[5]

Nowhere is the ban on seeing women stricter than in the synagogue. In Orthodox synagogues women are carefully segregated from the men and must confine themselves to a restricted zone where they are hidden behind a curtain, so that no man will accidentally see the shape of a woman as he says his prayers or reads scriptures. Yet if all this is backed by thousands of years of Jewish tradition and immutable divine laws, how to explain the fact that when archeologists excavated ancient synagogues in Israel from the time of the Mishnah and Talmud, they found no sign of gender segregation, and instead uncovered beautiful floor mosaics and wall paintings depicting women, some of them rather scantily dressed? The rabbis who wrote the Mishnah and Talmud regularly prayed and studied in these synagogues, but present-day Orthodox Jews would consider them blasphemous desecrations of ancient traditions.[6]

Similar distortions of ancient traditions characterize all religions. The Islamic State has boasted that it has reverted to the pure and original version of Islam, but in truth, their take on Islam is brand-new. Yes, they quote many venerable texts, but they exercise a lot of discretion in choosing which texts to quote, which to ignore, and how to interpret them. Indeed, their do-it-yourself attitude to interpreting the holy texts is itself very modern. Traditionally, interpretation was the monopoly of the learned *ulama*, scholars who studied Muslim law and theology in reputable institutions such as Cairo's Al-Azhar. Few of the Islamic State's leaders have had such credentials, and most respected *ulama* have dismissed Abu Bakr al-Baghdadi and his ilk as ignorant criminals.[7]

That does not mean that the Islamic State has been "un-Islamic" or "anti-Islamic," as some people argue. It is particularly ironic when Christian leaders such as Barack Obama have the temerity to tell self-professing Muslims such as Abu Bakr al-Baghdadi what it means to be Muslim.[8] The heated argument about the true essence of Islam is simply pointless. Islam has no fixed DNA. Islam is whatever Muslims make of it.[9]

GERMANS AND GORILLAS

There is an even deeper difference distinguishing human groups from animal species. Species often split, but they never merge. About seven million years ago chimpanzees and gorillas had common ancestors. This single ancestral species split into two populations that eventually went their separate evolutionary ways. Once this happened, there was no going back. Since individuals belonging to different species cannot produce fertile offspring together, species can never merge. Gorillas cannot merge with chimpanzees, giraffes cannot merge with elephants, and dogs cannot merge with cats.

Human tribes, in contrast, tend to coalesce over time into larger and larger groups. Modern Germans were created from the merger of Saxons, Prussians, Swabians, and Bavarians, who not so long ago wasted little love on one another. Otto von Bismarck allegedly remarked (having read Darwin's *On the Origin of Species*) that the Bavarian is the missing link between the Austrian and the human.[10] The French were created from the merger of Franks, Normans, Bretons, Gascons, and Provençals. Meanwhile, across the Channel, English, Scots, Welsh, and Irish were gradually welded together (willingly or not) to form Britons. In the not too distant future, Germans, French, and Britons might yet merge into Europeans.

Mergers don't always last, as people in London, Edinburgh, and Brussels are keenly aware these days. Brexit may well initiate the simultaneous unraveling of both the United Kingdom and the European Union, but over the long run, history's direction is clear-cut. Ten thousand years ago humankind was divided into countless isolated tribes. With each passing millennium, these fused into larger and larger groups, creating fewer and fewer distinct civilizations. In recent generations the few remaining civilizations have been blending into a single global civilization. Political, ethnic, cultural, and economic divisions endure, but they do not undermine the fundamental unity. Indeed, some divisions are made possible only by an overarching common structure. In the economy, for example, the division of labor cannot succeed unless everyone shares a single market. One country cannot specialize in producing cars or oil unless it can buy food from other countries that grow wheat and rice.

The process of human unification has taken two distinct forms: establishing links between distinct groups and homogenizing practices across groups. Links may be formed even between groups that continue to behave very differently. In fact, links may form even between sworn enemies. War itself can generate some of the strongest of all human bonds. Historians often argue that globalization reached a first peak in 1913, then went into a long decline during the era of the world wars and the Cold War, and recuperated only after 1989.[11] This may be true of economic globalization, but it ignores the different but equally important dynamic of military globalization. War spreads ideas, technologies, and people far more quickly than commerce does. In 1918 the United States was more closely linked to Europe than in 1913; the two then drifted apart in the interwar years, only to have their fates inextricably meshed together by the Second World War and the Cold War.

War also makes people far more interested in one another. The United States had never been more closely in touch with Russia than during the Cold War, when every cough in a Moscow corridor sent people scrambling up and down Washington staircases. People care far more about their enemies than about their trade partners. For every American film about Taiwan, there are probably fifty about Vietnam.

THE MEDIEVAL OLYMPICS

The world of the early twenty-first century has gone way beyond forming links between different groups. People across the globe are not only in touch with one another, they increasingly share identical beliefs and practices. A thousand years ago, planet Earth provided fertile ground to dozens of different political models. In Europe you could find feudal principalities vying with independent city-states and minuscule theocracies. The Muslim world had its caliphate, claiming universal sovereignty, but it also experimented with kingdoms, sultanates, and emirates. The Chinese empires believed themselves to be the sole legitimate political entity, while to the north and west tribal confederacies fought each other with glee. India and Southeast Asia contained a kaleidoscope of regimes, whereas polities in America, Africa, and Australasia ranged from tiny hunter-gatherer bands to sprawling empires. No wonder that even neighboring human groups had trouble agreeing on common diplomatic procedures, not to mention international laws. Each society had its own political paradigm and found it difficult to understand and respect alien political concepts.

Today, in contrast, a single political paradigm is accepted everywhere. The planet is divided between about two hundred sovereign states, which generally agree on the same diplomatic protocols and on common international laws. Sweden, Nigeria, Thailand, and Brazil are all marked on our atlases as the same kind of colorful shapes; they are all members of the United Nations; and despite myriad differences they are all recognized as sovereign states enjoying similar rights and privileges. Indeed, they share many more political ideas and practices than not, including at least a token belief in representative bodies, political parties, universal suffrage, and human rights. There are parliaments in Tehran, Moscow, Cape Town, and New Delhi as well as in London and Paris. When Israelis and Palestinians, Russians and Ukrainians, Kurds and Turks compete for the favors of global public opinion, they all use the same discourse of human rights, state sovereignty, and international law.

The world may be peppered with various types of "failed states," but it knows only one paradigm for a successful state. Global politics thus follows the Anna Karenina principle: successful states are all alike, but every failed state fails in its own way, by missing this or that ingredient of the dominant political package. The Islamic State has recently stood out in its complete rejection of this package and in its attempt to establish an entirely different kind of political entity—a universal caliphate. But precisely for this reason it has failed. Numerous guerrilla forces and terror organizations have managed to establish new countries or to conquer existing ones. But they have always done so by accepting the fundamental principles of the global political order. Even the Taliban sought international recognition as the legitimate government of the sovereign country of Afghanistan. No group rejecting the principles of global politics has so far gained any lasting control of any significant territory.

The strength of the global political paradigm can perhaps best be appreciated by considering not hard-core political questions of war and diplomacy but rather something like the 2016 Rio Olympics. Take a moment to reflect on the way the Games were organized. The eleven thousand athletes were grouped into delegations by nationality rather than by religion, class, or language. There was no Buddhist delegation, proletarian delegation, or English-speaking delegation. Except in a handful of cases—most notably Taiwan and Palestine—determining the athletes' nationality was a straightforward affair.

At the opening ceremony on August 5, 2016, the athletes marched in groups, each waving its national flag. Whenever Michael Phelps won another gold medal, the Stars and Stripes was raised to the sound of "The Star-Spangled Banner." When Emilie Andéol won the gold medal in judo, the French tricolor was hoisted and "La Marseillaise" was played.

Conveniently enough, each country in the world has an anthem that conforms to the same universal model. Almost all anthems are orchestral pieces of a few minutes in length, rather than a twenty-minute chant that can only be performed by a special caste of hereditary priests. Even countries such as Saudi Arabia, Pakistan, and Congo have adopted Western musical conventions for their anthems. Most of them sound like something composed by Beethoven on a rather mediocre day. (You can spend an evening with friends playing the various anthems on YouTube and trying to guess which is which.) Even the lyrics are almost the same throughout the world, indicating common conceptions of politics and group loyalty. For example, to which nation do you think the following anthem belongs? (I changed only the country's name into the generic "My country"):

My country, my homeland,
The land where I have shed my blood,
It is there I stand,
To be my motherland's guard.
My country, my nation,
My people and my homeland,
Let us proclaim
"My country unite!"
Long live my land, long live my state,
My nation, my homeland, in its entirety.
Build its soul, awaken its body,
For my great country!
My great country, independent and free
My home and my country which I love.
My great country, independent and free,
Long live my great country!

The answer is Indonesia. But would you have been surprised if I'd told you that the answer was actually Poland, Nigeria, or Brazil?

National flags display the same dreary conformity. With a single exception, all flags are rectangular pieces of cloth marked by an extremely limited repertoire of colors, stripes, and geometrical shapes. Nepal is the odd country out, with a flag consisting of two triangles. (But Nepal never won an Olympic medal.) The Indonesian flag consists of a red stripe above a white stripe. The Polish flag displays a white stripe above a red stripe. The flag of Monaco is identical to that of Indonesia. A color-blind person could hardly tell the difference between the flags of Belgium, Chad, Ivory Coast, France, Guinea, Ireland, Italy, Mali, and Romania—they all have three vertical stripes of various colors.

Some of these countries have been engaged in bitter war with one another, but during the tumultuous twentieth century only three Olympic Games were canceled due to war (in 1916, 1940, and

1944). In 1980 the United States and some of its allies boycotted the Moscow Olympics; in 1984 the Soviet bloc boycotted the Los Angeles Games; and on several other occasions the Olympics found themselves at the center of a political storm (most notably in 1936, when Nazi Berlin hosted the Games, and in 1972, when Palestinian terrorists massacred the Israeli delegation to the Munich Olympics). Yet on the whole, political controversies have not derailed the Olympic project.

Now let's go back a thousand years. Suppose you wanted to hold the Medieval Olympics in Rio in 1016. Forget for a moment that Rio was then a small village of Tupi Indians and that Asians, Africans, and Europeans were not even aware of America's existence.[12] Forget the logistical problems of bringing all the world's top athletes to Rio in the absence of airplanes. Forget too that few sports were shared throughout the world, and even if all humans could run, not everybody could agree on the same rules for a running competition. Just ask yourself how to group the competing delegations. Today's International Olympic Committee spends countless hours discussing the Taiwan question and the Palestine question. Multiply this by ten thousand to estimate the number of hours you would have to spend on the politics of the Medieval Olympics.

For starters, in 1016 the Chinese Song Empire recognized no political entity on earth as its equal. It would therefore be an unthinkable humiliation for the Olympic committee to give its Olympic delegation the same status as that granted to the delegations of the Korean kingdom of Koryo or of the Vietnamese kingdom of Dai Co Viet—not to mention the delegations of "primitive barbarians" from across the seas.

The caliph in Baghdad also claimed universal hegemony, and most Sunni Muslims recognized him as their supreme leader. In practical terms, however, the caliph barely ruled the city of Baghdad. So would all Sunni athletes be part of a single caliphate delegation, or would they be separated into dozens of delegations from the numerous emirates and sultanates of the Sunni world? But why stop with the emirates and sultanates? The Arabian Desert was teeming with free Bedouin tribes who recognized no overlord save Allah. Would each be entitled to send an independent delegation to compete in archery or camel racing? Europe would give you any number of similar headaches. Would an athlete from the Norman town of Ivry compete under the banner of the local Count of Ivry, of his lord the Duke of Normandy, or perhaps of the feeble King of France?

Many of these political entities appeared and disappeared within a matter of years. As you made your preparations for the 1016 Olympics, you would not be able to know in advance which delegations would show up, because nobody could be sure which political entities would still exist next year. If the kingdom of England had sent a delegation to the 1016 Olympics, by the time the athletes came home with their medals they would have discovered that the Danes had just captured London and that England was being absorbed into the North Sea Empire of King Cnut the Great, together with Denmark, Norway, and parts of Sweden. Within another twenty years, that empire disintegrated, but thirty years later England was conquered again, this time by the Duke of Normandy.

Needless to say, the vast majority of these ephemeral political entities had neither anthem to play nor flag to hoist. Political symbols were of great importance, of course, but the symbolic language of European politics was very different from the symbolic languages of Indonesian, Chinese, and Tupi politics. Agreeing on a common protocol to mark victory would have been all but impossible.

So when you watch the Tokyo Games in 2020, remember that this seeming competition between nations actually represents an astonishing global agreement. For all the national pride people feel when their delegation wins a gold medal and their flag is raised, there is far greater reason to feel pride that humankind is capable of organizing such an event.

ONE DOLLAR TO RULE THEM ALL

In premodern times humans experimented not only with diverse political systems but also with a mind-boggling variety of economic models. Russian boyars, Hindu maharajas, Chinese mandarins, and Amerindian tribal chiefs had very different ideas about money, trade, taxation, and employment. Nowadays, in contrast, almost everybody believes in a slightly different variation on the same capitalist theme, and we are all cogs within a single global production line. Whether you live in Congo or Mongolia, in New Zealand or Bolivia, your daily routines and economic fortunes depend on the same economic theories, the same corporations and banks, and the same currents of capital. If the finance ministers of Israel and Iran were to meet for lunch, they would have a common economic language, and could easily understand and sympathize with each other's woes.

When the Islamic State conquered large parts of Syria and Iraq, it murdered tens of thousands of people, demolished archeological sites, toppled statues, and systematically destroyed the symbols of previous regimes and of Western cultural influence.[13] But when its fighters entered the local banks and found stashes of American dollars there covered with the faces of American presidents and with slogans in English praising American political and religious ideals, they did not burn these symbols of American imperialism. For the dollar bill is universally venerated across all political and religious divides. Though it has no intrinsic value—you cannot eat or drink a dollar bill—trust in the dollar and in the wisdom of the Federal Reserve is so firm that it is shared even by Islamic fundamentalists, Mexican drug lords, and North Korean tyrants.

Yet the homogeneity of contemporary humanity is most apparent when it comes to our view of the natural world and of the human body. If you fell sick a thousand years ago, it mattered a great deal where you lived. In Europe, the resident priest would probably tell you that you had made God angry and that in order to regain your health you should donate something to the church, make a pilgrimage to a sacred site, and pray fervently for God's forgiveness. Alternatively, the village witch might explain that a demon had possessed you and that she could cast it out using song, dance, and the blood of a black cockerel.

In the Middle East, doctors brought up on classical traditions might explain that your four bodily humors were out of balance and that you should harmonize them with a proper diet and foul-smelling potions. In India, Ayurvedic experts would offer their own theories concerning the balance between the three bodily elements known as *doshas* and recommend a treatment of herbs, massages, and yoga postures. Chinese physicians, Siberian shamans, African witch doctors, Amerindian medicine men—every empire, kingdom, and tribe had its own traditions and experts, each espousing different views about the human body and the nature of sickness, and each offering their own cornucopia of rituals, concoctions, and cures. Some of them worked surprisingly well, whereas others were little short of a death sentence. The only thing that united European, Chinese, African, and American medical practices was that everywhere at least a third of all children died before reaching adulthood, and average life expectancy was far below fifty.[14]

Today, if you happen to be sick, it makes much less difference where you live. In Toronto, Tokyo, Tehran, or Tel Aviv, you will be taken to similar-looking hospitals, where you will meet doctors in white coats who learned the same scientific theories in the same medical colleges. They will follow identical protocols and use identical tests to reach very similar diagnoses. They will then dispense the same medicines produced by the same international drug companies. There are still some minor cultural differences, but Canadian, Japanese, Iranian, and Israeli physicians hold much the same views about the human body and human diseases. After the Islamic State captured Raqqa and Mosul, it did not tear down the local hospitals. Rather, it launched an appeal to Muslim doctors and nurses throughout the world to volunteer their services there.[15] Presumably even Islamist doctors and nurses believe that the body is made of cells, that diseases are caused by pathogens, and that antibiotics kill bacteria.

And what makes up these cells and bacteria? Indeed, what makes up the entire world? A thousand years ago every culture had its own story about the universe, and about the fundamental ingredients of the cosmic soup. Today, learned people throughout the world believe exactly the same things about matter, energy, time, and space. Take, for example, the Iranian and North Korean nuclear programs. The whole problem is that the Iranians and North Koreans have exactly the same view of physics as the Israelis and Americans. If the Iranians and North Koreans believed that $E = mc^4$, Israel and the United States would not care an iota about their nuclear programs.

People still have different religions and national identities. But when it comes to the practical stuff—how to build a state, an economy, a hospital, or a bomb—almost all of us belong to the same civilization. There are disagreements, no doubt, but then all civilizations have their internal disputes. Indeed, they are defined by these disputes. When trying to outline their identity, people often make a grocery list of common traits. That's a mistake. They would fare much better if they made a list of common conflicts and dilemmas. For example, in 1618 Europe didn't have a single religious identity—it was defined by religious conflict. To be a European in 1618 meant to obsess about tiny doctrinal differences between Catholics and Protestants or between Calvinists and Lutherans, and to be willing to kill and be killed because of these differences. If a human being in 1618 did not care about these conflicts, that person was perhaps a Turk or a Hindu, but definitely not a European.

Similarly in 1940 Britain and Germany had very different political values, yet they were both part and parcel of "European civilization." Hitler wasn't less European than Churchill. Rather, the very struggle between them defined what it meant to be European at that particular juncture in history. In contrast, a !Kung hunter-gatherer in 1940 wasn't European because the internal European clash about race and empire would have made little sense to him.

The people we fight most often are our own family members. Identity is defined by conflicts and dilemmas more than by agreement. What does it mean to be European in 2018? It doesn't mean to have white skin, to believe in Jesus Christ, or to uphold liberty. Rather, it means to argue vehemently about immigration, about the EU, and about the limits of capitalism. It also means to obsessively ask yourself "What defines my identity?" and to worry about an aging population, about rampant consumerism, and about global warming. In their conflicts and dilemmas, twenty-first-century Europeans are different from their ancestors in 1618 and 1940 but are increasingly similar to their Chinese and Indian trade partners.

Whatever changes await us in the future, they are likely to involve a fraternal struggle within a single civilization rather than a clash between alien civilizations. The big challenges of the twenty-first century will be global in nature. What will happen when climate change triggers ecological catastrophes? What will happen when computers outperform humans in more and more tasks, and replace them in an increasing number of jobs? What will happen when biotechnology enables us to upgrade humans and extend life spans? No doubt we will have huge arguments and bitter conflicts over these questions. But these arguments and conflicts are unlikely to isolate us from one another. Just the opposite. They will make us ever more interdependent. Though humankind is very far from constituting a harmonious community, we are all members of a single rowdy global civilization.

How, then, to explain the nationalistic wave sweeping over much of the world? Perhaps in our enthusiasm for globalization we have been too quick to dismiss the good old nations. Might a return to traditional nationalism be the solution to our desperate global crises? If globalization brings with it so many problems, why not just abandon it?

7

....

Nationalism

Global Problems Need Global Answers

Given that the whole of humankind now constitutes a single civilization, with all people sharing common challenges and opportunities, why do Britons, Americans, Russians, and numerous other groups turn toward nationalistic isolation? Does a return to nationalism offer real solutions to the unprecedented problems of our global world, or is it an escapist indulgence that may doom humankind and the entire biosphere to disaster?

In order to answer this question, we should first dispel a widespread myth. Contrary to common wisdom, nationalism is not a natural and eternal part of the human psyche, and it is not rooted in human biology. True, humans are social animals through and through, with group loyalty imprinted in their genes. However, for hundreds of thousands of years *Homo sapiens* and its hominid ancestors lived in small intimate communities numbering no more than a few dozen people. Humans easily develop loyalty to small intimate groups such as a tribe, an infantry company, or a family business, but it is hardly natural for humans to be loyal to millions of utter strangers. Such mass loyalties have appeared only in the last few thousand years—yesterday morning, in evolutionary terms—and they require immense efforts of social construction.

People went to the trouble of constructing national collectives because they confronted challenges that could not be solved by any single tribe. Take, for example, the ancient tribes that lived along the Nile River thousands of years ago. The river was their lifeblood. It watered their fields and carried their commerce. But it was an unpredictable ally. Too little rain and people starved to death; too much rain and the river overflowed its banks and destroyed entire villages. No tribe could solve this problem by itself, because each tribe commanded only a small section of the river and could mobilize no more than a few hundred laborers. Only a common effort to build huge dams and dig hundreds of miles of canals could hope to restrain and harness the mighty river. This was one of the reasons the tribes gradually coalesced into a single nation that had the power to build dams and canals, regulate the flow of the river, build grain reserves for lean years, and establish a countrywide system of transportation and communication.

Despite such advantages, transforming tribes and clans into a single nation was never easy, either in ancient times or today. To realize how difficult it is to identify with such a nation, you just need to ask yourself, "Do I know these people?" I can name my two sisters and eleven cousins and spend a whole day talking about their personalities, quirks, and relationships. I cannot name the eight million people who share my Israeli citizenship, I have never met most of them, and I am very unlikely to ever meet them in the future. My ability to nevertheless feel loyal to this nebulous mass is not a legacy from my hunter-gatherer ancestors but a miracle of recent history. A Martian biologist familiar only with the anatomy and evolution of *Homo sapiens* would never guess that these apes are capable of developing communal bonds with millions of strangers. In order to convince me to be loyal to "Israel" and its eight million inhabitants, the Zionist movement and the Israeli state had to create a mammoth apparatus of education, propaganda, and flag-waving, as well as national systems of security, health, and welfare.

That does not mean there is anything wrong with national bonds. Huge systems cannot function without mass loyalties, and expanding the circle of human empathy certainly has its merits. The milder forms of patriotism have been among the most benevolent of human creations. Believing that my nation is unique, that it deserves my allegiance, and that I have special obligations toward its members inspires me to care about others and make sacrifices on their behalf. It is a dangerous mistake to imagine that without nationalism we would all be living in a liberal paradise. More likely we would be living in tribal chaos. Peaceful, prosperous, and liberal countries such as Sweden, Germany, and Switzerland all enjoy a strong sense of nationalism. The list of countries lacking robust national bonds includes Afghanistan, Somalia, Congo, and most other failed states.[1]

The problem starts when benign patriotism morphs into chauvinistic ultranationalism. Instead of believing that my nation is unique—which is true of all nations—I might begin feeling that my nation is supreme, that I owe it my entire loyalty, and that I have no significant obligations to anyone else. This is fertile ground for violent conflicts. For generations the most basic criticism of nationalism was that it led to war. Yet the link between nationalism and violence hardly curbed nationalist excesses, particularly as each nation justified its own military expansion by the need to protect itself against the machinations of its neighbors. As long as the nation provided most of its citizens with unprecedented levels of security and prosperity, they were willing to pay the price in blood. In the nineteenth and early twentieth centuries the nationalist deal still looked very attractive. Though nationalism was leading to horrendous conflicts on an unprecedented scale, modern nation-states also built massive systems of healthcare, education, and welfare. National health services made Passchendaele and Verdun seem worthwhile.

Everything changed in 1945. The invention of nuclear weapons sharply tilted the balance of the nationalist deal. After Hiroshima people no longer feared that nationalism would lead to mere war; they began fearing it would lead to *nuclear* war. Total annihilation has a way of sharpening people's minds, and thanks in no small measure to the atom bomb, the impossible happened and the nationalist genie was squeezed at least halfway back into its bottle. Just as the ancient villagers of the Nile Basin redirected some of their loyalty from local clans to a much bigger kingdom that was able to restrain the dangerous river, so in the nuclear age a global community gradually developed over and above the various nations, because only such a community could restrain the nuclear demon.

In the 1964 U.S. presidential campaign, Lyndon B. Johnson aired the famous "Daisy" advertisement, one of the most successful pieces of propaganda in the annals of television. The advertisement opens with a little girl picking the petals of a daisy as she counts, but when she reaches ten, a metallic male voice takes over, counting back from ten to zero as in a missile countdown. Upon reaching zero, the bright flash of a nuclear explosion fills the screen. Then candidate Johnson addresses the American public and says: "These are the stakes. To make a world in which all of God's children can live, or to go into the dark. We must either love each other, or we must die."[2] We tend to associate the "make love, not war" slogan with the late 1960s counterculture, but in fact, in 1964 it was already accepted wisdom even among hard-nosed politicians such as Johnson.

Consequently, during the Cold War nationalism took a backseat to a more global approach to international politics, and when the Cold War ended, globalization seemed to be the irresistible wave of the future. It was expected that humankind would leave nationalistic politics completely behind, as a relic of more primitive times that might appeal at most to the ill-informed inhabitants of a few underdeveloped countries. Events in recent years have proved, however, that nationalism still has a powerful hold even on the citizens of

Europe and the United States, not to mention Russia, India, and China. Alienated by the impersonal forces of global capitalism, and fearing for the fate of national systems of health, education, and welfare, people all over the world seek reassurance and meaning in the bosom of the nation.

Yet the question raised by Johnson in the "Daisy" advertisement is even more pertinent today than it was in 1964. Will we make a world in which all humans can live together, or will we all go into the dark? Do Donald Trump, Theresa May, Vladimir Putin, Narendra Modi, and their colleagues save the world by fanning our national sentiments, or is the current nationalist spate a form of escapism from the intractable global problems we face?

THE NUCLEAR CHALLENGE

Let's start with humankind's familiar nemesis: nuclear war. When the "Daisy" advertisement aired in 1964, two years after the Cuban missile crisis, nuclear annihilation was a palpable threat. Pundits and laypeople alike feared that humankind did not have the wisdom to avert destruction, and that it was only a matter of time before the Cold War turned scorching hot. In fact, humankind successfully rose to the nuclear challenge. Americans, Soviets, Europeans, and Chinese changed the way geopolitics had been conducted for millennia, so the Cold War ended with little bloodshed, and a new internationalist world order fostered an era of unprecedented peace. Not only was nuclear war averted, but war of all kinds declined. Since 1945 surprisingly few borders have been redrawn through naked aggression, and most countries have ceased using war as a standard political tool. In 2016, despite wars in Syria, Ukraine, and several other hot spots, fewer people died from human violence than from obesity, car accidents, or suicide.[3] This may well have been the greatest political and moral achievement of our times.

Unfortunately, by now we are so used to this achievement that we take it for granted. This is partly why people allow themselves to play with fire. Russia and the United States have recently embarked on a new nuclear arms race, developing novel doomsday machines that threaten to undo the hard-won gains of the last decades and bring us back to the brink of nuclear annihilation.[4] Meanwhile, the public has learned to stop worrying and love the bomb (as suggested in *Dr. Strangelove*) or has just forgotten about its existence.

This is why the Brexit debate in Britain—a major nuclear power—revolved mainly around questions of economics and immigration, while the vital contribution of the EU to European and global peace has largely been ignored. After centuries of terrible bloodshed, French, Germans, Italians, and Britons have finally built a mechanism that ensures continental harmony—only to have the British public throw a wrench into the miracle machine.

It was extremely difficult to construct the internationalist regime that prevented nuclear war and safeguarded global peace. No doubt we need to adapt this regime to the changing conditions of the world, for example by relying less on the United States and granting a greater role to non-Western powers such as China and India.[5] But abandoning this regime altogether and reverting to nationalist power politics would be an irresponsible gamble. True, in the nineteenth century countries played the nationalist game without destroying human civilization. But that was in the pre-Hiroshima era. Since then, nuclear weapons have raised the stakes and changed the fundamental nature of war and politics. As long as humans know how to enrich uranium and plutonium, their survival depends on privileging the prevention of nuclear war over the interests of any particular nation. Zealous nationalists who cry "Our country first!" should ask themselves whether their country by itself, without a robust system of international cooperation, can protect the world—or even itself—from nuclear destruction.

THE ECOLOGICAL CHALLENGE

On top of nuclear war, in the coming decades humankind will face a new existential threat that hardly registered on political radars in 1964: ecological collapse. Humans are destabilizing the global biosphere on multiple fronts. We are taking more and more resources out of the environment while pumping back into it enormous quantities of waste and poison, thereby changing the composition of the soil, the water, and the atmosphere.

We are hardly even aware of the myriad ways in which we disrupt the delicate ecological balance that has been shaped over millions of years. Consider, for example, the use of phosphorus as a fertilizer. In small quantities it is an essential nutrient for the growth of plants. But in excessive amounts it becomes toxic. Modern industrial farming is based on artificially fertilizing the fields with plenty of phosphorus, but the high-phosphorus runoff from the farms subsequently poisons rivers, lakes, and oceans, with a devastating impact on marine life. A farmer growing corn in Iowa might thus inadvertently kill fish in the Gulf of Mexico.

As a result of such activities, habitats are degraded, animals and plants are becoming extinct, and entire ecosystems such as the Great Barrier Reef off Australia and the Amazon rainforest might be destroyed. For thousands of years *Homo sapiens* behaved as an ecological serial killer; now it is morphing into an ecological mass murderer. If we continue with our present course, it will not just cause the annihilation of a large percentage of all life-forms but also might sap the foundations of human civilization.[6]

Most threatening of all is the prospect of climate change. Humans have been around for hundreds of thousands of years and have survived numerous ice ages and warm spells. However, agriculture, cities, and complex societies have existed for no more than ten thousand years. During this period, known as the Holocene, Earth's climate has been relatively stable. Any deviation from Holocene standards will present human societies with enormous challenges they have never encountered before. It will be like conducting an open-ended experiment on billions of human guinea pigs. Even if human civilization eventually adapts to the new conditions, who knows how many victims might perish in the process of adaptation.

This terrifying experiment has already been set in motion. Unlike nuclear war—which is a future potential—climate change is a present reality. There is a scientific consensus that human activities, in particular the emission of greenhouse gases such as carbon dioxide, are causing the earth's climate to change at a frightening rate.[7] Nobody knows exactly how much carbon dioxide we can continue to pump into the atmosphere without triggering an irreversible cataclysm. But our best scientific estimates indicate that unless we dramatically cut the emission of greenhouse gases in the next twenty years, average global temperatures will increase by more than 3.6°F, resulting in expanding deserts, disappearing ice caps, rising oceans and more frequent extreme weather events such as hurricanes and typhoons.[8] These changes in turn will disrupt agricultural production, inundate cities, make much of the world uninhabitable, and send hundreds of millions of refugees in search of new homes.[9]

Moreover, we are rapidly approaching a number of tipping points, beyond which even a dramatic drop in greenhouse gas emissions will not be enough to reverse the trend and avoid a worldwide tragedy. For example, as global warming melts the polar ice sheets, less sunlight is reflected back from planet Earth to outer space. This means that the planet absorbs more heat, temperatures rise even higher, and the ice melts even faster. Once this feedback loop crosses a critical threshold it will gather an unstoppable momentum, and all the ice in the polar regions will melt even if humans stop burning coal, oil, and gas. Therefore it is not enough that we recognize the danger we face. It is critical that we actually do something about it *now*.

Unfortunately, as of 2018, instead of a reduction in greenhouse gas emissions, the global emission rate is still increasing. Humanity has very little time left to wean itself from fossil fuels. We need to enter rehab today. Not next year or next month, but today. "Hello, I am *Homo sapiens*, and I am a fossil-fuel addict."

Where does nationalism fit into this alarming picture? Is there a nationalist answer to the ecological menace? Can any nation, however powerful, stop global warming by itself? Individual countries can certainly adopt a variety of green policies, many of which make good economic as well as environmental sense. Governments can tax carbon emissions, add the cost of externalities to the price of oil and gas, adopt stronger environmental regulations, cut subsidies to polluting industries, and incentivize the switch to renewable energy. They can also invest more money in researching and developing revolutionary eco-friendly technologies, in a kind of ecological Manhattan Project. The internal combustion engine is to be thanked for many of the advancements of the last 150 years, but if we are to keep a stable physical and economic environment, it must now be retired and substituted by new technologies that do not burn fossil fuels.[10]

Technological breakthroughs can be helpful in many other fields besides energy. Consider, for example, the potential of developing "clean meat." At present the meat industry not only inflicts untold misery on billions of sentient beings but is also one of the chief causes of global warming, one of the main consumers of antibiotics and poison, and one of the foremost polluters of air, land, and water. According to a 2013 report by the Institution of Mechanical Engineers, it takes nearly four thousand gallons of fresh water to produce a little over two pounds of beef, compared to the seventy-five gallons needed to produce the same weight of potatoes.[11]

The pressure on the environment is likely to get worse as rising prosperity in countries such as China and Brazil allows hundreds of millions of additional people to switch from eating potatoes to eating beef on a regular basis. It would be difficult to persuade the Chinese and the Brazilians—not to mention the Americans and the Germans—to stop eating steaks, hamburgers, and sausages. But what if engineers could find a way to grow meat from cells? If you want a hamburger, just grow a hamburger, instead of raising and slaughtering an entire cow (and transporting the carcass thousands of miles).

This might sound like science fiction, but the world's first clean hamburger was grown from cells—and then eaten—in 2013. It cost $330,000. Four years of research and development brought the price down to $11 per unit, and within another decade industrially pro-duced clean meat is expected to be cheaper than slaughtered meat. This technological development could save billions of animals from a life of abject misery, could help feed billions of malnourished hu-mans, and could simultaneously help to prevent ecological melt-down.[12]

There are many things that governments, corporations, and indi-viduals can do to avoid climate change. But to be effective, they must be done on a global level. When it comes to climate, countries are just not sovereign. They are at the mercy of actions taken by people on the other side of the planet. The Republic of Kiribati, an island nation in the Pacific Ocean, could reduce its greenhouse gas emissions to zero and nevertheless be submerged under the rising waves if other countries don't follow suit. Chad could put a solar panel on every roof in the country and yet become a barren desert due to the irresponsible environmental policies of distant foreign-ers. Even powerful nations such as China and Japan are not ecologi-cally sovereign. To protect Shanghai, Hong Kong, and Tokyo from destructive floods and typhoons, the Chinese and Japanese will have to persuade the Russian and American governments to abandon their "business as usual" approach.

Nationalist isolationism is probably even more dangerous in the context of climate change than nuclear war. An all-out nuclear war threatens to destroy all nations, so all nations have an equal stake in preventing it. Global warming, in contrast, will probably have dif-ferent impacts on different nations. Some countries, most notably Russia, might actually benefit from it. Because Russia has relatively few coastline assets, it is far less worried than China or Kiribati about rising sea levels. And whereas higher temperatures are likely to turn Chad into a desert, they might simultaneously turn Siberia into the breadbasket of the world. Moreover, as the ice melts in the far north, the Russian-dominated Arctic sea lanes might become the artery of global commerce, and Kamchatka might replace Singapore as the crossroad of the world.[13]

Similarly, replacing fossil fuels with renewable energy sources is likely to appeal to some countries more than to others. China, Japan, and South Korea depend on importing huge quantities of oil and gas. They will be delighted to be free of that burden. Russia, Iran, and Saudi Arabia depend on exporting oil and gas. Their economies will collapse if oil and gas suddenly give way to solar and wind.

Consequently, while some nations such as China, Japan, and Kiribati are likely to push hard for reducing global carbon emissions as soon as possible, other nations such as Russia and Iran might be far less enthusiastic. Even in countries that stand to lose much from global warming, such as the United States, nationalists might be too shortsighted and self-absorbed to appreciate the danger. A small but telling example occurred in January 2018, when the United States announced a 30 percent tariff on foreign-made solar panels and solar equipment, preferring to support American solar producers even at a cost of slowing the switch to renewable energy.[14]

An atom bomb is such an obvious and immediate threat that nobody can ignore it. Global warming, in contrast, is a more vague and protracted menace. Therefore whenever long-term environmental considerations demand some painful short-term sacrifice, nationalists might be tempted to put immediate national interests first, and reassure themselves that they can worry about the environment later, or just leave it to people elsewhere. Alternatively, they may simply deny the problem. It isn't a coincidence that skepticism about climate change tends to be the preserve of the nationalist right. You rarely see left-wing socialists tweet that "climate change is a Chinese hoax." Since there is no national answer to the problem of global warming, some nationalist politicians prefer to believe the problem does not exist.[15]

THE TECHNOLOGICAL CHALLENGE

The same dynamics are likely to spoil any nationalist antidote to the third existential threat of the twenty-first century: technological disruption. As we saw in earlier chapters, the merger of infotech and biotech opens the door to a cornucopia of doomsday scenarios, ranging from digital dictatorships to the creation of a global useless class.

What is the nationalist answer to these menaces?

There is no nationalist answer. As in the case of climate change, so also with technological disruption; the nation-state is simply the wrong framework with which to address the threat. Since research and development are not the monopoly of any one country, even a superpower such as the United States cannot restrict them by itself. If the U.S. government forbids genetically engineering human embryos, this doesn't prevent Chinese scientists from doing so. And if the resulting developments confer on China some crucial economic or military advantage, the United States will be tempted to break its own ban. Particularly in a xenophobic dog-eats-dog world, if even a single country chooses to pursue a high-risk, high-gain technological path, other countries will be forced to do the same, because nobody can afford to remain behind. In order to avoid such a race to the bottom, humankind will probably need some kind of global identity and loyalty.

Moreover, whereas nuclear war and climate change threaten only the physical survival of humankind, disruptive technologies might change the very nature of humanity, and are therefore entangled with humans' deepest ethical and religious beliefs. While everyone agrees that we should avoid nuclear war and ecological meltdown, people have widely different opinions about using bioengineering and AI to upgrade humans and to create new life-forms. If humankind fails to devise and administer globally accepted ethical guidelines, it will be open season for Dr. Frankenstein.

When it comes to formulating such ethical guidelines, nationalism suffers above all from a failure of the imagination. Nationalists think in terms of territorial conflicts lasting centuries, while the technological revolutions of the twenty-first century should really be understood in cosmic terms. After four billion years of organic life evolving by natural selection, science is ushering in the era of inorganic life shaped by intelligent design.

In the process, *Homo sapiens* itself will likely disappear. Today we are still apes of the hominid family. We still share most of our bodily structures, physical abilities, and mental faculties with Neanderthals and chimpanzees. Not only are our hands, eyes, and brains distinctly hominid, but so are our lust, our love, our anger, and our social bonds. Within a century or two, the combination of biotechnology and AI might result in physical and mental traits that completely break free of the hominid mold. Some believe that consciousness might even be severed from any organic structure and could surf cyberspace free of all biological and physical constraints. On the other hand, we might witness the complete decoupling of intelligence from consciousness, and the development of AI might result in a world dominated by superintelligent but completely nonconscious entities.

What does Israeli, Russian, or French nationalism have to say about this? In order to make wise choices about the future of life we need to go way beyond the nationalist viewpoint and look at things from a global or even a cosmic perspective.

SPACESHIP EARTH

Each of these three problems—nuclear war, ecological collapse, and technological disruption—is enough to threaten the future of human civilization. But taken together, they add up to an unprecedented existential crisis, especially because they are likely to reinforce and compound one another.

For example, although the ecological crisis threatens the survival of human civilization as we have known it, it is unlikely to stop the development of AI and bioengineering. If you are counting on rising oceans, dwindling food supplies, and mass migrations to divert our attention from algorithms and genes, think again. As the ecological crisis deepens, the development of high-risk, high-gain technologies will probably only accelerate.

Indeed, climate change may well come to perform the same function as the two world wars. Between 1914 and 1918, and again between 1939 and 1945, the pace of technological development skyrocketed, because nations engaged in total war threw caution and economy to the wind and invested immense resources in all kinds of audacious and fantastic projects. Many of these projects failed, but some produced tanks, radar, poison gas, supersonic jets, intercontinental ballistic missiles, and nuclear bombs. Similarly, nations facing a climate cataclysm might be tempted to invest their hopes in desperate technological gambles. Humankind has a lot of justifiable concerns about AI and bioengineering, but in times of crisis people do risky things. Whatever you think about regulating disruptive technologies, ask yourself whether these regulations are likely to hold even if climate change causes global food shortages, floods cities all over the world, and sends hundreds of millions of refugees across borders.

In turn, technological disruptions might increase the danger of apocalyptic wars, not just by increasing global tensions but also by destabilizing the nuclear balance of power. Since the 1950s, superpowers avoided conflicts with one another because they all knew that war meant mutually assured destruction. But as new kinds of offensive and defensive weapons appear, a rising technological superpower might conclude that it can destroy its enemies with impunity. Conversely, a declining power might fear that its traditional nuclear weapons might soon become obsolete and that it had better use them before it loses them. Traditionally, nuclear confrontations resembled a hyperrational chess game. What would happen when players could use cyberattacks to wrest control of a rival's pieces, when anonymous third parties could move a pawn without anyone knowing who was making the move—or when AlphaZero graduates from ordinary chess to nuclear chess?

Just as the different challenges are likely to compound one another, so also the goodwill necessary to confront one challenge may be sapped by problems on another front. Countries locked in armed competition are unlikely to agree on restricting the development of AI, and countries striving to outstrip the technological achievements of their rivals will find it very difficult to agree on a common plan to stop climate change. As long as the world remains divided into rival nations, it will be very hard to simultaneously overcome all three challenges—and failure on even a single front might prove catastrophic.

To conclude, the nationalist wave sweeping across the world cannot return the world to 1939 or 1914. Technology has changed everything by creating a set of global existential threats that no nation can solve on its own. A common enemy is the best catalyst for forging a common identity, and humankind now has at least three such enemies—nuclear war, climate change, and technological disruption. If despite these common threats humans choose to privilege their particular national loyalties above everything else, the results may be far worse than in 1914 and 1939.

A much better path is the one outlined in the European Union's Constitution, which says that "while remaining proud of their own national identities and history, the peoples of Europe are determined to transcend their former divisions and, united ever more closely, to forge a common destiny."[16] This does not mean abolishing all national identities, abandoning all local traditions, and turning humanity into homogeneous gray goo. Nor does it mean vilifying all expressions of patriotism. Indeed, by providing a continental military and economic protective shell, the European Union arguably fostered local patriotism in places such as Flanders, Lombardy, Catalonia, and Scotland. The idea of establishing an independent Scotland or Catalonia looks more attractive when you don't have to fear a German invasion and when you can count on a common European front against global warming and global corporations.

European nationalists are therefore taking it easy. For all the talk of the return of the nation, few Europeans are actually willing to kill and be killed for it. When the Scots sought to break away from London's grip in the days of William Wallace and Robert Bruce, they had to raise an army to do so. In contrast, not a single person was killed during the 2014 Scottish referendum, and if next time Scots do vote for independence, it is highly unlikely that they will have to restage the Battle of Bannockburn. The Catalan attempt to break away from Spain has resulted in considerably more violence, but it too falls far short of the carnage Barcelona experienced in 1939 or in 1714.

The rest of the world can learn from the European example. Even on a united planet there will be plenty of room for the kind of patriotism that celebrates the uniqueness of my nation and stresses my special obligations toward it. Yet if we want to survive and flourish, humankind has little choice but to complement such local loyalties with substantial obligations toward a global community. A person can and should be loyal simultaneously to her family, her neighborhood, her profession, and her nation—so why not add humankind and planet Earth to that list? True, when you have multiple loyalties, conflicts are sometimes inevitable. But then who said life was simple? Deal with it.

In previous centuries national identities were forged because humans faced problems and opportunities that were far beyond the scope of local tribes and which only countrywide cooperation could hope to handle. In the twenty-first century, nations find themselves in the same situation as the old tribes: they are no longer the right framework to manage the most important challenges of the age. We need a new global identity because national institutions are incapable of handling a set of unprecedented global predicaments. We now have a global ecology, a global economy, and a global science—but we are still stuck with only national politics. This mismatch prevents the political system from effectively countering our main problems. To have effective politics, either we must deglobalize the ecology, the economy, and the march of science or we must globalize our politics. Since it is impossible to deglobalize the ecology and the march of science, and since the cost of deglobalizing the economy would probably be prohibitive, the only real solution is to globalize politics. This does not mean establishing a "global government"—a doubtful and unrealistic vision. Rather, to globalize politics means that political dynamics within countries and even cities should give far more weight to global problems and interests.

Nationalist sentiments are unlikely to be of much help in that. Perhaps, then, we can rely on the universal religious traditions of humankind to help us unite the world? Hundreds of years ago, religions such as Christianity and Islam already thought in global rather than local terms, and they were always keenly interested in the big questions of life rather than just in the political struggles of this or that nation. But are traditional religions still relevant? Do they retain the power to shape the world, or are they just inert relics from our past, tossed here and there by the mighty forces of modern states, economies, and technologies?

8

....

Religion

God Now Serves the Nation

So far, modern ideologies, scientific experts, and national governments have failed to create a viable vision for the future of humanity. Can such a vision be drawn from the deep wells of human religious traditions? Maybe the answer has been waiting for us all along in the pages of the Bible, the Quran, or the Vedas.

Secular people are likely to react to this idea with ridicule or apprehension. Holy scriptures may have been relevant in the Middle Ages, but how can they guide us in an era of artificial intelligence, bioengineering, global warming, and cyberwarfare? Yet secular people are a minority. Billions of humans still profess greater faith in the Quran and the Bible than in the theory of evolution; religious movements shape the politics of countries as diverse as India, Turkey, and the United States; and religious animosities fuel conflicts from Nigeria to the Philippines.

So how relevant are religions such as Christianity, Islam, and Hinduism? Can they help us solve the major problems we face? To understand the role of traditional religions in the world of the twenty-first century, we need to distinguish between three types of problems:

1. Technical problems. For example, how should farmers in arid countries deal with severe droughts caused by global warming?
2. Policy problems. For example, what measures should governments adopt to prevent global warming in the first place?
3. Identity problems. For example, should I even care about the problems of farmers on the other side of the world, or should I care only about problems of people from my own tribe and country?

As we shall see in the following pages, traditional religions are largely irrelevant to technical and policy problems. In contrast, they are extremely relevant to identity problems—but in most cases they constitute a major part of the problem rather than a potential solution.

TECHNICAL PROBLEMS: CHRISTIAN AGRICULTURE

In premodern times religions were responsible for solving a wide range of technical problems in mundane areas such as agriculture. Divine calendars determined when to plant and when to harvest, while temple rituals secured rainfall and protected against pests. When an agricultural crisis loomed due to drought or a plague of locusts, farmers turned to the priests to intercede with the gods. Medicine too fell within the religious domain. Almost every prophet, guru, and shaman doubled as a healer. Jesus, for example, spent much of his time healing the sick, helping the blind to see, granting speech to the mute, and making the mad sane. Whether you lived in ancient Egypt or in medieval Europe, if you were ill you were likely to go to the witch doctor rather than to the doctor, and to make a pilgrimage to a renowned temple rather than to a hospital.

In recent times biologists and surgeons have taken over from priests and miracle workers. If Egypt is now struck by a plague of locusts, Egyptians may well ask Allah for help—why not?—but they will not forget to call upon chemists, entomologists, and geneticists to develop stronger pesticides and insect-resistant wheat strains. If the child of a devout Hindu suffers from a severe case of measles, the father will say a prayer to Dhanvantari and offer flowers and sweets at the local temple—but only after he has rushed the toddler to the nearest hospital and entrusted him to the care of the doctors there. Even mental illness—the last bastion of religious healers—is gradually passing into the hands of scientists, as neurology replaces demonology and Prozac supplants exorcism.

The victory of science has been so complete that our very idea of religion has changed. We no longer associate religion with farming and medicine. Even many zealots now suffer from collective amnesia and prefer to forget that traditional religions ever laid claim to those domains. "So what if we turn to engineers and doctors?" say the zealots. "That proves nothing. What has religion got to do with agriculture or medicine in the first place?"

Traditional religions have lost so much turf because, frankly, they just weren't very good at farming or healthcare. The true expertise of priests and gurus has never really been rainmaking, healing, prophecy, or magic. Rather, it has always been interpretation. A priest is not somebody who knows how to perform the rain dance and end the drought. A priest is somebody who knows how to justify why the rain dance failed, and why we must keep believing in our god even though he seems deaf to all our prayers.

Yet it is precisely their genius for interpretation that puts religious leaders at a disadvantage when they compete against scientists. Scientists too know how to cut corners and twist the evidence, but in the end, the mark of science is the willingness to admit failure and try a different tack. That's why scientists gradually learn how to grow better crops and make better medicines, whereas priests and gurus learn only how to make better excuses. Over the centuries, even the true believers have noticed the difference, which is why religious authority has been dwindling in more and more technical fields. This is also why the entire world has increasingly become a single civilization. When things really work, everybody adopts them.

POLICY PROBLEMS: MUSLIM ECONOMICS

While science provides us with clear-cut answers to technical questions such as how to cure measles, there is considerable disagreement among scientists about questions of policy. Almost all scientists concur that global warming is a fact, but there is no consensus regarding the best economic reaction to this threat. That does not mean, however, that traditional religions can help us resolve the issue. Ancient scriptures are just not good guides for modern economics, and the main fault lines—for example, between capitalists and socialists—don't correspond to the divisions between traditional religions.

True, in countries such as Israel and Iran rabbis and ayatollahs have a direct say about the government's economic policy, and even in more secular countries such as the United States and Brazil religious leaders influence public opinion on matters ranging from taxation to environmental regulations. Yet a closer look reveals that in most of these cases, traditional religions really play second fiddle to modern scientific theories. When Ayatollah Khamenei needs to make a crucial decision about the Iranian economy, he will not be able to find the necessary answer in the Quran, because seventh-century Arabs knew very little about the problems and opportunities of modern industrial economies and global financial markets. So he, or his aides, must turn to Karl Marx, Milton Friedman, Friedrich Hayek, and the modern science of economics to get answers. Having made up his mind to raise interest rates, lower taxes, privatize government monopolies, or sign an international tariff agreement, Khamenei can then use his religious knowledge and authority to wrap the scientific answer in the garb of this or that Quranic verse and present it to the masses as the will of Allah. But the garb matters little. When you compare the economic policies of Shiite Iran, Sunni Saudi Arabia, Jewish Israel, Hindu India, and Christian America, you just don't see that much of a difference.

During the nineteenth and twentieth centuries, Muslim, Jewish, Hindu, and Christian thinkers railed against modern materialism, soulless capitalism, and the excesses of the bureaucratic state. They promised that if only they were given a chance, they would solve all the ills of modernity and establish a completely different socioeconomic system based on the eternal spiritual values of their creed. Well, they have been given quite a few chances, and the only noticeable change they have made to the edifice of modern economies is to redo the paint and place a huge crescent, cross, Star of David, or om on the roof.

Just as in the case of rainmaking, so also when it comes to economics: it is the long-honed expertise of religious scholars in reinterpreting texts that makes religion irrelevant. No matter which economic policy Khamenei chooses, he can always square it with the Quran. Therefore the Quran is degraded from a source of true knowledge to a source of mere authority. When you face a difficult economic dilemma, you read Marx and Hayek closely, and they help you understand the economic system better, see things from a new angle, and think about potential solutions. Having formulated an answer, you then turn to the Quran and read it closely in search of some surah that, if interpreted imaginatively enough, can justify the solution you got from Hayek or Marx. No matter what solution you find there, if you are a good Quranic scholar you will always be able to justify it.

The same is true of Christianity. A Christian may be a capitalist as easily as a socialist, and even though a few things Jesus said smack of downright communism, during the Cold War good American capitalists went on reading the Sermon on the Mount without taking much notice. There is just no such thing as "Christian economics," "Muslim economics," or "Hindu economics."

Not that there aren't any economic ideas in the Bible, the Quran, or the Vedas—it is just that these ideas are not up to date. Mahatma Gandhi's reading of the Vedas caused him to envision independent India as a collection of self-sufficient agrarian communities, each spinning its own khadi cloth, exporting little and importing even less. The most famous photograph of him shows him spinning cotton with his own hands, and he made the humble spinning wheel the symbol of the Indian nationalist movement.[1] Yet this Arcadian vision was simply incompatible with the realities of modern economics, and for that reason not much has remained of it save for Gandhi's radiant image on billions of rupee notes.

Modern economic theories are so much more relevant than traditional dogmas that it has become common to interpret even ostensibly religious conflicts in economic terms, whereas nobody thinks of doing the reverse. For example, some argue that the Troubles in Northern Ireland between Catholics and Protestants were fueled largely by class conflict. Due to various historical accidents, in Northern Ireland the upper classes were mostly Protestant and the lower classes were mostly Catholic. Therefore what seems at first sight to have been a theological conflict about the nature of Christ was in fact a typical struggle between haves and have-nots. In contrast, very few people would claim that the conflicts between communist guerrillas and capitalist landowners in South America in the 1970s were really just a cover for a far deeper disagreement about Christian theology.

So what difference would religion make when facing the big questions of the twenty-first century? Take the question of whether to grant AI the authority to make decisions about people's lives— choosing what you should study, where you should work, and whom you should marry. What is the Muslim position on that question? What is the Jewish position? There are no "Muslim" or "Jewish" positions here. Humankind is likely to be divided into two main camps—those in favor of giving AI significant authority, and those opposed to it. Muslims and Jews are likely to be found in *both* camps, and to justify whichever position they espouse through imaginative interpretations of the Quran and the Talmud.

Of course, religious groups might harden their views on particular issues and turn them into allegedly sacred and eternal dogmas. In the 1970s theologians in Latin America came up with liberation theology, which made Jesus look a bit like Che Guevara. Similarly, Jesus can easily be recruited to the debate on global warming, with the result that current political positions look as if they are eternal religious principles.

This is already beginning to happen. Opposition to environmental regulations is incorporated into the fire-and-brimstone sermons of some American evangelical pastors, while Pope Francis is leading the charge against global warming, in the name of Christ (as witnessed in his second encyclical, "Laudato sí").[2] So perhaps by 2070, on the environmental question it will make all the difference in the world whether you are evangelical or Catholic. It goes without saying that evangelicals will object to any cap on carbon emissions, while Catholics will believe that Jesus preached that we must protect the environment.

You will see the difference even in their cars. Evangelicals will drive huge gasoline-guzzling SUVs, while devout Catholics will go around in slick electric cars with a bumper sticker reading "Burn the Planet—and Burn in Hell!" But though they might quote various biblical passages in defense of their positions, the real source of their difference will be in modern scientific theories and political movements, not in the Bible. From this perspective, religion doesn't really have much to contribute to the great policy debates of our time. As Karl Marx argued, it is just a veneer.

IDENTITY PROBLEMS: THE LINES IN THE SAND

Yet Marx exaggerated when he dismissed religion as a mere super-structure hiding powerful technological and economic forces. Even if Islam, Hinduism, or Christianity is just a set of colorful decorations over a modern economic structure, people often identify with the decor, and people's identities are a crucial historical force. Human power depends on mass cooperation, and mass cooperation depends on manufacturing mass identities—and all mass identities are based on fictional stories, not on scientific facts or even on economic necessities. In the twenty-first century, the division of humans into Jews and Muslims or into Russians and Poles still depends on religious myths. Attempts by Nazis and communists to scientifically determine human identities based on race and class proved to be dangerous pseudoscience, and since then scientists have been extremely reluctant to help define any "natural" identities for human beings.

So in the twenty-first century religions don't bring rain, they don't cure illnesses, they don't build bombs—but they do get to determine who are "us" and who are "them," whom we should cure and whom we should bomb. As noted earlier, in practical terms there are surprisingly few differences between Shiite Iran, Sunni Saudi Arabia, and Jewish Israel. All are bureaucratic nation-states, all pursue more or less capitalist policies, all vaccinate kids against polio, and all rely on chemists and physicists to make bombs. There is no such thing as Shiite bureaucracy, Sunni capitalism, or Jewish physics. So how do we make people feel loyal to one human tribe and hostile to another?

In order to draw firm lines in the shifting sands of humanity, religions use rites, rituals, and ceremonies. Shiites, Sunnis, and Orthodox Jews wear different clothes, chant different prayers, and observe different taboos. These differing religious traditions often fill daily life with beauty and encourage people to behave more kindly and more charitably. Five times a day, the muezzin's melodious voice rises above the noise of bazaars, offices, and factories, calling Muslims to take a break from the hustle and bustle of mundane pursuits and try to connect to an eternal truth. Their Hindu neighbors may reach for the same goal with the help of daily pujas and the recitation of mantras. Every week on Friday night, Jewish families sit for a special meal of joy, thanksgiving, and togetherness. Two days later, on Sunday morning, Christian gospel choirs bring hope to the lives of millions, helping to forge community bonds of trust and affection.

Other religious traditions fill the world with a lot of ugliness and make people behave meanly and cruelly. There is little to be said, for example, in favor of religiously inspired misogyny or caste discrimination. But whether beautiful or ugly, all such religious traditions unite certain people while distinguishing them from their neighbors. Looked at from the outside, the religious traditions that divide people often seem trifling, and Freud ridiculed the obsession people have about such matters as "the narcissism of small differences."[3] But in history and in politics, small differences can go a very long way. For example, if you happen to be gay or lesbian, it is literally a matter of life and death whether you live in Israel, Iran, or Saudi Arabia. In Israel, LGBT people enjoy the protection of the law, and there are even some rabbis who would bless the marriage of two women. In Iran, gays and lesbians are systematically persecuted and occasionally even executed. In Saudi Arabia, a lesbian could not even drive a car until 2018—just for being a woman, never mind being a lesbian.

Perhaps the best example of the continuing power and importance of traditional religions in the modern world comes from Japan. In 1853 an American fleet forced Japan to open itself to the modern world. In response, the Japanese state embarked on a rapid and extremely successful process of modernization. Within a few decades it became a powerful bureaucratic state relying on science, capitalism, and the latest military technology to defeat China and

Russia, occupy Taiwan and Korea, and ultimately sink much of the American fleet at Pearl Harbor and destroy the European empires in the Far East. Yet Japan did not blindly copy the Western blueprint. It was fiercely determined to protect its unique identity and to ensure that modern Japanese citizens would be loyal to Japan rather than to science, modernity, or some nebulous global community.

To that end, Japan upheld the native religion, Shinto, as the cornerstone of Japanese identity. In truth, the Japanese state reinvented Shinto. Traditional Shinto was a hodgepodge of animist beliefs in various deities, spirits, and ghosts, and every village and temple had its own favorite spirits and local customs. In the late nineteenth and early twentieth centuries, the Japanese state created an official version of Shinto, while discouraging many local traditions. This "state Shinto" was fused with very modern ideas about nationality and race, which the Japanese elite selected from the European imperialists. Any element in Buddhism, Confucianism, and the samurai feudal ethos that could be helpful in cementing loyalty to the state was added to the mix. To top it all off, state Shinto enshrined as its supreme principle the worship of the Japanese emperor, who was considered a direct descendant of the sun goddess Amaterasu, and himself no less than a living god.[4]

On first sight, this odd concoction of old and new seemed an extremely inappropriate choice for a state embarking on a crash course of modernization. A living god? Animist spirits? Feudal ethos? That sounds more like a Neolithic chieftainship than a modern industrial power.

Yet it worked like magic. The Japanese modernized at a breathtaking pace while simultaneously developing a fanatical loyalty to their state. The best-known sign of the success of state Shinto is the fact that Japan was the first power to develop and use precision-guided missiles. Decades before the United States fielded the smart bomb, and at a time when Nazi Germany was only beginning to deploy dumb V-2 rockets, Japan sank dozens of allied ships with precision-guided missiles—better known as kamikaze. Whereas in present-day precision-guided munitions the guidance is provided by computers, the kamikaze were ordinary airplanes loaded with explosives and guided by human pilots willing to go on one-way missions. This willingness was the product of the death-defying spirit of sacrifice cultivated by state Shinto. The kamikaze thus relied on combining state-of-the-art technology with state-of-the-art religious indoctrination.[5]

Knowingly or not, numerous governments today follow the Japanese example. They adopt the universal tools and structures of modernity while relying on traditional religions to preserve a unique national identity. The role of state Shinto in Japan is fulfilled to a lesser or greater degree by Orthodox Christianity in Russia, Catholicism in Poland, Shiite Islam in Iran, Wahhabism in Saudi Arabia, and Judaism in Israel. No matter how archaic a religion might look, with a bit of imagination and reinterpretation it can almost always be married to the latest technological gadgets and the most sophisticated modern institutions.

In some cases states might create a completely new religion to bolster their unique identity. The most extreme example can be seen today in Japan's former colony of North Korea. The North Korean regime indoctrinates its subjects with a fanatical state religion called Juche. Juche is a mix of Marxism-Leninism, some ancient Korean traditions, a racist belief in the unique purity of the Korean race, and the deification of Kim Il-Sung's family line. Though nobody claims that the Kims are descendants of a sun goddess, they are worshipped with more fervor than almost any god in history. Perhaps mindful of how the Japanese Empire was eventually defeated, North Korean Juche has also long insisted on adding nuclear weapons to the mix, depicting their development as a sacred duty worthy of supreme sacrifices.[6]

THE HANDMAID OF NATIONALISM

No matter how technology will develop, we can expect that arguments about religious identities and rituals will continue to influence the use of new technologies, and might well retain the power to set the world ablaze. The most up-to-date nuclear missiles and cyber bombs might well be employed to settle a doctrinal argument about medieval texts. Religions, rites, and rituals will remain important as long as the power of humankind rests on mass cooperation and as long as mass cooperation rests on belief in shared fictions.

Unfortunately, all of this really makes traditional religions part of humanity's problem, not part of the remedy. Religions still have a lot of political power, inasmuch as they can cement national identities and even ignite the Third World War. But when it comes to solving rather than stoking the global problems of the twenty-first century, they don't seem to offer much. Though many traditional religions espouse universal values and claim cosmic validity, at present they are used mainly as the handmaid of modern nationalism, whether in North Korea, Russia, Iran, or Israel. They therefore make it even harder to transcend national differences and find a global solution to the threats of nuclear war, ecological collapse, and technological disruption.

For example, when dealing with global warming or nuclear proliferation, Shiite clerics encourage Iranians to see these problems from a narrow Iranian perspective, Jewish rabbis inspire Israelis to care mainly about what's good for Israel, and Orthodox priests urge Russians to think first and foremost about Russian interests. After all, we are God's chosen nation, the argument goes, so what's good for our nation is pleasing to God too. There certainly are religious sages who reject nationalist excesses and adopt far more universal visions. Unfortunately, such sages don't wield much political power these days.

We are trapped, then, between a rock and a hard place. Human-

kind now constitutes a single civilization, and problems such as nuclear war, ecological collapse, and technological disruption can only
be solved on the global level. On the other hand, nationalism and
religion still divide our human civilization into different and often
hostile camps. This collision between global problems and local
identities manifests itself in the crisis that now besets the greatest
multicultural experiment in the world—the European Union. Built
on the promise of universal liberal values, the EU is teetering on the
verge of disintegration due to the difficulties of integration and immigration.

9

....

Immigration

Some Cultures Might Be Better than Others

Though globalization has greatly reduced cultural differences across the planet, it has simultaneously made it far easier to encounter strangers and become upset by their oddities. The difference between Anglo-Saxon England and the Indian Pala Empire was far greater than the difference between modern Britain and modern India—but British Airways didn't offer direct flights between Delhi and London in the days of King Alfred the Great.

As more and more humans cross more and more borders in search of jobs, security, and a better future, the need to confront, assimilate, or expel strangers strains political systems and collective identities that were shaped in less fluid times. Nowhere is the problem more poignant than in Europe. The European Union was built on the promise of transcending the cultural differences between French, Germans, Spaniards, and Greeks. It might collapse due to its inability to contain the cultural differences between Europeans and migrants from Africa and the Middle East. Ironically, it has been Europe's very success in building a prosperous multicultural system that drew so many migrants in the first place. Syrians want to immigrate to Germany rather than to Saudi Arabia, Iran, Russia, or Japan not because Germany is closer or wealthier than all the other potential destinations but because Germany has a far better record of welcoming and absorbing immigrants.

The growing wave of refugees and immigrants produces mixed reactions among Europeans and sparks bitter discussions about Europe's identity and future. Some Europeans demand that Europe slam its gates shut; are they betraying Europe's multicultural and tolerant ideals, or are they just taking sensible steps to prevent disaster? Others call for opening the gates wider; are they faithful to core European values, or are they guilty of saddling the European project with impossible expectations? This discussion about immigration often degenerates into a shouting match in which neither side hears the other. To clarify matters, it would perhaps be helpful to view immigration as a deal with three basic conditions or terms:

TERM 1: The host country allows the immigrants in.

TERM 2: In return, the immigrants must embrace at least the core norms and values of the host country, even if that means giving up some of their traditional norms and values.

TERM 3: If the immigrants assimilate to a sufficient degree, over time they become equal and full members of the host country. "They" become "us."

These three terms give rise to three distinct debates about the exact meaning of each term. A fourth debate concerns the fulfillment of the terms. When people argue about immigration, they often confuse the four debates, so that nobody understands what the argument is really about. It is therefore best to look at each of these debates separately.

★   ★   ★

DEBATE 1: The first clause of the immigration deal says simply that the host country allows immigrants in. But should this be understood as a duty or a favor? Is the host country obliged to open its gates to everybody, or does it have the right to pick and choose, and even to halt immigration altogether? Pro-immigrationists seem to think that countries have a moral duty to accept not just refugees but also people from poverty-stricken lands who seek jobs and a better future. Especially in a globalized world, all humans have moral obligations toward all other humans, and those shirking these obligations are egoists or even racists.

In addition, many pro-immigrationists stress that it is impossible to completely stop immigration: no matter how many walls and fences we build, desperate people will always find a way through. So it is better to legalize immigration and deal with it openly than create a vast underworld of human trafficking, illegal workers, and undocumented children.

Anti-immigrationists reply that if you use sufficient force, you can completely stop immigration, and except perhaps in the case of refugees fleeing brutal persecution in a neighboring country, you are never obliged to open your door. Turkey may have a moral duty to allow desperate Syrian refugees to cross its border, but if these refugees then try to move on to Sweden, the Swedes are not bound to accept them. As for migrants who seek jobs and welfare, it is totally up to the host country whether it wants them in or not, and under what conditions.

Anti-immigrationists stress that one of the most basic rights of every human collective is to defend itself against invasion, whether in the form of armies or migrants. The Swedes have worked very hard and made numerous sacrifices in order to build a prosperous liberal democracy, and if the Syrians have failed to do the same, this is not the Swedes' fault. If Swedish voters don't want more Syrian immigrants—for whatever reason—it is their right to refuse them entry. And if they do accept some immigrants, it should be abso-

lutely clear that this is a favor Sweden extends rather than an obligation it fulfills. Which means that immigrants who are allowed into
Sweden should feel extremely grateful for whatever they get, instead of arriving with a list of demands as if they own the place.

Moreover, say the anti-immigrationists, a country can have whatever immigration policy it wants. It can screen immigrants not just
for their criminal records or professional talents but even for things
like religion. If a country like Israel wants to allow in only Jews and
a country like Poland agrees to absorb Middle Eastern refugees on
the condition that they are Christians, this may seem distasteful, but
it is perfectly within the rights of the Israeli or Polish voters.

What complicates matters is that in many cases people want to
eat their cake and have it too. Numerous countries turn a blind eye
to illegal immigration or even accept foreign workers on a temporary basis because they want to benefit from the foreigners' energy,
talents, and cheap labor. But the countries then refuse to legalize
the status of these people, saying that they don't want immigration.
In the long run, this could create hierarchical societies in which an
upper class of full citizens exploits an underclass of powerless foreigners, as happens today in Qatar and several other Gulf states.

As long as this debate isn't settled, it is extremely difficult to
answer all subsequent questions about immigration. Since pro-
immigrationists think that people have a right to immigrate to another land if they so wish, and host countries have a duty to absorb
them, they react with moral outrage when people's right to immigrate is violated and when countries fail to perform their duty of
absorption. Anti-immigrationists are astounded by such views.
They see immigration as a privilege and absorption as a favor. Why
accuse people of being racists or fascists just because they refuse
entry into their own country?

Of course, even if allowing immigrants in constitutes a favor
rather than a duty, once the immigrants settle in, the host country
gradually incurs numerous duties toward them and their descen-

dants. Therefore you cannot justify anti-Semitism in the United States today by arguing that "we did your great-grandmother a favor by letting her into this country in 1910, so we can now treat you any way we like."

DEBATE 2: The second clause of the immigration deal says that if they are allowed in, the immigrants have an obligation to assimilate into the local culture. But how far should assimilation go? If immigrants move from a patriarchal society to a liberal society, must they become feminists? If they come from a deeply religious society, need they adopt a secular worldview? Should they abandon their traditional dress codes and food taboos? Anti-immigrationists tend to place the bar high, whereas pro-immigrationists place it much lower.

Pro-immigrationists argue that Europe itself is extremely diverse, and its native populations have a wide spectrum of opinions, habits, and values. This is exactly what makes Europe vibrant and strong. Why should immigrants be forced to adhere to some imaginary European identity that few Europeans actually live up to? Do you want to force Muslim immigrants to the United Kingdom to become Christian when many British citizens hardly go to church? Do you want to demand that immigrants from the Punjab give up their curry and masala in favor of fish and chips and Yorkshire pudding? If Europe has any real core values, then they are the liberal values of tolerance and freedom, which imply that Europeans should show tolerance toward the immigrants too, and allow them as much freedom as possible to follow their own traditions, provided these do not harm the freedoms and rights of other people.

Anti-immigrationists agree that tolerance and freedom are the most important European values, and accuse many immigrant groups—especially from Muslim countries—of intolerance, misogyny, homophobia, and anti-Semitism. Precisely because Europe cherishes tolerance, it cannot allow in too many intolerant people. While a tolerant society can manage small illiberal minorities, if the number of such extremists exceeds a certain threshold, the whole nature of society changes. If Europe allows in too many immigrants from the Middle East, it will end up looking like the Middle East.

Other anti-immigrationists go much further. They point out that a national community is far more than a collection of people who tolerate each other. Therefore it is not enough that immigrants adhere to European standards of tolerance. They must also adopt many of the unique characteristics of British, German, or Swedish culture, whatever these may be. By allowing them in, the local culture is taking upon itself a big risk and a huge expense. There is no reason it should destroy itself as well. It offers eventual full equality, so it demands full assimilation. If the immigrants have an issue with certain quirks of British, German, or Swedish culture, they are welcome to go elsewhere.

The two key issues of this debate are the disagreement about immigrant intolerance and the disagreement about European identity. If immigrants are indeed guilty of incurable intolerance, many liberal Europeans who currently favor immigration will sooner or later come around to oppose it bitterly. Conversely, if most immigrants prove to be liberal and broad-minded in their attitudes toward religion, gender, and politics, this will disarm some of the most effective arguments against immigration.

This will still leave open, however, the question of Europe's unique national identities. Tolerance is a universal value. Are there any unique French norms and values that should be accepted by someone immigrating to France, and are there unique Danish norms and values that immigrants to Denmark must embrace? As long as Europeans are bitterly divided about this question, they can hardly have a clear policy about immigration. Conversely, once Europeans know who they are, five hundred million Europeans should have no difficulty absorbing a few million refugees—or turning them away.

DEBATE 3: The third clause of the immigration deal says that if immigrants indeed make a sincere effort to assimilate—and in particular to adopt the value of tolerance—the host country is duty-bound to treat them as first-class citizens. But exactly how much time needs to pass before the immigrants become full members of society? Should immigrants from Algeria feel aggrieved if they are still not seen as fully French after twenty years in the country? How about second-generation immigrants whose grandparents came to France in the 1970s?

Pro-immigrationists tend to demand a speedy acceptance, whereas anti-immigrationists want a much longer probation period. For pro-immigrationists, if third-generation immigrants are not seen and treated as equal citizens, this means that the host country is not fulfilling its obligations, and if this results in tensions, hostility, and even violence, the host country has nobody to blame but its own bigotry. For anti-immigrationists, these inflated expectations are a large part of the problem. The immigrants should be patient. If your grandparents arrived here just forty years ago and you now riot in the streets because you think you are not being treated as a native, then you have failed the test.

The root issue of this debate concerns the gap between personal timescale and collective timescale. From the viewpoint of human collectives, forty years is a short time. It is hard to expect society to fully absorb foreign groups within a few decades. Past civilizations that assimilated foreigners and made them equal citizens—such as imperial Rome, the Muslim caliphate, the Chinese empires, and the United States—all took centuries rather than decades to accomplish the transformation.

From a personal viewpoint, however, forty years can be an eternity. For a teenager born in France twenty years after her grandparents immigrated there, the journey from Algiers to Marseilles is ancient history. She was born here, all her friends were born here, she speaks French rather than Arabic, and she has never even been to Algeria. France is the only home she has ever known. And now people say to her it's not her home, and that she should go "back" to a place she never inhabited?

It's as if you take a seed of a eucalyptus tree from Australia and plant it in France. From an ecological perspective, eucalyptus trees are an invading species, and it will take generations before botanists reclassify them as native European plants. Yet from the viewpoint of the individual tree, it is French. If you don't water it with French water, it will wither. If you try to uproot it, you will discover it has struck its roots deep in the French soil, just like the local oaks and pines.

DEBATE 4: On top of all these disagreements regarding the exact definition of the immigration deal, the ultimate question is whether the deal is actually working. Are both sides living up to their obligations?

Anti-immigrationists tend to argue that the immigrants are not fulfilling term number 2. They are not making a sincere effort to assimilate, and too many of them stick to intolerant and bigoted worldviews. Therefore, the host country has no reason to fulfill term number 3 (to treat them as first-class citizens), and has every reason to reconsider term number 1 (to allow them in). If people from a particular culture have consistently proven themselves unwilling to live up to the immigration deal, why allow more of them in and create an even bigger problem?

Pro-immigrationists reply that it is the host country that fails to fulfill its side of the deal. Despite the honest efforts of the vast majority of immigrants to assimilate, the hosts are making it difficult for them to do so; worse still, those immigrants who successfully assimilate are still treated as second-class citizens even in the second and third generations. It is of course possible that both sides are not living up to their commitments, thereby fueling each other's suspicions and resentments in an escalating vicious circle.

This fourth debate cannot be resolved before clarifying the exact definition of the three terms. As long as we don't know whether absorption is a duty or a favor, what level of assimilation is required from immigrants, and how quickly host countries should treat them as equal citizens, we cannot judge whether the two sides are fulfilling their obligations. An additional problem concerns accounting. When evaluating the immigration deal, both sides give far more weight to violations than to compliance. If a million immigrants are law-abiding citizens but one hundred join terrorist groups and attack the host country, does it mean that the immigrants are complying with the terms of the deal or violating them? If a third-generation immigrant walks down the street a thousand times without being molested but once in a while some racist shouts abuse at her, does it mean that the native population is accepting or rejecting the immigrants?

Yet underneath all these debates lurks a far more fundamental question, which concerns our understanding of human culture. Do we enter the immigration debate with the assumption that all cultures are inherently equal, or do we think that some cultures might well be superior to others? When Germans argue over the absorption of a million Syrian refugees, can they ever be justified in thinking that German culture is in some way better than Syrian culture?

FROM RACISM TO CULTURISM

A century ago Europeans took it for granted that some races—most notably the white race—were inherently superior to others. After 1945 such views increasingly became anathema. Racism was seen not only as morally abysmal but also as scientifically bankrupt. Life scientists, and in particular geneticists, have produced very strong scientific evidence that the biological differences between Europeans, Africans, Chinese, and Native Americans are negligible.

At the same time, however, anthropologists, sociologists, historians, behavioral economists, and even brain scientists have accumulated a wealth of data for the existence of significant differences between human cultures. After all, if all human cultures were essentially the same, why would we even need anthropologists and historians? Why invest resources in studying trivial differences? At the very least, we should stop financing all those expensive field excursions to the South Pacific and the Kalahari Desert and be content with studying people in Oxford or Boston. If cultural differences are insignificant, then whatever we discover about Harvard undergraduates should be true of Kalahari hunter-gatherers too.

Upon reflection, most people concede the existence of at least some significant differences between human cultures, in things ranging from sexual mores to political habits. How then should we treat these differences? Cultural relativists argue that difference doesn't imply hierarchy, and we should never prefer one culture over another. Humans may think and behave in various ways, but we should celebrate this diversity and give equal value to all beliefs and practices. Unfortunately, such broad-minded attitudes cannot stand the test of reality. Human diversity may be great when it comes to cuisine and poetry, but few would see witch-burning, infanticide, or slavery as fascinating human idiosyncrasies that should be protected against the encroachments of global capitalism and Coca-Colonialism.

Or consider the way different cultures relate to strangers, immigrants, and refugees. Not all cultures are characterized by exactly the same level of acceptance. German culture in the early twenty-first century is more tolerant of strangers and more welcoming of immigrants than Saudi culture. It is far easier for a Muslim to immigrate to Germany than it is for a Christian to immigrate to Saudi

Arabia. Indeed, it is probably easier for even a Muslim refugee from Syria to immigrate to Germany than to Saudi Arabia, and since 2011 Germany has taken in many more Syrian refugees than has Saudi Arabia.[1] Similarly, the weight of evidence suggests that the culture of California in the early twenty-first century is more immigrant-friendly than the culture of Japan. Therefore, if you think that it is good to tolerate strangers and welcome immigrants, shouldn't you also think that at least in this regard, German culture is superior to Saudi culture, and Californian culture is better than Japanese culture?

Moreover, even when two cultural norms are equally valid in theory, in the practical context of immigration it might still be justified to judge the host culture as better. Norms and values that are appropriate in one country just don't work well under different circumstances. Let's look closely at a concrete example. In order not to fall prey to well-established prejudices, let's imagine two fictional countries: Coldia and Warmland. The two countries have many cultural differences, among which is their attitude to human relations and interpersonal conflict. Coldians are educated from infancy that if you get into conflict with somebody at school, at work, or even in your family, the best thing to do is to repress it. You should avoid shouting, expressing rage, or confronting the other person—angry outbursts just make things worse. It's better to work with your own feelings while allowing things to cool down. In the meantime, limit your contact with the person in question, and if contact is unavoidable, be terse but polite, and avoid sensitive issues.

Warmlanders, by contrast, are educated from infancy to externalize conflicts. If you find yourself in conflict, they believe, don't let it simmer and don't repress anything. Use the first opportunity you get to vent your emotions openly. It is okay to get angry, to shout, and to tell the other person exactly how you feel. This is the only way to work things through together, in an honest and direct way. One day of shouting can resolve a conflict that might otherwise fester for years, and though head-on confrontation is never pleasant, you will all feel much better afterward.

Both these methods have their pros and cons, and it is hard to say that one is always better than the other. What might happen, though, when a Warmlander immigrates to Coldia and gets a job in a Coldian firm?

Whenever a conflict arises with a coworker, the Warmlander bangs on the table and yells at the top of his voice, expecting that this will focus attention on the problem and help to resolve it quickly. Several years later a senior position falls vacant. Though the Warmlander has all the necessary qualifications, the boss prefers to give the promotion to a Coldian employee. When asked about it, she explains: "Yes, the Warmlander has many talents, but he also has a serious problem with human relations. He is hot-tempered, creates unnecessary tensions around him, and disturbs our corporate culture." The same fate befalls other Warmlander immigrants to Coldia. Most of them remain in junior positions, or fail to find any job at all, because managers presuppose that if they are Warmlanders, they will probably be hot-tempered and problematic employees. Since the Warmlanders never reach senior positions, it is difficult for them to change the Coldian corporate culture.

Much the same thing happens to Coldians who immigrate to Warmland. A Coldian starting to work in a Warmland firm quickly acquires the reputation of a snob or a cold fish, and makes few if any friends. People think that he is insincere or that he lacks basic human-relation skills. He never advances to senior positions, and he therefore never gets the opportunity to change the corporate culture. Warmland managers conclude that most Coldians are unfriendly or shy, and prefer not to hire them for positions that require contact with customers or close cooperation with other employees.

Both of these cases may seem to smack of racism. But in fact, they are not racist. They are "culturist." People continue to conduct a heroic struggle against traditional racism without noticing that the battlefront has shifted. Traditional racism is waning, but the world is now full of "culturists."

Traditional racism was firmly grounded in biological theories. In the 1890s or 1930s it was widely believed in countries such as Britain, Australia, and the United States that some heritable biological trait made Africans and Chinese people innately less intelligent, less enterprising, and less moral than Europeans. The problem was in their blood. Such views enjoyed political respectability as well as widespread scientific backing. Today, in contrast, while many individuals still make such racist assertions, they have lost all of their scientific backing and most of their political respectability—unless they are rephrased in cultural terms. Saying that black people tend to commit crimes because they have substandard genes is out; saying that they tend to commit crimes because they come from dysfunctional subcultures is very much in.

In the United States, for instance, some political parties and leaders openly support discriminatory policies and often make denigrating remarks about African Americans, Latinos, and Muslims—but they will rarely if ever say that there is something wrong with the DNA of those groups. The problem is alleged to be with their culture. Thus when President Trump described Haiti, El Salvador, and some parts of Africa as "shithole countries," he was apparently offering the public a reflection on the culture of these places rather than on their genetic makeup.[2] On another occasion Trump said about Mexican immigrants to the United States that "when Mexico sends its people, they're not sending the best. They're sending people that have lots of problems and they're bringing those problems. They're bringing drugs, they're bringing crime. They're rapists and some, I assume, are good people." This is a very offensive claim to make, but it is sociologically rather than biologically offensive. Trump was not implying that Mexican blood is a bar to goodness—only that good Mexicans tend to stay south of the Rio Grande.[3]

The human body—the Latino body, the African body, the Chinese body—still stands at the center of the debate. Skin color matters a lot. Walking down a New York street with lots of melanin pigment in your skin means that wherever you are heading, the police might view you with extra suspicion. But the likes of both President Trump and President Obama will explain the significance of skin color in cultural and historical terms. The police view your skin color with suspicion not due to any biological reason but rather due to history. Presumably the Obama camp will explain that police prejudice is an unfortunate legacy of historical crimes such as slavery, while the Trump camp will explain that black criminality is an unfortunate legacy of historical errors committed by white liberals and black communities. In any case, even if you are a tourist from Delhi who knows nothing about American history, you will have to deal with the consequences of that history.

The shift from biology to culture is not just a meaningless change of jargon. It is a profound shift with far-reaching practical consequences, some good, some bad. For starters, culture is more malleable than biology. This means, on one hand, that present-day culturists might be more tolerant than traditional racists—if only the "others" adopt our culture, we will accept them as our equals. On the other hand, that could result in far stronger pressures on the "others" to assimilate, and in far harsher criticism of their failure to do so.

You can hardly blame a dark-skinned person for not whitening his skin, but people can and do accuse Africans or Muslims of failing to adopt the norms and values of Western culture. Which is not to say that such accusations are necessarily justified. In many cases there is little reason to adopt the dominant culture, and in many other cases it is an all but impossible mission. African Americans from a poverty-stricken slum who honestly try to fit into the hegemonic American culture might first find their way blocked by institutional discrimination—only to be accused later of not having made sufficient effort, and so they have nobody but themselves to blame for their troubles.

A second key difference between talking about biology and talking about culture is that unlike traditional racist bigotry, culturist arguments might occasionally make good sense, as in the case of Warmland and Coldia. Warmlanders and Coldians really have different cultures, characterized by different styles of human relations. Since human relations are crucial to many jobs, is it unethical for a Warmlander firm to penalize Coldians for behaving in accordance with their cultural legacy?

Anthropologists, sociologists, and historians feel extremely uneasy about this issue. On one hand, it all sounds dangerously close to racism. On the other hand, culturism has a much firmer scientific basis than racism, and particularly scholars in the humanities and social sciences cannot deny the existence and importance of cultural differences.

Of course, even if we accept the validity of some culturist claims, we do not have to accept all of them. Many culturist claims suffer from three common flaws. First, culturists often confuse local superiority with objective superiority. Thus in the local context of Warmland, the Warmland method of conflict resolution may well be superior to the Coldian method, in which case a Warmland firm operating in Warmland has a good reason to discriminate against introverted employees (which will disproportionately penalize Coldian immigrants). However, that does not mean that the Warmland method is objectively superior. The Warmlanders could perhaps learn a thing or two from the Coldians, and if circumstances change—for example, the Warmland firm goes global and opens branches in many different countries—diversity could suddenly become an asset.

Second, when you clearly define a yardstick, a time, and a place, culturist claims may well be empirically sound. But all too often people adopt very general culturist claims that make little sense. For instance, saying that "Coldian culture is less tolerant of public angry outbursts than Warmland culture" is a reasonable claim, but it is far less reasonable to say that "Muslim culture is very intolerant." The latter claim is just far too vague. What do we mean by "intolerant"? Intolerant of whom, or what? A culture can be intolerant toward religious minorities and unusual political views while simultaneously being very tolerant toward obese people or the elderly. And what do we mean by "Muslim culture"? Are we talking about the Arabian peninsula in the seventh century? The Ottoman Empire in the sixteenth century? Pakistan in the early twenty-first century? Finally, what is the benchmark? If we care about tolerance toward religious minorities and compare the Ottoman Empire in the sixteenth century with Western Europe in the sixteenth century, we would conclude that Muslim culture is extremely tolerant. If we compare Afghanistan under the Taliban to contemporary Denmark, we would reach a very different conclusion.

Yet the worst problem with culturist claims is that despite their statistical nature they are all too often used to prejudge *individuals*. When a Warmlander native and a Coldian immigrant apply for the same position in a Warmlander firm, the manager may prefer to hire the Warmlander because "Coldians are frosty and unsociable." Even if this is statistically true, maybe this particular Coldian is actually far more warm and outgoing than that particular Warmlander. While culture is important, people are also shaped by their genes and their unique personal history. Individuals often defy statistical stereotypes. It makes sense for a firm to prefer sociable employees to stony ones, but it does not make sense to prefer Warmlanders to Coldians.

All this, however, modifies particular culturist claims without discrediting culturism as a whole. Unlike racism, which is an unscientific prejudice, culturist arguments may sometimes be quite sound. If we look at statistics and discover that Warmlander firms have few Coldians in senior positions, this may result not from racist discrimination but from good judgment. Should Coldian immigrants feel resentment at this situation and claim that Warmland is reneging on the immigration deal? Should we force Warmlander firms to hire more Coldian managers through affirmative action laws, in the hope of cooling down Warmland's hot-tempered business culture? Or does the fault perhaps lie with Coldian immigrants failing to assimilate into the local culture, and we should therefore make a greater effort to inculcate Coldian children with Warmlander norms and values?

Coming back from the realm of fiction to the realm of facts, we see that the European debate about immigration is far from being a clear-cut battle between good and evil. It would be wrong to tar all anti-immigrationists as "fascists," just as it would be wrong to depict all pro-immigrationists as committed to "cultural suicide." Therefore, the debate about immigration should not be conducted as an uncompromising struggle over some nonnegotiable moral imperative. Rather, it must be a discussion between two legitimate political positions, with the ultimate choice decided through standard democratic procedures.

At present, it is far from clear whether Europe can find a middle path that will enable it to keep its gates open to strangers without being destabilized by people who don't share its values. If Europe succeeds in finding such a path, perhaps its formula could be copied on the global level. If the European project fails, however, it would indicate that belief in the liberal values of freedom and tolerance is not enough to resolve the cultural conflicts of the world and to unite humankind in the face of nuclear war, ecological collapse, and technological disruption. If Greeks and Germans cannot agree on a common destiny, and if five hundred million affluent Europeans cannot absorb a few million impoverished refugees, what chance does humanity have of overcoming the far deeper conflicts that beset our global civilization?

One thing that might help Europe and the world as a whole to integrate better and to keep borders and minds open is to downplay the hysteria regarding terrorism. It would be extremely unfortunate if the European experiment in freedom and tolerance unraveled due to an overblown fear of terrorists. That would not only realize the terrorists' own goals but also give this handful of fanatics far too great a say about the future of humankind. Terrorism is the weapon of a marginal and weak segment of humanity. How did it come to dominate global politics?

PART III

....

Despair and Hope

Though the challenges are unprecedented, and though the disagreements are intense, human-kind can rise to the occasion if we keep our fears under control and be a bit more humble about our views.

10

....

Terrorism

Don't Panic

Terrorists are masters of mind control. They kill very few people but nevertheless manage to terrify billions and rattle huge political structures such as the European Union or the United States. Since September 11, 2001, each year terrorists have killed about 50 people in the European Union, about 10 people in the United States, about 7 people in China, and up to 25,000 people elsewhere in the globe (mostly in Iraq, Afghanistan, Pakistan, Nigeria, and Syria).[1] In contrast, each year traffic accidents kill about 80,000 Europeans, 40,000 Americans, 270,000 Chinese, and 1.25 million people altogether.[2] Diabetes and high sugar levels kill up to 3.5 million people annually, while air pollution kills about 7 million people per year.[3] So why do we fear terrorism more than sugar, and why do governments lose elections because of sporadic terrorist attacks but not because of chronic air pollution?

As the literal meaning of the word indicates, terrorism is a military strategy that hopes to change the political situation by spreading fear rather than by causing material damage. This strategy is almost always adopted by very weak parties who cannot inflict much material damage on their enemies. Of course every military action spreads fear. But in conventional warfare, fear is just a by-product of the material losses, and it is usually proportional to the force inflicting the losses. In terrorism, fear is the main story, and there is an astounding disproportion between the actual strength of the terrorists and the fear they manage to inspire.

It is not always easy to change the political situation through violence. On the first day of the Battle of the Somme, July 1, 1916, 19,000 British soldiers were killed and another 40,000 wounded. By the time the battle ended in November, both sides together suffered more than a million casualties, including 300,000 dead.[4] Yet this horrific carnage hardly altered the political balance of power in Europe. It took another two years and millions of additional casualties for something to finally snap.

Compared to the Somme offensive, terrorism is a puny matter. The Paris attacks of November 2015 killed 130 people, the Brussels bombings of March 2016 killed 32 people, and the Manchester Arena bombing in May 2017 killed 22 people. In 2002, at the height of the Palestinian terror campaign against Israel, when buses and restaurants were bombed on a daily basis, the yearly toll reached 451 dead Israelis.[5] In the same year, 542 Israelis were killed in car accidents.[6] A few terrorist attacks, such as the bombing of Pan Am flight 103 over Lockerbie in 1988, kill hundreds.[7] The 9/11 attacks set a new record, killing almost 3,000 people.[8] Yet even this tragedy is dwarfed by the price of conventional warfare. If you add up all the people killed and wounded in Europe by terrorist attacks since 1945—including victims of nationalist, religious, leftist, and rightist groups alike—the total will still fall far short of the casualties in any number of obscure First World War battles, such as the third Battle of the Aisne (250,000 casualties) or the tenth Battle of the Isonzo (225,000).[9]

How, then, can terrorists hope to achieve much? Following an act of terrorism, the enemy continues to have the same number of soldiers, tanks, and ships as before. The enemy's communication network, roads, and railways are largely intact. His factories, ports, and bases remain untouched. However, the terrorists hope that even though they can barely make a dent in the enemy's material power, fear and confusion will cause the enemy to misuse his intact strength and overreact. Terrorists calculate that when the enraged enemy uses his massive power against them, he will raise a much more violent military and political storm than the terrorists themselves could ever create. During every storm, many unforeseen things happen. Mistakes are made, atrocities are committed, public opinion wavers, neutrals change their stance, and the balance of power shifts.

In this respect, terrorists resemble a fly that tries to destroy a china shop. The fly is so weak that it cannot move even a single teacup. So how does a fly destroy a china shop? It finds a bull, gets inside its ear, and starts buzzing. The bull goes wild with fear and anger, and destroys the china shop. This is what happened after 9/11, as Islamic fundamentalists incited the American bull to destroy the Middle Eastern china shop. Now they flourish in the wreckage. And there is no shortage of short-tempered bulls in the world.

RESHUFFLING THE CARDS

Terrorism is a very unattractive military strategy, because it leaves all the important decisions in the hands of the enemy. Since all the options the enemy had prior to a terrorist attack are at his disposal afterward as well, he is completely free to choose among them. Armies normally try to avoid such a situation at all costs. When they attack, they don't want to stage a frightening spectacle that would anger the enemy and provoke him to hit back. Rather, they seek to inflict significant material damage and reduce the enemy's ability to retaliate. In particular, they seek to eliminate his most dangerous weapons and options.

That is, for example, what Japan did in December 1941 when it launched a surprise attack on the United States and sank much of the U.S. Pacific Fleet in Pearl Harbor. This wasn't terrorism. It was war. The Japanese could not be certain how the Americans would retaliate for the attack, except about one thing: no matter what the Americans decided to do, they would not be able to send a fleet to the Philippines or Hong Kong in 1942.

Provoking the enemy to action without eliminating any of his weapons or options is an act of desperation, taken only when there is no other option. Whenever it is possible to inflict serious material damage, nobody gives that up in favor of mere terrorism. If in December 1941 the Japanese torpedoed a civilian passenger ship in order to provoke the United States but left the Pacific Fleet in Pearl Harbor intact, this would have been madness.

But the terrorists have little choice. They are so weak that they cannot wage war. So they opt instead to produce a theatrical spectacle that they hope will provoke the enemy and cause him to overreact. Terrorists stage a terrifying spectacle of violence that captures our imagination and turns it against us. By killing a handful of people the terrorists cause millions to fear for their lives. In order to calm these fears, governments react to the theater of terror with a show of security, orchestrating immense displays of force such as the persecution of entire populations or the invasion of foreign countries. In most cases, this overreaction to terrorism poses a far greater threat to our security than the terrorists themselves.

Terrorists don't think like army generals. Instead, they think like theater producers. The public memory of the 9/11 attacks testifies that everyone understands this intuitively. If you ask people what happened on 9/11, they are likely to say that al-Qaeda knocked down the twin towers of the World Trade Center. Yet the attack involved not merely the towers but two other actions, in particular a successful attack on the Pentagon. Why do fewer people remember that?

If the 9/11 operation had been a conventional military campaign, the Pentagon attack would have received most of the attention.

After all, al-Qaeda managed to destroy part of the enemy's central headquarters, killing and wounding senior commanders and analysts. Why is it that public memory grants far more importance to the destruction of two civilian buildings and the killing of brokers, accountants, and clerks?

It is because the Pentagon is a relatively flat and unassuming building, whereas the World Trade Center was a tall phallic totem whose collapse created an immense audiovisual effect. Nobody who saw the images of its collapse could ever forget them. Because we intuitively understand that terrorism is theater, we judge it by its emotional rather than material impact.

Like terrorists, those combating terrorism should also think more like theater producers and less like army generals. Above all, if we want to combat terrorism effectively, we must realize that nothing the terrorists do can defeat us. We are the only ones who can defeat ourselves, if we overreact in a misguided way to their provocations.

Terrorists undertake an impossible mission: to change the political balance of power through violence, despite having no army. To achieve their aim, they present the state with an impossible challenge of its own: to prove that it can protect all of its citizens from political violence, anywhere, anytime. The terrorists hope that when the state tries to fulfill this impossible mission, it will reshuffle the political cards and hand them some unforeseen ace.

True, when the state rises to the challenge, it usually succeeds in crushing the terrorists. Hundreds of terrorist organizations were wiped out over the last few decades by various states. In 2002–4 Israel proved that even the most ferocious terrorist campaigns can be suppressed by brute force.[10] Terrorists know full well that the chances in such a confrontation are against them. But since they are very weak and have no other military option, they have nothing to lose and much to gain. And once in a while the political storm created by counterterrorist campaigns does benefit the terrorists. A terrorist is like a gambler who is holding a particularly bad hand and tries to convince his rivals to reshuffle the cards. He cannot lose anything, and he could win everything.

A SMALL COIN IN A BIG EMPTY JAR

Why should the state agree to reshuffle the cards? Since the material damage caused by terrorism is negligible, the state could theoretically do nothing about it, or take strong but discreet measures far from the cameras and microphones. In fact, states often do exactly that. But every now and then a state loses its temper and reacts far too forcefully and publicly, thus playing into the hands of the terrorists. Why are states so sensitive to terrorist provocations?

States find it difficult to withstand these provocations because the legitimacy of the modern state is based on its promise to keep the public sphere free of political violence. A regime can withstand terrible catastrophes, and even ignore them, provided its legitimacy is not based on preventing them. On the other hand, a regime may collapse due to a minor problem if that issue is seen as undermining its legitimacy. In the fourteenth century the Black Death killed between a quarter and a half of European populations, yet no king lost his throne as a result, and no king made much of an effort to overcome the plague. Nobody back then thought that preventing plagues was part of a king's job. On the other hand, rulers who allowed religious heresy to spread in their dominions risked losing their crown, and even their head.

Today, a government might take a softer approach to domestic and sexual violence than to terrorism, because despite the impact of movements such as #MeToo, rape does not undermine a government's legitimacy. In France, for example, more than ten thousand rape cases are reported to the authorities each year, with an estimated tens of thousands of additional cases left unreported.[11] Rapists and abusive husbands, however, are not perceived as an existential threat to the French state, because historically the state did not build itself on the promise to eliminate sexual violence. In contrast, the much rarer cases of terrorism are viewed as a deadly threat to the French Republic, because over the last few centuries modern Western states have gradually established their legitimacy on the explicit promise to tolerate no political violence within their borders.

Back in the Middle Ages, the public sphere was full of political violence. In fact, the ability to use violence was the entry ticket to the political game, and whoever lacked this ability had no political voice. Numerous noble families retained armed forces, as did towns, guilds, churches, and monasteries. When a former abbot died and a dispute arose about succession, the rival factions—comprising monks, local strongmen, and concerned neighbors—often used armed force to decide the issue.

Terrorism had no place in such a world. Anybody who was not strong enough to cause substantial material damage was of no consequence. If in 1150 a few Muslim fanatics murdered a handful of civilians in Jerusalem, demanding that the Crusaders leave the Holy Land, the reaction would have been ridicule more than terror. If you wanted to be taken seriously, you should have at least gained control of a fortified castle or two. Terrorism did not bother our medieval ancestors because they had much bigger problems to deal with.

During the modern era, centralized states gradually reduced the level of political violence within their territories, and in the last few decades Western countries have managed to eradicate it almost entirely. The citizens of France, Britain, or the United States can struggle for control of towns, corporations, organizations, and even the government itself without any need of an armed force. Command of trillions of dollars, millions of soldiers, and thousands of ships, airplanes, and nuclear missiles passes from one group of politicians to another without a single shot being fired. People quickly got used to this and now consider it their natural right. Consequently, sporadic acts of political violence that kill a few dozen people are seen as a deadly threat to the legitimacy and even survival of the state. A small coin in a big empty jar makes a lot of noise.

This is why the theater of terrorism is so successful. The state has created a huge space empty of political violence, which now acts as a sounding board, amplifying the impact of any armed attack, however small. The less political violence in a particular state, the greater the public shock at an act of terrorism. Killing a few people in Belgium draws far more attention than killing hundreds in Nigeria or Iraq. Paradoxically, then, the very success of modern states in preventing political violence makes them particularly vulnerable to terrorism.

The state has stressed many times that it will not tolerate political violence within its borders. The citizens, for their part, have become used to zero political violence. That is why the theater of terror generates visceral fears of anarchy, making people feel as if the social order is about to collapse. After centuries of bloody struggles we have crawled out of the black hole of violence, but we sense that the black hole is still there, patiently waiting to swallow us again. A few gruesome atrocities, and we imagine that we are falling back in.

In order to assuage these fears, the state is driven to respond to the theater of terror with its own theater of security. The most efficient answer to terrorism might be good intelligence and clandestine action against the financial networks that feed terrorism. But this is not something citizens can watch on television. The citizens have seen the terrorist drama of the World Trade Center collapsing. The state feels compelled to stage an equally spectacular counterdrama, with even more fire and smoke. So instead of acting quietly and efficiently, the state unleashes a mighty storm, which not infrequently fulfills the terrorists' most cherished dreams.

How then should the state deal with terrorism? A successful counterterrorism struggle should be conducted on three fronts. First, governments should focus on clandestine actions against the terrorist networks. Second, the media should keep things in perspective and avoid hysteria. The theater of terror cannot succeed without publicity. Unfortunately, the media all too often provides this publicity for free. It obsessively reports terrorist attacks and greatly inflates their danger, because reports on terrorism sell newspapers much better than reports on diabetes or air pollution.

The third front is the imagination of each and every one of us. Terrorists hold our imagination captive and use that against us. Again and again we rehearse the terrorist attack on the stage of our mind, remembering 9/11 or the latest suicide bombings. The terrorists kill a hundred people—and cause a hundred million to imagine that there is a murderer lurking behind every tree. It is the responsibility of all citizens to liberate our imagination from the terrorists and to remind ourselves of the true dimensions of the threat. It is our own inner terror that prompts the media to obsess about terrorism and the government to overreact.

The success or failure of terrorism therefore depends on us. If we allow our imagination to be captured by the terrorists and then we overreact to our own fears, terrorism will succeed. If we free our imagination from the terrorists and then we react in a balanced and cool way, terrorism will fail.

TERRORISM GOES NUCLEAR

The preceding analysis holds true of terrorism as we have known it in the last two centuries, and as it currently manifests itself in the streets of New York, London, Paris, and Tel Aviv. However, if terrorists acquire weapons of mass destruction, the nature not just of terrorism but of state and global politics will change dramatically. If tiny organizations representing a handful of fanatics have the ability to destroy entire cities and kill millions, there will no longer be a public sphere free of political violence.

So while present-day terrorism is mostly theater, future nuclear terrorism, cyberterrorism, or bioterrorism would pose a much more serious threat and would demand a far more drastic reaction from governments. Precisely because of this, we should be very careful to differentiate such hypothetical future scenarios from the actual terrorist attacks we have so far witnessed. Fear that terrorists might one day get their hands on a nuclear bomb and destroy New York or London does not justify a hysterical overreaction to a terrorist who kills a dozen passersby with an automatic rifle or a runaway truck. States should be even more careful not to start persecuting all dissident groups on the grounds that they might one day try to obtain nuclear weapons or that they might hack our self-driving cars and turn them into a fleet of killer robots.

Likewise, though governments must certainly monitor radical groups and take action to prevent them from gaining control of weapons of mass destruction, they need to balance the fear of nuclear terrorism against other threatening scenarios. In the last two decades the United States wasted trillions of dollars and much political capital on its War on Terror. George W. Bush, Tony Blair, Barack Obama, and their administrations can argue with some justification that by hounding terrorists they forced them to think more about survival than about acquiring nuclear bombs. They might thereby have saved the world from a nuclear 9/11. Since this is a counterfactual claim—"if we hadn't launched the War on Terror, al-Qaeda would have acquired nuclear weapons"—it is difficult to judge whether it is true or not.

We can be certain, however, that in pursuing the War on Terror the Americans and their allies not only caused immense destruction across the globe but also incurred what economists call "opportunity costs." The money, time, and political capital invested in fighting terrorism were not invested in fighting global warming, AIDS, and poverty; in bringing peace and prosperity to sub-Saharan Africa; or in forging better ties with Russia and China. If New York or London eventually sinks under the rising Atlantic Ocean, or if tensions with Russia erupt into open warfare, people might well accuse Bush, Blair, and Obama of focusing on the wrong front.

It is hard to set priorities in real time, while it is all too easy to second-guess priorities with hindsight. We accuse leaders of failing to prevent the catastrophes that happened, while we remain blissfully unaware of the disasters that never materialized. For example, people look back at the Clinton administration in the 1990s and blame it for neglecting the al-Qaeda threat. But in the 1990s few people imagined that Islamic terrorists would ignite a global conflict by plunging passenger airliners into New York skyscrapers. In contrast, many feared that Russia might collapse entirely and lose control not just of its vast territory but also of thousands of nuclear and biological bombs. An additional concern was that the bloody wars in the former Yugoslavia might spread to other parts of Eastern Europe, resulting in conflicts between Hungary and Romania, between Bulgaria and Turkey, or between Poland and Ukraine.

Many felt even more uneasy about the reunification of Germany. Just four and a half decades after the fall of the Third Reich, many people still harbored visceral fears of German power. Free of the Soviet menace, wouldn't Germany become a superpower dominating the European continent? And what about China? Alarmed by the collapse of the Soviet bloc, China might abandon its reforms, return to hard-line Maoist policies, and end up as a larger version of North Korea.

Today we can ridicule these scary scenarios because we know they didn't materialize. The situation in Russia stabilized, most of Eastern Europe was peacefully absorbed into the EU, reunified Germany is hailed today as the leader of the free world, and China has become the economic engine of the entire globe. All this was achieved, at least in part, thanks to constructive U.S. and EU policies. Would it have been wiser if the United States and the European Union had focused in the 1990s on Islamic extremists rather than on the situation in the former Soviet bloc or in China?

We cannot prepare for every eventuality. Accordingly, while we must surely prevent nuclear terrorism, this cannot be the number one item on humanity's agenda. And we certainly shouldn't use the theoretical threat of nuclear terrorism as a justification for overreaction to run-of-the-mill terrorism. These are different problems that demand different solutions.

If despite our efforts terrorist groups eventually do lay their hands on weapons of mass destruction, it is hard to know how political struggles will be conducted, but they will be very different from the terror and counterterror campaigns of the early twenty-first century. If in 2050 the world is full of nuclear terrorists and bioterrorists, their victims will look back at the world of 2018 with longing tinged with disbelief: how could people who lived such secure lives nevertheless have felt so threatened?

Of course, our current sense of danger is fueled not just by terrorism. Many pundits and laypeople fear that the Third World War is just around the corner, and that the world of 2018 is eerily reminiscent of the world of 1914. Now as then, rising tensions between the great powers coupled with intractable global problems seem to be dragging us toward a global war. Is this anxiety more justified than our overblown fear of terrorism?

11

War

Never Underestimate Human Stupidity

The last few decades have been the most peaceful era in human history. Whereas in early agricultural societies human violence caused up to 15 percent of all human deaths, and in the twentieth century it caused 5 percent, today it is responsible for only 1 percent.[1] Yet since the global financial crisis of 2008 the international situation is rapidly deteriorating, warmongering is back in vogue, and military expenditures are ballooning.[2] Both laypeople and experts fear that just as in 1914 the murder of an Austrian archduke sparked the First World War, so in 2018 some incident in the Syrian desert or an unwise move in the Korean peninsula might ignite a global conflict.

Given the growing tensions in the world and the personality of leaders in Washington, Pyongyang, and several other places, there is definitely cause for concern. Yet there are several key differences between 2018 and 1914. In particular, in 1914 war had great appeal to elites across the world because they had many concrete examples of how successful wars contributed to economic prosperity and political power. In contrast, in 2018 successful wars seem to be an endangered species.

From the days of the Assyrians and the Qin, great empires were usually built through violent conquest. In 1914 too, all the major powers owed their status to successful wars. For instance, imperial Japan had become a regional power due to its victories over China and Russia; Germany had become Europe's top dog after its triumphs over Austria-Hungary and France; and Britain had created the world's largest and most prosperous empire through a series of splendid little wars all over the planet—in 1882, when Britain invaded and occupied Egypt, it lost a mere fifty-seven soldiers in the decisive Battle of Tel el-Kebir.[3] Whereas today occupying a Muslim country is the stuff of Western nightmares, following Tel el-Kebir the British faced little armed resistance and for more than six decades controlled the Nile Valley and the vital Suez Canal. Other European powers emulated the British, and whenever governments in Paris, Rome, or Brussels contemplated putting boots on the ground in Vietnam, Libya, or Congo, their only fear was that somebody else might get there first.

Even the United States owed its great-power status to military action rather than economic enterprise alone. In 1846 it invaded Mexico and conquered California, Nevada, Utah, Arizona, New Mexico, and parts of Colorado, Kansas, Wyoming, and Oklahoma. The peace treaty also confirmed the previous U.S. annexation of Texas. About thirteen thousand American soldiers died in the war, which added 888,000 square miles to the United States (more than the combined size of France, Britain, Germany, Spain, and Italy).[4] It was the bargain of the millennium.

In 1914 the elites in Washington, London, and Berlin knew exactly what a successful war looked like and how much could be gained from it. In contrast, in 2018 global elites have good reason to suspect that this type of war might have become extinct. Though some Third World dictators and nonstate actors still manage to flourish through war, it seems that major powers no longer know how to do so.

The greatest victory in living memory—of the United States over the Soviet Union—was achieved without any major military confrontation. The United States then got a fleeting taste of old-fashioned military glory in the First Gulf War, but this only tempted it to waste trillions of dollars on humiliating military fiascos in Iraq and Afghanistan. China, the rising power of the early twenty-first century, has assiduously avoided all armed conflicts since its failed invasion of Vietnam in 1979, and it owes its ascent strictly to economic factors. In this it has emulated not the Japanese, German, and Italian empires of the pre-1914 era but rather the Japanese, German, and Italian economic miracles of the post-1945 era. In all these cases economic prosperity and geopolitical clout were achieved without firing a shot.

Even in the Middle East—the fighting arena of the world—regional powers don't know how to wage successful wars. Iran gained nothing from the long bloodbath of the Iran-Iraq War and subsequently avoided all direct military confrontations. The Iranians finance and arm local movements from Iraq to Yemen and have sent their Revolutionary Guards to help their allies in Syria and Lebanon, but so far they have been careful not to invade any country. Iran has recently become the regional hegemon not by dint of any brilliant battlefield victory but rather by default. Its two main enemies—the United States and Iraq—became embroiled in a war that destroyed both Iraq and the American appetite for Middle Eastern quagmires, thereby leaving Iran to enjoy the spoils.

Much the same can be said of Israel. Its last successful war was waged in 1967. Since then Israel prospered despite its many wars, not thanks to them. Most of its occupied territories saddle it with heavy economic burdens and crippling political liabilities. Much like Iran, Israel has lately improved its geopolitical position not by waging successful wars but by avoiding military adventures. While war has ravaged Israel's erstwhile enemies in Iraq, Syria, and Libya, Israel has remained aloof. Not getting sucked into the Syrian civil war has arguably been Israeli prime minister Benjamin Netanyahu's greatest political achievement (as of March 2018). If it had wanted to, the Israel Defense Forces could have seized Damascus within a week, but what would Israel have gained from that? It would be even easier for the IDF to conquer Gaza and topple the Hamas regime, but Israel has repeatedly declined to do so. For all its military prowess and for all the hawkish rhetoric of Israeli politicians, Israel knows there is little to be won from war. Like the United States, China, Germany, Japan, and Iran, Israel seems to understand that in the twenty-first century the most successful strategy is to sit on the fence and let others do the fighting for you.

THE VIEW FROM THE KREMLIN

So far the only successful invasion mounted by a major power in the twenty-first century has been the Russian conquest of the Crimea. In February 2014 Russian forces invaded neighboring Ukraine and occupied the Crimean peninsula, which was subsequently annexed to Russia. With hardly any fighting, Russia gained strategically vital territory, struck fear into its neighbors, and reestablished itself as a world power. However, the conquest succeeded due to an extraordinary set of circumstances. Neither the Ukrainian army nor the local population showed much resistance to the Russians, while other powers refrained from directly intervening in the crisis. These circumstances will be hard to reproduce elsewhere around the world. If the precondition for a successful war is the absence of enemies willing to resist the aggressor, it seriously limits the available opportunities.

Indeed, when Russia sought to reproduce its Crimean success in other parts of Ukraine, it encountered substantially stiffer opposition, and the war in eastern Ukraine bogged down into an unproductive stalemate. Even worse (from Moscow's perspective), the war has stoked anti-Russian feelings in Ukraine and turned that country from an ally into a sworn enemy. Just as success in the First Gulf War tempted the United States to overreach itself in Iraq, success in Crimea may have tempted Russia to overreach itself in Ukraine.

Taken together, Russia's wars in the Caucasus and Ukraine in the early twenty-first century can hardly be described as very successful. Though they have boosted Russia's prestige as a great power, they have also increased distrust and animosity toward Russia, and in economic terms they have been a losing enterprise. Tourist resorts in the Crimea and decrepit Soviet-era factories in Luhansk and Donetsk hardly balance the price of financing the war, and they certainly do not offset the costs of capital flight and international sanctions. To realize the limitations of the Russian policy, one just needs to compare the immense economic progress of peaceful China in the last twenty years to the economic stagnation of "victorious" Russia during the same period.[5]

The brave talk from Moscow notwithstanding, the Russian elite itself is probably well aware of the real costs and benefits of its military adventures, which is why it has so far been very careful not to escalate them. Russia has been following the schoolyard-bully principle: pick on the weakest kid, and don't beat him up too much, lest the teacher intervene. If Putin had conducted his wars in the spirit of Stalin, Peter the Great, or Genghis Khan, then Russian tanks would have long ago made a dash for Tbilisi and Kiev, if not for Warsaw and Berlin. But Putin is neither Genghis nor Stalin. He seems to know better than anyone else that military power cannot go far in the twenty-first century, and that waging a successful war means waging a limited war. Even in Syria, despite the ruthlessness of Russian aerial bombardments, Putin has been careful to minimize the Russian footprint, to let others do all the serious fighting, and to prevent the war from spilling over into neighboring countries.

Indeed, from Russia's perspective, all its supposedly aggressive moves in recent years were not the opening gambits of a new global war but rather an attempt to shore up exposed defenses. Russians can justifiably point out that after their peaceful retreats in the late 1980s and early 1990s they were treated like a defeated enemy. The United States and NATO took advantage of Russian weakness and, despite promises to the contrary, expanded NATO to Eastern Europe and even to some former Soviet republics. The West went on to ignore Russian interests in the Middle East, invaded Serbia and Iraq on doubtful pretexts, and generally made it very clear to Russia that it can count only on its own military power to protect its sphere of influence from Western incursions. From this perspective, recent Russian military moves can be blamed on Bill Clinton and George W. Bush as much as on Vladimir Putin.

Of course, Russian military actions in Georgia, Ukraine, and Syria may yet turn out to be the opening salvoes of a far bolder imperial drive. Even if Putin has not harbored serious plans so far for global conquests, success might fan his ambitions. However, we would also do well to remember that Putin's Russia is far weaker than Stalin's USSR, and unless it is joined by other countries such as China, it cannot support a new Cold War, let alone a full-blown world war. Russia has a population of 150 million people and a GDP of $4 trillion. In both population and production it is dwarfed by the United States (325 million people and a $19 trillion GDP) and the European Union (500 million people and a $21 trillion GDP).[6] Together, the United States and the European Union have five times more people than Russia, and ten times more dollars.

Recent technological developments have made this gap even bigger than it seems. The USSR reached its zenith in the mid-twentieth century, when heavy industry was the locomotive of the global economy and the Soviet centralized system excelled in the mass production of tractors, trucks, tanks, and intercontinental missiles. Today, information technology and biotechnology are more important than heavy industry, but Russia excels in neither. Though it has impressive cyberwarfare capabilities, it lacks a civilian IT sector, and its economy relies overwhelmingly on natural resources, particularly oil and gas. This may be good enough to enrich a few oligarchs and keep Putin in power, but it is not enough to win a digital or biotechnological arms race.

Even more important, Putin's Russia lacks a universal ideology. During the Cold War the USSR relied on the global appeal of communism as much as on the global reach of the Red Army. Putinism, in contrast, has little to offer Cubans, Vietnamese, or French intellectuals. Authoritarian nationalism may indeed be spreading in the world, but by its very nature it is not conducive to the establishment of cohesive international blocs. Whereas Polish communism and Russian communism were both committed, at least in theory, to the universal interests of an international working class, Polish nationalism and Russian nationalism are by definition committed to opposing interests. As Putin's rise sparks an upsurge of Polish nationalism, this will only make Poland more anti-Russian than before.

Therefore, although Russia has embarked on a global campaign of disinformation and subversion that aims to break up NATO and the EU, it does not seem likely that it is about to embark on a global campaign of physical conquest. One can hope—with some justification—that the takeover of the Crimea and the Russian incursions in Georgia and eastern Ukraine will remain isolated examples rather than harbingers of a new era of war.

THE LOST ART OF WINNING WARS

Why is it so difficult for major powers to wage successful wars in the twenty-first century? One reason is the change in the nature of the economy. In the past, economic assets were mostly material; therefore, it was relatively straightforward to enrich yourself by conquest. If you defeated your enemies on the battlefield, you could cash in by looting their cities, selling their civilians in the slave markets, and occupying valuable wheat fields and gold mines. Romans prospered by selling captive Greeks and Gauls, and nineteenth-century Americans thrived by occupying the gold mines of California and the cattle ranches of Texas.

Yet in the twenty-first century only puny profits can be made that way. Today the main economic assets consist of technical and institutional knowledge rather than wheat fields, gold mines, or even oil fields, and you just cannot conquer knowledge through war. An organization such as the Islamic State may still flourish by looting cities and oil wells in the Middle East—it seized more than $500 million from Iraqi banks and in 2015 made an additional $500 million from selling oil—but for a major power such as China or the United States, these are trifling sums.[7] With an annual GDP of more than $20 trillion, China is unlikely to start a war for a paltry billion. As for spending trillions of dollars on a war against the United States, how could China repay these expenses and balance all the war damages and lost trade opportunities? Would the victorious People's Liberation Army loot the riches of Silicon Valley? True, corporations such as Apple, Facebook, and Google are worth hundreds of billions of dollars, but you cannot seize these fortunes by force. There are no silicon mines in Silicon Valley.

A successful war could theoretically still bring huge profits by enabling the victor to rearrange the global trade system in its favor, as Britain did after its victory over Napoleon and as the United States did after its victory over Hitler. However, changes in military technology make it difficult to repeat this feat in the twenty-first century. The atom bomb has turned victory in a world war into collective suicide. It is no coincidence that ever since Hiroshima, superpowers have never fought one another directly, instead engaging only in what (for them) were low-stakes conflicts, in which the temptation to use nuclear weapons to avert defeat was small. Indeed, even attacking a second-rate nuclear power such as North

Korea is an extremely unattractive proposition. It is scary to think what the Kim family might do if it faces military defeat.

Cyberwarfare makes things even worse for would-be imperialists. In the good old days of Queen Victoria and the Maxim gun, the British army could massacre the fuzzy-wuzzies in some far-off desert without endangering the peace of Manchester and Birmingham. Even in the days of George W. Bush, the United States could wreak havoc in Baghdad and Fallujah while the Iraqis had no means of retaliating against San Francisco or Chicago. But if the United States now attacks a country possessing even moderate cyberwarfare capabilities, the war could be brought to California or Illinois within minutes. Malwares and logic bombs could stop air traffic in Dallas, cause trains to collide in Philadelphia, and bring down the electric grid in Michigan.

In the great age of conquerors warfare was a low-damage, high-profit affair. At the Battle of Hastings in 1066 William the Conqueror gained the whole of England in a single day for the cost of a few thousand dead. Nuclear weapons and cyberwarfare, by contrast, are high-damage, low-profit technologies. You can use such tools to destroy entire countries but not to build profitable empires.

Therefore, in a world filling up with saber-rattling and bad vibes, perhaps our best guarantee of peace is that major powers aren't familiar with recent examples of successful wars. While Genghis Khan or Julius Caesar would invade a foreign country at the drop of a hat, present-day nationalist leaders such as Recep Tayyip Erdogan of Turkey, India's Narendra Modi, and Israel's Benjamin Netanyahu talk loudly but are very careful about actually launching wars. Of course, if somebody does find a formula with which to wage successful wars under twenty-first-century conditions, the gates of hell might open with a rush. This is what makes the Russian success in the Crimea a particularly frightening omen. Let's hope it remains an exception.

THE MARCH OF FOLLY

Alas, even if it remains impossible to wage successful wars in the twenty-first century, that would not give us an absolute guarantee of peace. We should never underestimate human stupidity. Both on the personal and on the collective level, humans are prone to engage in self-destructive activities.

In 1939 war was probably a counterproductive move for the Axis powers—yet that likelihood did not save the world from conflict. One of the astounding things about the Second World War is that following the war the defeated powers prospered as never before. Twenty years after the complete annihilation of their armies and the utter collapse of their empires, Germans, Italians, and Japanese were enjoying unprecedented levels of affluence. Why, then, did they go to war in the first place? Why did they inflict unnecessary death and destruction on countless millions? It was all just a stupid miscalculation. In the 1930s Japanese generals, admirals, economists, and journalists concurred that without control of Korea, Manchuria, and the Chinese coast, Japan was doomed to economic stagnation.[8] They were all wrong. In fact, the famed Japanese economic miracle began only after Japan lost all of its mainland conquests.

Human stupidity is one of the most important forces in history, yet we often tend to discount it. Politicians, generals, and scholars treat the world as a great chess game, where every move follows careful rational calculation. This is correct up to a point. Few leaders in history have been mad in the narrow sense of the word, moving pawns and knights at random. Hideki Tojo, Saddam Hussein, and Kim Jong-Il had rational reasons for every move they played. The problem is that the world is far more complicated than a chessboard, and human rationality is not up to the task of really understanding it. For that reason even rational leaders frequently end up doing very stupid things.

So how much should we fear a world war? On one hand, war is definitely not inevitable. The peaceful termination of the Cold War proves that when humans make the right decisions, even super-power conflicts can be resolved peacefully. Moreover, it is exceedingly dangerous to assume that a new world war is inevitable. That would be a self-fulfilling prophecy. Once countries assume that war is inevitable, they beef up their armies, embark on spiraling arms races, refuse to compromise in any conflict, and suspect that good-will gestures are just traps. That guarantees the eruption of war.

On the other hand, it would be naive to assume that war is impossible. Even if war is catastrophic for everyone, no god and no law of nature protect us from human stupidity.

One potential remedy for human stupidity is a dose of humility. National, religious, and cultural tensions are made worse by the grandiose feeling that my nation, my religion, and my culture are the most important in the world—and therefore my interests should come before the interests of anyone else, or of humankind as a whole. How can we make nations, religions, and cultures a bit more realistic and modest about their true place in the world?

12

....

Humility

You Are Not the Center of the World

Most people tend to believe they are the center of the world, and their culture is the linchpin of human history. Many Greeks believe that history began with Homer, Sophocles, and Plato and that all important ideas and inventions were born in Athens, Sparta, Alexandria, or Constantinople. Chinese nationalists retort that history really began with the Yellow Emperor and the Xia and Shang dynasties, and that whatever Westerners, Muslims, or Indians achieved is but a pale copy of original Chinese breakthroughs.

Hindu nativists dismiss these Chinese boasts and argue that even airplanes and nuclear bombs were invented by ancient sages in the Indian subcontinent long before Confucius and Plato, not to mention Einstein and the Wright brothers. Did you know, for example, that it was Maharishi Bhardwaj who invented rockets and airplanes, that Vishwamitra not only invented but also used missiles, that Acharya Kanad was the father of atomic theory, and that the Mahabharata accurately describes nuclear weapons?[1]

Pious Muslims regard all history prior to the Prophet Muhammad as largely irrelevant, and they consider all history after the revelation of the Quran to revolve around the Muslim *ummah*. The main exceptions are Turkish, Iranian, and Egyptian nationalists, who argue that even prior to Muhammad their particular nation was the fountainhead of all that was good about humanity, and that even after the revelation of the Quran, it was mainly their people who preserved the purity of Islam and spread its glory.

Needless to say, the British, French, Germans, Americans, Russians, Japanese, and countless other groups are similarly convinced that humankind would have lived in barbarous and immoral ignorance if it hadn't been for the spectacular achievements of their nation. Some people in history went so far as to imagine that their political institutions and religious practices were essential to the very laws of physics. Thus the Aztecs firmly believed that without the sacrifices they performed each year, the sun would not rise and the entire universe would disintegrate.

All these claims are false. They combine a willful ignorance of history with more than a hint of racism. None of the religions or nations of today existed when humans colonized the world, domesticated plants and animals, built the first cities, or invented writing and money. Morality, art, spirituality, and creativity are universal human abilities embedded in our DNA. Their genesis was in Stone Age Africa. It is therefore crass egotism to ascribe to them a more recent place and time, be it China in the age of the Yellow Emperor, Greece in the age of Plato, or Arabia in the age of Muhammad.

Personally, I am all too familiar with such crass egotism, because the Jews, my own people, also think that they are the most important thing in the world. Name any human achievement or invention, and they will quickly claim credit for it. Knowing them intimately, I also know they are genuinely convinced of such claims. I once took a class with a yoga teacher in Israel who in the introductory session explained in all seriousness that yoga was invented by Abraham and that all the basic yoga postures derive from the shape of the letters of the Hebrew alphabet! (Thus the *trikonasana* posture imitates the shape of the Hebrew letter *aleph*, *tuladandasana* imitates the letter *dalet*, etc.) Abraham taught these postures to the son of one of his concubines, who went to India and taught yoga to the Indians. When I asked for some evidence, the master quoted a biblical passage: "And to the sons of his concubines Abraham gave gifts, and while he was still living he sent them away from his son Isaac, eastward to the east country" (Genesis 25:6). What else could these gifts be? So you see, even yoga was actually invented by the Jews.

Considering Abraham to be the inventor of yoga is a fringe notion. Yet mainstream Judaism solemnly maintains that the entire cosmos exists just so that Jewish rabbis can study their holy scriptures, and that if Jews cease this practice, the universe will come to an end. China, India, Australia, and even the distant galaxies will all be annihilated if the rabbis in Jerusalem and Brooklyn stop debating the Talmud. This is a central article of faith of Orthodox Jews, and anyone who dares doubt it is considered an ignorant fool. Secular Jews may be a bit more skeptical about this grandiose claim, but they too believe that the Jewish people are the central heroes of history and the ultimate wellspring of human morality, spirituality, and learning.

What my people lack in numbers and real influence, they more than compensate for in chutzpah. Since it is more polite to criticize one's own people than to criticize foreigners, I will use the example of Judaism to illustrate how ludicrous such self-important narratives are, and I will leave it to readers around the world to puncture the hot-air balloons inflated by their own tribes.

FREUD'S MOTHER

I originally wrote my book *Sapiens: A Brief History of Humankind* in Hebrew, for an Israeli public. After the Hebrew edition was published in 2011, the most common question I received from Israeli readers was why I hardly mentioned Judaism in my history of the human race. Why did I write extensively about Christianity, Islam, and Buddhism but devote just a few words to the Jewish religion and the Jewish people? Was I deliberately ignoring their immense contribution to human history? Was I motivated by some sinister political agenda?

Such questions come naturally to Israeli Jews, who are educated from kindergarten to think that Judaism is the superstar of human history. Israeli children usually finish twelve years of school without receiving any clear picture of global historical processes. They are taught almost nothing about China, India, or Africa, and though they learn about the Roman Empire, the French Revolution, and the Second World War, these isolated jigsaw pieces do not add up to any overarching narrative. Instead, the only coherent history offered by the Israeli educational system begins with the Hebrew Old Testament, continues to the Second Temple era, skips between various Jewish communities in the Diaspora, and culminates with the rise of Zionism, the Holocaust, and the establishment of the state of Israel. Most students leave school convinced that this must be the main plotline of the entire human story. For even when they hear about the Roman Empire or the French Revolution, the discussion in class focuses on the way the Roman Empire treated the Jews or on the legal and political status of Jews in the French Republic. People fed on such a historical diet have a very hard time digesting the idea that Judaism had relatively little impact on the world as a whole.

Yet the truth is that Judaism played only a modest role in the annals of our species. Unlike such universal religions as Christianity, Islam, and Buddhism, Judaism has always been a tribal creed. It focuses on the fate of one small nation and one tiny land, and it has little interest in the fate of all other people and all other countries. For example, it cares little about events in Japan or about the people of the Indian subcontinent. It is no wonder, therefore, that its historical role was limited.

It is certainly true that Judaism begat Christianity and influenced the birth of Islam—two of the most important religions in history.

However, the credit for the global achievements of Christianity and Islam—as well as the guilt for their many crimes—belongs to the Christians and Muslims themselves rather than to the Jews. Just as it would be unfair to blame Judaism for the mass killings of the Crusades (Christianity is 100 percent culpable), there is also no reason to credit Judaism with the important Christian idea that all human beings are equal before God (an idea that stands in direct contradiction to Jewish orthodoxy, which even today holds that Jews are intrinsically superior to all other humans).

The role of Judaism in the story of humankind is a bit like the role of Freud's mother in modern Western history. For better or worse, Sigmund Freud had immense influence on the science, culture, art, and folk wisdom of the modern West. It is also true that without Freud's mother we wouldn't have had Freud, and that Freud's personality, ambitions, and opinions were likely shaped to a significant extent by his relations with his mother—as he would be the first to admit. But when writing the history of the modern West, nobody expects to find an entire chapter on Freud's mother. Similarly, without Judaism you would not have had Christianity, but that doesn't merit granting much importance to Judaism when writing the history of the world. The crucial issue is what Christianity did with the legacy of its Jewish mother.

It goes without saying that the Jewish people are a unique people with an astonishing history (though this is true of most peoples). It similarly goes without saying that the Jewish tradition is full of deep insights and noble values (though it is also full of questionable ideas and of racist, misogynist, and homophobic attitudes). It is further true that, relative to their numbers, the Jewish people have had a disproportionate impact on the history of the last two thousand years. But when you look at the big picture of our history as a species, since the emergence of *Homo sapiens* more than a hundred thousand years ago, it is obvious that the Jewish contribution to history has been very limited. Humans settled the entire planet, adopted agriculture, built the first cities, and invented writing and money thousands of years before the appearance of Judaism.

Even in the last two millennia, if you look at history from the perspective of the Chinese or of the Native Americans, it is hard to see any major Jewish contribution except through the mediation of Christians or Muslims. The Hebrew Old Testament eventually became a cornerstone of global human culture because it was warmly embraced by Christianity and incorporated into their Bible. In contrast, the Talmud—whose importance to Jewish culture far surpasses that of the Old Testament—was rejected by Christianity, and consequently remains an esoteric text hardly known to the Arabs, Poles, or Dutch, not to mention the Japanese and the Maya. (Which is a great pity, because the Talmud is a far more thoughtful and compassionate book than the Old Testament.)

Can you name a great work of art inspired by the Old Testament? Oh, that's easy: Michelangelo's *David*, Verdi's *Nabucco*, Cecil B. DeMille's *The Ten Commandments*. Do you know of any famous work inspired by the New Testament? Piece of cake: Leonardo's *Last Supper*, Bach's *St. Matthew Passion*, Monty Python's *Life of Brian*. Now for the real test: can you list a few masterpieces inspired by the Talmud?

Though Jewish communities that studied the Talmud spread over large parts of the world, they did not play an important role in the building of the Chinese empires, in the European voyages of discovery, in the establishment of the democratic system, or in the Industrial Revolution. The coin, the university, parliament, the bank, the compass, the printing press, and the steam engine were all invented by Gentiles.

ETHICS BEFORE THE BIBLE

Israelis often use the term "the three great religions," thinking that these religions are Christianity (2.3 billion adherents), Islam (1.8 billion), and Judaism (15 million). Hinduism, with its 1 billion believers, and Buddhism, with its 500 million followers—not to mention the Shinto religion (50 million) and the Sikh religion (25 million)—don't make the cut.[2] This warped concept of "the three great religions" often implies in the mind of Israelis that all major religious and ethical traditions emerged out of the womb of Judaism, which was the first religion to preach universal ethical rules—as if humans prior to the days of Abraham and Moses lived in a Hobbesian state of nature without any moral commitments, and as if all of contemporary morality derives from the Ten Commandments. This is a baseless and insolent idea, which ignores many of the world's most important ethical traditions.

Stone Age hunter-gatherer tribes had moral codes tens of thousands of years before Abraham. When the first European settlers reached Australia in the late eighteenth century, they encountered Aboriginal tribes that had a well-developed ethical worldview despite being totally ignorant of Moses, Jesus, and Muhammad. It would be difficult to argue that the Christian colonists who violently dispossessed the natives exhibited superior moral standards.

Scientists nowadays point out that morality in fact has deep evolutionary roots predating the appearance of humankind by millions of years. All social mammals, such as wolves, dolphins, and monkeys, have ethical codes, adapted by evolution to promote group cooperation.[3] For example, when wolf pups play with one another, they have "fair game" rules. If a pup bites too hard or continues to bite an opponent that has rolled on his back and surrendered, the other pups will stop playing with him.[4]

In chimpanzee bands dominant members are expected to respect the property rights of weaker members. If a junior female chimpanzee finds a banana, even the alpha male will usually avoid stealing it for himself. If he breaks this rule, he is likely to lose status.[5] Apes not only avoid taking advantage of weak group members but sometimes actively help them. A pygmy chimpanzee male called Kidogo, who lived in the Milwaukee County Zoo, suffered from a serious heart condition that made him feeble and confused. When he was first moved to the zoo, he could neither orient himself nor understand the instructions of the human caretakers. When the other chimpanzees understood his predicament, they intervened. They often took Kidogo by the hand and led him wherever he needed to go. If Kidogo became lost, he would utter loud distress signals, and some ape would rush to help.

One of Kidogo's main helpers was the highest-ranking male in the band, Lody, who not only guided Kidogo but also protected him. While almost all group members treated Kidogo with kindness, one juvenile male called Murph would often tease him mercilessly. When Lody noticed such behavior, he often chased the bully away, or alternatively put a protective arm around Kidogo.[6]

An even more touching case occurred in the jungles of Ivory Coast. After a young chimpanzee named Oscar lost his mother, he struggled to survive on his own. None of the other females was willing to adopt and take care of him, because they were burdened with their own young. Oscar gradually lost weight, health, and vitality. But when all seemed lost, Oscar was "adopted" by the band's alpha male, Freddy. The alpha made sure that Oscar ate well, and even carried him around on his back. Genetic tests proved that Freddy was not related to Oscar.[7] We can only speculate what drove the gruff old leader to take care of the orphaned toddler, but apparently ape leaders developed the tendency to help the poor, the needy, and the fatherless millions of years before the Bible instructed ancient Israelites that they should not "mistreat any widow or fatherless child" (Exodus 22:21), and before the prophet Amos complained about social elites "who oppress the poor and crush the needy" (Amos 4:1).

Even among *Homo sapiens* living in the ancient Middle East, the biblical prophets were hardly original in their moral views. "Thou shalt not kill" and "Thou shalt not steal" were well known in the legal and ethical codes of Sumerian city-states, pharaonic Egypt, and the Babylonian Empire. Periodic rest days long predated the Jewish Sabbath. A thousand years before the prophet Amos reprimanded Israelite elites for their oppressive behavior, the Babylonian king Hammurabi explained that the great gods had instructed him "to demonstrate justice within the land, to destroy evil and wickedness, to stop the mighty exploiting the weak."[8]

Meanwhile, in Egypt—centuries before the birth of Moses— scribes wrote down "the story of the eloquent peasant," which tells of a poor peasant whose property was stolen by a greedy landowner. The peasant came before Pharaoh's corrupt officials, and when they failed to protect him, he explained to them why it was necessary that they provide justice and in particular defend the poor from the rich. In one colorful allegory, this Egyptian peasant explained that the meager possessions of the poor are like their very breath, and official corruption suffocates them by plugging their nostrils.[9]

Many biblical laws copy rules that were accepted in Mesopotamia, Egypt, and Canaan centuries and even millennia prior to the establishment of the kingdoms of Judah and Israel. If biblical Judaism gave these laws any unique twist, it was by turning them from universal rulings applicable to all humans into tribal codes aimed primarily at the Jewish people. Jewish morality was initially shaped as an exclusive, tribal affair, and has remained so to some extent to this day. The Old Testament, the Talmud, and many (though not all) rabbis maintained that the life of a Jew is more valuable than the life of a Gentile, which is why, for example, Jews are allowed to desecrate the Sabbath in order to save a Jew from death but are forbidden to do so merely in order to save a Gentile (Babylonian Talmud, Yoma 84:2).[10]

Some Jewish sages have argued that even the famous commandment "Love your neighbor as yourself" refers only to Jews, and that there is absolutely no commandment to love Gentiles. Indeed, the original text from Leviticus says: "Do not seek revenge or bear a grudge against anyone among your people, but love your neighbor as yourself" (Leviticus 19:18), which raises the suspicion that "your neighbor" refers only to members of "your people." This suspicion is greatly strengthened by the fact that the Bible commands Jews to exterminate certain people such as the Amalekites and the Canaanites. "Do not leave alive a single soul," decrees the holy book. "Completely destroy them—the Hittites, Amorites, Canaanites, Perizzites, Hivites and Jebusites—as the Lord your God has commanded you" (Deuteronomy 20:16–17). This is one of the first recorded instances in human history when genocide was presented as a binding religious duty.

It was only the Christians who selected some choice morsels of the Jewish moral code, turned them into universal commandments, and spread them throughout the world. Indeed, Christianity split from Judaism precisely on this account. While many Jews to this day believe that the so-called chosen people are closer to God than other nations are, the founder of Christianity, the Apostle Paul, stipulated in his famous Epistle to the Galatians that "there is neither Jew nor Gentile, neither slave nor free, nor is there male and female, for you are all one in Christ Jesus" (Galatians 3:28).

And we must again emphasize that despite the enormous impact of Christianity, this was definitely not the first time a human preached a universal ethic. The Bible is far from being the exclusive font of human morality (and luckily so, given the many racist, misogynist, and homophobic attitudes it contains). Confucius, Laozi, Buddha, and Mahavira established universal ethical codes long before Paul and Jesus, without knowing anything about the land of Canaan or the prophets of Israel. Confucius taught that every person must love others as he loves himself about five hundred years before Rabbi Hillel the Elder said that this was the essence of the Torah. And at a time when Judaism still mandated the sacrifice of animals and the systematic extermination of entire human populations, Buddha and Mahavira were already instructing their followers to avoid harming not only all human beings but any sentient being whatsoever, even including insects. It therefore makes absolutely no sense to credit Judaism and its Christian and Muslim offspring with the creation of human morality.

THE BIRTH OF BIGOTRY

What about monotheism, then? Doesn't Judaism at least deserve special praise for pioneering the belief in a single God, which was unparalleled anywhere else in the world (even if this belief was then spread to the four corners of the earth by Christians and Muslims more than Jews)? We can quibble even about that, since the first clear evidence for monotheism comes from the religious revolution of Pharaoh Akhenaten around 1350 BCE, and documents such as the Mesha Stele (erected by the Moabite king Mesha) indicate that the religion of biblical Israel was not all that different from the religion of neighboring kingdoms such as Moab. Mesha describes his great god Chemosh in almost the same way that the Old Testament describes Yahweh. But the real problem with the idea that Judaism contributed monotheism to the world is that this is hardly something to be proud of. From an ethical perspective, monotheism was arguably one of the worst ideas in human history.

Monotheism did little to improve the moral standards of humans— do you really think Muslims are inherently more ethical than Hindus just because Muslims believe in a single god while Hindus believe in many gods? Were Christian conquistadores more ethical than pagan Native American tribes? What monotheism undoubtedly did was to make many people far more intolerant than before, thereby contributing to the spread of religious persecutions and holy wars. Polytheists found it perfectly acceptable that different people worshipped different gods and performed diverse rites and rituals. They rarely if ever fought, persecuted, or killed people just because of their religious beliefs. Monotheists, in contrast, believed that their God was the only god, and that He demanded universal obedience. Consequently, as Christianity and Islam spread around the world, so did the incidence of crusades, jihads, inquisitions, and religious discrimination.[11]

Compare, for example, the attitude of Emperor Ashoka of India in the third century BCE to that of the Christian emperors of the late Roman Empire. Emperor Ashoka ruled an empire teeming with myriad religions, sects, and gurus. He gave himself the official titles of "Beloved-of-the-Gods" and "the king who regards everyone with affection." Sometime around 250 BCE, he issued an imperial edict of tolerance that proclaimed:

> Beloved-of-the-Gods, the king who regards everyone with affection, honors both ascetics and the householders of all religions . . . and values that there should be growth in the essentials of all religions. Growth in essentials can be done in different ways, but all of them have as their root restraint in speech, that is, not praising one's own religion, or condemning the religion of others without good cause. . . . Whoever praises his own religion, due to excessive devotion, and condemns others with the thought "Let me glorify my own religion," only harms his own religion. Therefore contact between religions is good. One should listen to and respect the doctrines professed by others. Beloved-of-the-Gods, the king who regards everyone with affection, desires that all should be well learned in the good doctrines of other religions.[12]

Five hundred years later, the late Roman Empire was as diverse as Ashoka's India, but when Christianity took over, the emperors adopted a very different approach to religion. Beginning with Constantine the Great and his son Constantius II, the emperors closed all non-Christian temples and forbade so-called pagan rituals on pain of death. The persecution culminated under the reign of Emperor Theodosius—whose name means "given by God"—who in 391 issued the Theodosian Decrees, which effectively made all religions except Christianity and Judaism illegal (Judaism too was persecuted in numerous ways, but it remained legal to practice it).[13] According to the new laws, one could be executed even for worshipping Jupiter or Mithras in the privacy of one's own home.[14] As part of their campaign to cleanse the empire of all infidel heritage, the Christian emperors also suppressed the Olympic Games. Having been celebrated for more than a thousand years, the last ancient Olympiad was held sometime in the late fourth or early fifth century.[15]

Of course, not all monotheist rulers were as intolerant as Theodosius, whereas numerous rulers rejected monotheism without adopting the broad-minded policies of Ashoka. Nevertheless, by insisting that "there is no god but our God," the monotheist idea tended to encourage bigotry. Jews would do well to downplay their part in disseminating this dangerous meme and let the Christians and Muslims carry the blame for it.

JEWISH PHYSICS, CHRISTIAN BIOLOGY

Only in the nineteenth and twentieth centuries do we see Jews make an extraordinary contribution to humankind as a whole, through their outsized role in modern science. In addition to such well-known names as Einstein and Freud, about 20 percent of all Nobel Prize laureates in science have been Jews, though Jews constitute less than 0.2 percent of the world's population.[16] But it should be stressed that this has been a contribution of individual Jews rather than of Judaism as a religion or a culture. Most of the important Jewish scientists of the past two hundred years acted outside the Jewish religious sphere. Indeed, Jews began to make their remarkable contribution to science only once they had abandoned the yeshiva in favor of the laboratory.

Prior to 1800, the Jewish impact on science was limited. Naturally enough, Jews played no significant role in the progress of science in China, in India, or in the Maya civilization. In Europe and the Middle East some Jewish thinkers such as Maimonides had considerable influence on their Gentile colleagues, but the overall Jewish impact was more or less proportional to their demographic weight. During the sixteenth, seventeenth, and eighteenth centuries Judaism was hardly instrumental to the outbreak of the Scientific Revolution. Except for Spinoza (who was excommunicated for his trouble by the Jewish community), you can hardly name a single Jew who was critical to the birth of modern physics, chemistry, biology, or the social sciences. We don't know what Einstein's ancestors were doing in the days of Galileo and Newton, but in all likelihood they were far more interested in studying the Talmud than in studying the properties of light.

The great change occurred only in the nineteenth and twentieth centuries, when secularization and the Jewish Enlightenment caused many Jews to adopt the worldview and lifestyle of their Gentile neighbors. Jews then began to join the universities and research centers of countries such as Germany, France, and the United States. Jewish scholars brought from the ghettos and shtetls important cultural legacies. The central value of education in Jewish culture was one of the main reasons for the extraordinary success of Jewish scientists. Other factors included the desire of a persecuted minority to prove its worth, and the barriers that prevented talented Jews from advancement in more anti-Semitic institutions such as the army and the state administration.

Yet while Jewish scientists brought with them from the yeshivas strong discipline and a deep faith in the value of knowledge, they did not bring any helpful baggage of concrete ideas and insights. Einstein was Jewish, but the theory of relativity wasn't "Jewish physics." What does faith in the sacredness of the Torah have to do with the insight that energy equals mass multiplied by the speed of light squared? For the sake of comparison, Darwin was a Christian and even began his studies at Cambridge intending to become an Anglican priest. Does it imply that the theory of evolution is a Christian theory? It would be ridiculous to list the theory of relativity as a Jewish contribution to humankind, just as it would be ridiculous to credit Christianity with the theory of evolution.

Similarly, it is hard to see anything particularly Jewish about the invention of the process for synthesizing ammonia by Fritz Haber (Nobel Prize in Chemistry, 1918), the discovery of the antibiotic streptomycin by Selman Waksman (Nobel Prize in Physiology or Medicine, 1952), or the discovery of quasicrystals by Dan Shechtman (Nobel Prize in Chemistry, 2011). In the case of scholars from the humanities and social sciences—such as Freud—their Jewish heritage probably had a deeper impact on their insights. Yet even in these cases, the discontinuities are more glaring than the surviving links. Freud's views about the human psyche were very different from those of Rabbi Joseph Caro or Rabbi Yochanan ben Zakkai, and he did not discover the Oedipus complex by carefully perusing the Shulhan Arukh (the code of Jewish law).

To summarize, although the Jewish emphasis on learning probably made an important contribution to the exceptional success of Jewish scientists, it was Gentile thinkers who laid the groundwork for the achievements of Einstein, Haber, and Freud. The Scientific Revolution wasn't a Jewish project, and Jews found their place in it only when they moved from the yeshivas to the universities. Indeed, the Jewish habit of seeking the answers to all questions by reading ancient texts was a significant obstacle to Jewish integration into the world of modern science, where answers come from observations and experiments. If there was anything about the Jewish religion itself that necessarily leads to scientific breakthroughs, why is it that between 1905 and 1933 ten secular German Jews won Nobel Prizes in chemistry, medicine, and physics, but during the same period not a single ultra-Orthodox Jew or a single Bulgarian or Yemenite Jew won any Nobel Prize?

Lest I be suspected of being a "self-hating Jew" or an anti-Semite,

I would like to emphasize that I am not saying Judaism is a particularly evil or benighted religion. All I am saying is that it wasn't particularly important to the history of humankind. For many centuries Judaism was the humble religion of a small persecuted minority that preferred to read and contemplate rather than to conquer faraway countries and burn heretics at the stake.

Anti-Semites usually think that Jews are very important. Anti-Semites imagine that the Jews control the world, or the banking system, or at least the media, and that they are to blame for everything from global warming to the 9/11 attacks. Such anti-Semitic paranoia is as ludicrous as Jewish megalomania. Jews may be a very interesting people, but when you look at the big picture, you must realize that they have had a very limited impact on the world.

Throughout history, humans have created hundreds of different religions and sects. A handful of them—Christianity, Islam, Hinduism, Confucianism, and Buddhism—influenced billions of people (not always for the best). The vast majority of creeds, such as the Bon religion, the Yoruba religion, and the Jewish religion, had a far smaller impact. Personally I like the idea of descending not from brutal world conquerors but from insignificant people who seldom poked their noses into other people's business. Many religions praise the value of humility but then imagine themselves to be the most important thing in the universe. They mix calls for personal meekness with blatant collective arrogance. Humans of all creeds would do well to take humility more seriously.

And among all forms of humility, perhaps the most important is to have humility before God. Whenever they talk of God, humans all too often profess abject self-effacement, but then use the name of God to lord it over their brethren.

13

. . . .

God

Don't Take the Name of God in Vain

Does God exist? That depends on which God you have in mind: the cosmic mystery, or the worldly lawgiver? Sometimes when people talk about God, they talk about a grand and awesome enigma, about which we know absolutely nothing. We invoke this mysterious God to explain the deepest riddles of the cosmos. Why is there something rather than nothing? What shaped the fundamental laws of physics? What is consciousness, and where does it come from? We do not know the answers to these questions, and we give our ignorance the grand name of God. The most fundamental characteristic of this mysterious God is that we cannot say anything concrete about Him. This is the God of the philosophers, the God we talk about when we sit around a campfire late at night and wonder what life is all about.

On other occasions people see God as a stern and worldly lawgiver about whom we know only too much. We know exactly what He thinks about fashion, food, sex, and politics, and we invoke this angry man in the sky to justify a million regulations, decrees, and conflicts. He gets upset when women wear short-sleeved shirts,

when two men have sex with each other, or when teenagers mastur-
bate. Some people say He does not like us to ever drink alcohol,
whereas according to others He positively demands that we drink
wine every Friday night or every Sunday morning. Entire libraries
have been written to explain in the minutest details exactly what He
wants and what He dislikes. The most fundamental characteristic
of this worldly lawgiver is that we can say extremely concrete things
about Him. This is the God of the Crusaders and jihadists, of the
inquisitors, misogynists, and homophobes. This is the God we talk
about when we stand around a burning pyre, hurling stones and
abuses at the heretics being grilled there.

When the faithful are asked whether God really exists, they often
begin by talking about the enigmatic mysteries of the universe and
the limits of human understanding. "Science cannot explain the Big
Bang," they exclaim, "so that must be God's doing." Yet like a magi-
cian fooling an audience by imperceptibly replacing one card with
another, the faithful quickly replace the cosmic mystery with the
worldly lawgiver. After giving the name of "God" to the unknown
secrets of the cosmos, they then use this to somehow condemn bi-
kinis and divorce. "We do not understand the Big Bang—therefore
you must cover your hair in public and vote against gay marriage."
Not only is there no logical connection between the two, but they
are in fact contradictory. The deeper the mysteries of the universe,
the less likely it is that whatever is responsible for them gives a damn
about female dress codes or human sexual behavior.

The missing link between the cosmic mystery and the worldly
lawgiver is usually provided through some holy book. The book is
full of the most trifling regulations but is nevertheless attributed to
the cosmic mystery. The creator of space and time supposedly composed it, but He bothered to enlighten us mainly about some arcane
temple rituals and food taboos. In truth, we don't have any evidence
whatsoever that the Bible or the Quran or the Book of Mormon or
the Vedas or any other holy book was composed by the force that
determined that energy equals mass multiplied by the speed of light

squared, and that protons are 1,837 times more massive than electrons. To the best of our scientific knowledge, all of these sacred texts were written by imaginative *Homo sapiens*. They are just stories invented by our ancestors in order to legitimize social norms and political structures.

I personally never cease to wonder about the mystery of existence. But I have never understood what it has to do with the niggling laws of Judaism, Christianity, or Hinduism. These laws were certainly very helpful in establishing and maintaining the social order for thousands of years. But in that, they are not fundamentally different from the laws of secular states and institutions.

The third of the biblical Ten Commandments instructs humans never to make wrongful use of the name of God. Many understand this in a childish way, as a prohibition on uttering the explicit name of God (as in the famous Monty Python scene "If you say Jehovah . . ."). Perhaps the deeper meaning of this commandment is that we should never use the name of God to justify our political interests, our economic ambitions, or our personal hatreds. People hate somebody and say, "God hates him"; people covet a piece of land and say, "God wants it." The world would be a much better place if we followed the third commandment more devotedly. You want to wage war on your neighbors and steal their land? Leave God out of it and find yourself some other excuse.

When all is said and done, it is a matter of semantics. When I use the word "God," I think of the God of the Islamic State, of the Crusades, of the Inquisition, and of the "God hates fags" banners. When I think of the mystery of existence, I prefer to use other words, so as to avoid confusion. And unlike the God of the Islamic State and the Crusades—who cares a lot about names and above all about His most holy name—the mystery of existence doesn't care an iota what names we apes give it.

GODLESS ETHICS

Of course the cosmic mystery doesn't help us at all in maintaining the social order. People often argue that we must believe in a god that gave some very concrete laws to humans, or else morality will disappear and society will collapse into primeval chaos.

It is certainly true that belief in gods was vital to various social orders, and that it sometimes had positive consequences. Indeed, the very same religions that inspire hate and bigotry in some people inspire love and compassion in others. For example, in the early 1960s the Methodist minister Ted McIlvenna became aware of the plight of LGBT people in his community. He began exploring the situation of gays and lesbians in society in general, and in May 1964 convened a pioneering three-day dialogue between clergymen and gay and lesbian activists at the White Memorial Retreat Center in California. The participants subsequently set up the Council on Religion and the Homosexual, which in addition to the activists included Methodist, Episcopal, Lutheran, and United Church of Christ ministers. This was the first American organization to dare use the word "homosexual" in its official title.

In the following years CRH activities ranged from organizing costume parties to taking legal actions against unjust discrimination and persecution. The CRH became the seed of the gay rights movement in California. Reverend McIlvenna and the other men of God who joined him were well aware of the biblical injunctions against homosexuality. But they thought that it was more important to be true to the compassionate spirit of Christ than to the strict word of the Bible.[1]

Yet though gods can inspire us to act compassionately, religious faith is not a necessary condition for moral behavior. The idea that we need a supernatural being to make us act morally assumes that there is something unnatural about morality. But why? Morality of some kind is natural. All social mammals from chimpanzees to rats have ethical codes that limit behavior like theft and murder. Among humans, morality is present in all societies, even though not all of them believe in the same god, or in any god. Christians act with charity even without believing in the Hindu pantheon, Muslims value honesty despite rejecting the divinity of Christ, and secular countries such as Denmark and the Czech Republic aren't more violent than devout countries such as Iran and Pakistan.

Morality doesn't mean "following divine commands." It means "reducing suffering." Therefore in order to act morally, you don't need to believe in any myth or story. You just need to develop a deep appreciation of suffering. If you really understand how an action causes unnecessary suffering to yourself or to others, you will naturally abstain from it. People nevertheless murder, rape, and steal because they have only a superficial appreciation of the misery this causes. They are fixated on satisfying their immediate lust or greed, without concern for the impact on others—or even for the long-term impact on themselves. Even inquisitors who deliberately inflict as much pain as possible on their victim usually use various desensitizing and dehumanizing techniques in order to distance themselves from what they are doing.[2]

You might object that every human naturally seeks to avoid feeling miserable, but why would a human care about the misery of others unless some god demands it? One obvious answer is that humans are social animals, and therefore their happiness depends to a very large extent on their relations with others. Without love, friendship, and community, who could be happy? If you live a lonely, self-centered life, you are almost guaranteed to be miserable. So at the very least, to be happy you need to care about your family, your friends, and your community members.

What, then, about complete strangers? Why not murder strangers and take their possessions to enrich myself and my tribe? Many thinkers have constructed elaborate social theories, explaining why in the long run such behavior is counterproductive. You would not like to live in a society where strangers are routinely robbed and murdered. Not only would you be in constant danger, but you would lack the benefit of things like commerce, which depends on trust between strangers. Merchants don't usually visit dens of thieves. That's how secular theoreticians from ancient China to modern Europe have justified the golden rule of "don't do to others what you would not like them to do to you."

Yet we do not really need such complex, long-term theories to find a natural basis for universal compassion. Forget about commerce for a moment. On a much more immediate level, hurting others always hurts me too. Every violent act in the world begins with a violent desire in somebody's mind, which disturbs that person's own peace and happiness before it disturbs the peace and happiness of anyone else. Thus people seldom steal unless they first develop a lot of greed and envy in their minds. People don't usually murder unless they first generate anger and hatred. Emotions such as greed, envy, anger, and hatred are very unpleasant. You cannot experience joy and harmony when you are boiling with anger or envy. Long before you murder anyone, your anger has already killed your own peace of mind.

Indeed, you might keep boiling with anger for years, without ever actually murdering the object of your hatred. In which case you haven't hurt anyone else, but you have nevertheless hurt yourself. It is therefore your natural self-interest—and not the command of some god—that should induce you to do something about your anger. If you were completely free of anger, you would feel far better than if you murdered an obnoxious enemy.

For some people, a strong belief in a compassionate god that commands us to turn the other cheek may help in curbing anger. That's been an enormous contribution of religious belief to the peace and harmony of the world. Unfortunately, for other people religious belief actually stokes and justifies their anger, especially if someone dares to insult their god or ignores His wishes. So the value of the lawgiver god ultimately depends on the behavior of His devotees. If they act well, they can believe anything they like.

Similarly, the value of religious rites and sacred places depends on the type of feelings and behaviors they inspire. If visiting a temple makes people experience peace and harmony, that's wonderful. But if a particular temple causes violence and conflicts, what do we need it for? It is clearly a dysfunctional temple. Just as it is pointless to fight over a sick tree that produces thorns rather than fruits, it is also pointless to fight over a defective temple that produces enmity rather than harmony.

Not visiting any temples and not believing in any god is also a viable option. As the last few centuries have proved, we don't need to invoke God's name in order to live a moral life. Secularism can provide us with all the values we need.

14

....

Secularism

Acknowledge Your Shadow

What does it mean to be secular? Secularism is sometimes defined as the negation of religion, and secular people are therefore characterized by what they *don't* believe and *don't* do. According to this definition, secular people do not believe in any gods or angels, do not go to churches and temples, and do not perform rites and rituals. As such, the secular world appears to be hollow, nihilistic, and amoral—an empty box waiting to be filled with something.

Few people would adopt such a negative identity. Self-professing secularists view secularism in a very different way. For them, secularism is a very positive and active worldview, defined by a coherent code of values rather than by opposition to this or that religion. In fact, many of the secular values are shared by various religious traditions. Unlike some sects that insist they have a monopoly over all wisdom and goodness, one of the chief characteristics of secular people is that they claim no such monopoly. They don't think that morality and wisdom came down from heaven in one particular place and time. Rather, they view morality and wisdom as the natural legacy of all humans. Therefore it is only to be expected that at least some values would pop up in human societies all over the world and would be common to Muslims, Christians, Hindus, and atheists.

Religious leaders often present their followers with a stark either/ or choice—either you are Muslim or you are not. And if you are Muslim, you should reject all other doctrines. In contrast, secular people are comfortable with multiple, hybrid identities. As far as secularism is concerned, you can go on calling yourself a Muslim and continue to pray to Allah, eat halal food, and make the haj to Mecca, yet also be a good member of secular society, provided you adhere to the secular ethical code. This ethical code—which is in fact accepted by millions of Muslims, Christians, and Hindus as well as by atheists—enshrines the values of truth, compassion, equality, freedom, courage, and responsibility. It forms the foundation of modern scientific and democratic institutions.

Like all ethical codes, the secular code is an ideal to aspire to rather than a social reality. Just as Christian societies and Christian institutions often deviate from the Christian ideal, so too secular societies and institutions often fall far short of the secular ideal. Medieval France was a self-proclaimed Christian kingdom, but it dabbled in all kinds of not-very-Christian activities—just ask the downtrodden peasantry. Modern France is a self-proclaimed secular state, but from the days of Robespierre onward it took some troubling liberties with the very definition of liberty (just ask women). That does not mean that secular people—in France or elsewhere— lack a moral compass or an ethical commitment. It just means that it is not easy to live up to an ideal.

THE SECULAR IDEAL

What then is the secular ideal? The most important secular commitment is to the truth, which is based on observation and evidence rather than on mere faith. Secularists strive not to confuse truth with belief. If you have a very strong belief in some story, that may tell us a lot of interesting things about your psychology, about your childhood, and about your brain structure—but it does not prove that the story is true. (Often, strong beliefs are needed precisely when the story isn't true.)

In addition, secularists do not sanctify any group, person, or book as if it and it alone has sole custody of the truth. Instead, secular people sanctify the truth wherever it may reveal itself—in ancient fossilized bones, in images of far-off galaxies, in tables of statistical data, or in the writings of various human traditions. This commitment to the truth underlies modern science, which has enabled humankind to crack the atom, decipher the genome, track the evolution of life, and understand the history of humanity itself.

The other chief commitment of secular people is to compassion. Secular ethics relies not on obeying the edicts of this or that god, but rather on a deep appreciation of suffering. For example, secular people abstain from murder not because some ancient book forbids it but because killing inflicts immense suffering on sentient beings. There is something deeply troubling and dangerous about people who avoid killing just because "God says so." Such people are motivated by obedience rather than compassion, and what will they do if they come to believe that their god commands them to kill heretics, witches, adulterers, or foreigners?

Of course, in the absence of absolute divine commandments, secular ethics often face difficult dilemmas. What happens when the same action hurts one person but helps another? Is it ethical to levy high taxes on the rich in order to help the poor? To wage a bloody war in order to remove a brutal dictator? To allow an unlimited number of refugees into our country? When secular people encounter such dilemmas, they do not ask, "What does God command?" Rather, they carefully weigh the feelings of all concerned parties, examine a wide range of observations and possibilities, and search for a middle path that will cause as little harm as possible.

Consider, for example, attitudes toward sexuality. How do secular people decide whether to endorse or oppose rape, homosexuality, bestiality, and incest? By examining feelings. Rape is obviously unethical, not because it breaks some divine commandment but because it hurts people. In contrast, a loving relationship between two men harms no one, so there is no reason to forbid it.

What about bestiality? I have participated in numerous private and public debates about gay marriage, and all too often some wise guy asks, "If marriage between two men is okay, why not allow marriage between a man and a goat?" From a secular perspective the answer is obvious. Healthy relationships require emotional, intellectual, and even spiritual depth. A marriage lacking such depth will make you frustrated, lonely, and psychologically stunted. Whereas two men can certainly satisfy the emotional, intellectual, and spiritual needs of each other, a relationship with a goat cannot. Therefore if you see marriage as an institution aimed at promoting human well-being—as secular people do—you would not dream of even raising such a bizarre question. Only people who see marriage as some kind of miraculous ritual might do so.

So how about relations between a father and his daughter? Both are humans, so what's wrong with that? Well, numerous psychological studies have demonstrated that such relations inflict immense and usually irreparable harm on the child. In addition, they reflect and intensify destructive tendencies in the parent. Evolution has shaped the psyche of *Homo sapiens* in such a way that romantic bonds just don't mix well with parental bonds. Therefore you don't need God or the Bible to oppose incest—you just need to read the relevant psychological studies.[1]

This is the deep reason secular people cherish scientific truth: not in order to satisfy their curiosity, but in order to know how best to reduce the suffering in the world. Without the guidance of scientific studies, our compassion is often blind.

The twin commitments to truth and compassion result also in a commitment to equality. Though opinions differ regarding questions of economic and political equality, secular people are fundamentally suspicious of all a priori hierarchies. Suffering is suffering, no matter who experiences it, and knowledge is knowledge, no matter who discovers it. Privileging the experiences or the discoveries of a particular nation, class, or gender is likely to make us both callous and ignorant. Secular people are certainly proud of the uniqueness of their particular nation, country, and culture—but they don't confuse uniqueness with superiority. Therefore, though they acknowledge their special duties toward their nation and their country, secular people don't think these duties are exclusive, and they simultaneously acknowledge their duties toward humanity as a whole.

We cannot search for the truth and for the way out of suffering without the freedom to think, investigate, and experiment. For that reason secular people cherish freedom, and refrain from investing supreme authority in any text, institution, or leader as the ultimate judge of what's true and what's right. Humans should always retain the freedom to doubt, to check again, to hear a second opinion, to try a different path. Secular people admire Galileo Galilei, who dared to question whether the Earth really sits motionless at the center of the universe; they admire the masses of common people who stormed the Bastille in 1789 and brought down the despotic regime of Louis XVI; and they admire Rosa Parks, who had the courage to sit down on a bus seat reserved for white passengers only.

It takes a lot of courage to fight biases and oppressive regimes, but it takes even greater courage to admit ignorance and venture into the unknown. Secular education teaches us that if we don't know something, we shouldn't be afraid of acknowledging our ignorance and looking for new evidence. Even if we think we know something, we shouldn't be afraid of doubting our opinions and checking ourselves again. Many people are afraid of the unknown and want clear-cut answers for every question. Fear of the unknown can paralyze us more than any tyrant. People throughout history worried that unless we put all our faith in some set of absolute answers, human society would crumble. In fact, modern history has demonstrated that a society of courageous people willing to admit ignorance and raise difficult questions is usually not just more prosperous but also more peaceful than societies in which everyone must unquestioningly accept a single answer. People afraid of losing their truth tend to be more violent than people who are used to looking at the world from several different viewpoints. Questions you cannot answer are usually far better for you than answers you cannot question.

Finally, secular people cherish responsibility. They don't believe in any higher power that takes care of the world, punishes the wicked, rewards the just, and protects us from famine, plague, or war. Therefore we flesh-and-blood mortals must take full responsibility for whatever we do—or don't do. If the world is full of misery, it is our duty to find solutions. Secular people take pride in the immense achievements of modern societies, such as curing epidemics, feeding the hungry, and bringing peace to large parts of the world. We need not credit any divine protector with these achievements—they resulted from humans developing their own knowledge and compassion. Yet for exactly the same reason, we need to take full responsibility for the crimes and failings of modernity, from genocides to ecological degradation. Instead of praying for miracles, we need to ask what we can do to help.

These are the chief values of the secular world. As noted earlier, none of these values is exclusively secular. Jews value the truth, Christians value compassion, Muslims value equality, Hindus value responsibility, and so forth. Secular societies and institutions are happy to acknowledge these links and to embrace religious Jews, Christians, Muslims, and Hindus, provided that when the secular code collides with religious doctrine, the latter gives way. For example, to be accepted into secular society, Orthodox Jews are expected to treat non-Jews as their equal, Christians should avoid burning heretics at the stake, Muslims must respect freedom of expression, and Hindus have to relinquish caste-based discrimination.

In contrast, there is no expectation that religious people should deny God or abandon traditional rites and rituals. The secular world judges people on the basis of their behavior rather than their favorite clothes and ceremonies. A person can follow the most bizarre sectarian dress code and practice the strangest of religious ceremonies, yet act out of a deep commitment to the core secular values. There are plenty of Jewish scientists, Christian environmentalists, Muslim feminists, and Hindu human rights activists. If they are loyal to scientific truth, to compassion, to equality, and to freedom, they are full members of the secular world, and there is absolutely no reason to demand that they take off their yarmulkes, crosses, hijabs, or tilakas.

For similar reasons, secular education does not mean a negative indoctrination that teaches kids not to believe in God and not to take part in any religious ceremonies. Rather, secular education teaches children to distinguish truth from belief, to develop compassion for all suffering beings, to appreciate the wisdom and experiences of all the earth's denizens, to think freely without fearing the unknown, and to take responsibility for their actions and for the world as a whole.

WAS STALIN SECULAR?

It is therefore groundless to criticize secularism for lacking ethical commitments or social responsibility. In fact, the main problem with secularism is just the opposite. It probably sets the ethical bar too high. Most people just cannot live up to such a demanding code, and large societies cannot be run on the basis of the open-ended quest for truth and compassion. Especially in times of emergency, such as war or economic crisis, societies must act promptly and forcefully, even if they are not sure what is the truth and what is the most compassionate thing to do. They need clear guidelines, catchy slogans, and inspiring battle cries. Since it is difficult to send soldiers into battle or impose radical economic reforms in the name of doubtful conjectures, secular movements repeatedly mutate into dogmatic creeds.

For example, Karl Marx began by claiming that all religions were oppressive frauds, and he encouraged his followers to investigate for themselves the true nature of the global order. In the following decades the pressures of revolution and war hardened Marxism, and by the time of Stalin the official line of the Soviet Communist Party said that because the global order was too complicated for ordinary people to understand, it was best to always trust the wisdom of the party and do whatever it told you to do, even when it orchestrated the imprisonment and extermination of tens of millions of innocent people. It might look ugly but, as party ideologues never got tired of explaining, revolution isn't a picnic, and if you want an omelette you need to break a few eggs.

Whether one should view Stalin as a secular leader is therefore a matter of how we define secularism. If we use the minimalist negative definition—"secular people don't believe in God"—then Stalin was definitely secular. If we use a positive definition—"secular people reject all unscientific dogmas and are committed to truth, compassion, and freedom"—then Marx was a secular luminary and Stalin was anything but. He was the prophet of the godless but extremely dogmatic religion of Stalinism.

Stalinism is not an isolated example. On the other side of the political spectrum, capitalism too began as a very open-minded scientific theory but gradually solidified into a dogma. Many capitalists keep repeating the mantra "free markets and economic growth" irrespective of realities on the ground. No matter what awful consequences occasionally result from modernization, industrialization, or privatization, capitalist true believers dismiss them as mere "growing pains" and promise that everything will be made good through a bit more growth.

Middle-of-the-road liberal democrats have been more loyal to the secular pursuit of truth and compassion, but even they sometimes abandon it in favor of comforting dogmas. When confronted by the mess of brutal dictatorships and failed states, liberals often put their unquestioning faith in the awesome ritual of general elections. They fight wars and spend billions in places such as Iraq, Afghanistan, and the Congo in the firm belief that holding general elections will magically turn these places into sunnier versions of Denmark— this despite repeated failures, and despite the fact that even in places with an established tradition of general elections these rituals occasionally bring to power authoritarian populists and result in nothing grander than majority dictatorships. If you try to question the alleged wisdom of general elections, you won't be sent to the gulag, but you are likely to get a very cold shower of dogmatic abuse.

Of course, not all dogmas are equally harmful. Just as some religious beliefs have benefited humanity, so also have some secular dogmas. This is particularly true of the doctrine of human rights. The only place rights exist is in the stories humans invent and tell one another. These stories were enshrined as self-evident dogma during the struggle against religious bigotry and autocratic governments. Though it isn't true that humans have a natural right to life or liberty, belief in this story curbed the power of authoritarian regimes, protected minorities from harm, and safeguarded billions from the worst consequences of poverty and violence. It thereby contributed to the happiness and welfare of humanity probably more than any other doctrine in history.

Yet it is still a dogma. As is Article 19 of the United Nations' Declaration of Human Rights, which says, "Everyone has the right to freedom of opinion and expression." If we understand this as a political demand ("everyone *should* have the right to freedom of opinion"), this is perfectly sensible. But if we believe that each and every human being is naturally endowed with a "right to freedom of opinion" and that censorship therefore violates some law of nature, we miss the truth about humanity. As long as you define yourself as "an individual possessing inalienable natural rights," you will not know who you really are, and you will not understand the historical forces that shaped your society and your own mind (including your belief in "natural rights").

Such ignorance perhaps mattered little in the twentieth century, when people were busy fighting Hitler and Stalin. But it might become fatal in the twenty-first century, because biotechnology and artificial intelligence now seek to change the very meaning of humanity. If we are committed to the right to life, does that imply we should use biotechnology to overcome death? If we are committed to the right to liberty, should we empower algorithms that decipher and fulfill our hidden desires? If all humans enjoy equal human rights, do superhumans enjoy superrights? Secular people will find it difficult to engage with such questions as long as they are committed to a dogmatic belief in "human rights."

The dogma of human rights was shaped in previous centuries as a weapon against the Inquisition, the ancien régime, the Nazis, and the Ku Klux Klan. It is hardly equipped to deal with superhumans, cyborgs, and superintelligent computers. While human rights movements have developed a very impressive arsenal of arguments and defenses against religious biases and human tyrants, this arsenal hardly protects us against consumerist excesses and technological utopias.

ACKNOWLEDGING THE SHADOW

Secularism should not be equated with Stalinist dogmatism or with the bitter fruits of Western imperialism and runaway industrialization. Yet it cannot shirk all responsibility for them either. Secular movements and scientific institutions have mesmerized billions with promises to perfect humanity and to utilize the bounty of planet Earth for the benefit of our species. Such promises resulted not just in overcoming plagues and famines but also in gulags and melting ice caps. You might well argue that this is all the fault of people misunderstanding and distorting the core secular ideals and the true facts of science. And you are absolutely right. But that is a common problem for all influential movements.

For example, Christianity has been responsible for great crimes such as the Inquisition, the Crusades, the oppression of native cultures across the world, and the disempowerment of women. A Christian might take offense at this and retort that all of these crimes resulted from a complete misunderstanding of Christianity. Jesus preached only love, and the Inquisition was based on a horrific distortion of his teachings. We can sympathize with this claim, but it would be a mistake to let Christianity off the hook so easily. Christians appalled by the Inquisition and by the Crusades cannot just wash their hands of these atrocities; they should rather ask themselves some very tough questions. How exactly did their "religion of love" allow itself to be distorted in such a way, and not once but numerous times? Protestants who try to blame it all on Catholic fanaticism are advised to read a book about the behavior of Protestant colonists in Ireland or in North America. Similarly, Marxists should ask themselves what it was about the teachings of Marx that paved the way to the gulag, scientists should consider how the scientific project lent itself so easily to destabilizing the global ecosystem, and geneticists in particular should take warning from the way the Nazis hijacked Darwinian theories.

Every religion, ideology, and creed has its shadow, and no matter which creed you follow you should acknowledge your shadow and avoid the naive reassurance that "it cannot happen to us." Secular science has at least one big advantage over most traditional religions—namely, that it is not inherently terrified of its shadow, and it is in principle willing to admit its mistakes and blind spots. If you believe in an absolute truth revealed by a transcendent power, you cannot allow yourself to admit any error, for that would nullify your whole story. But if you believe in a quest for truth by fallible humans, admitting blunders is part of the game.

This is also why undogmatic secular movements tend to make relatively modest promises. Aware of their imperfections, they hope to effect small incremental changes, raising the minimum wage by a few dollars or reducing child mortality by a few percentage points. It is the mark of dogmatic ideologies that due to their excessive self-confidence they routinely vow the impossible. Their leaders speak all too freely about "eternity," "purity," and "redemption," as if by enacting some law, building some temple, or conquering some piece of territory they will save the entire world in one grand gesture.

As we come to make the most important decisions in the history of life, I personally would trust more in those who admit ignorance than in those who claim infallibility. If you want your religion, ideology, or worldview to lead the world, my first question to you is: "What was the biggest mistake your religion, ideology, or worldview committed? What did it get wrong?" If you cannot come up with something serious, I for one would not trust you.

PART IV

....

Truth

If you feel overwhelmed and confused by the global predicament, you are on the right track. Global processes have become too complicated for any single person to understand. How then can you know the truth about the world, and avoid falling victim to propaganda and misinformation?

15

Ignorance

You Know Less than You Think

The preceding chapters surveyed some of the most important problems and developments of the present era, from the overhyped threat of terrorism to the underappreciated threat of technological disruption. If you are left with the nagging feeling that this is too much, that you cannot process it all, you are absolutely right. No person can.

In the last few centuries, liberal thought developed immense trust in the rational individual. It depicted individual humans as independent rational agents and has made these mythical creatures the basis of modern society. Democracy is founded on the idea that the voter knows best, free-market capitalism believes that the customer is always right, and liberal education teaches students to think for themselves.

It is a mistake, however, to put so much trust in the rational individual. Postcolonial and feminist thinkers have pointed out that this "rational individual" may well be a chauvinistic Western fantasy, glorifying the autonomy and power of upper-class white men. As noted earlier, behavioral economists and evolutionary psychologists have demonstrated that most human decisions are based on emotional reactions and heuristic shortcuts rather than on rational analysis, and that while our emotions and heuristics were perhaps suitable for dealing with life in the Stone Age, they are woefully inadequate in the Silicon Age.

Not only rationality, but individuality too is a myth. Humans rarely think for themselves. Rather, we think in groups. Just as it takes a tribe to raise a child, it also takes a tribe to invent a tool, solve a conflict, or cure a disease. No individual knows everything it takes to build a cathedral, an atom bomb, or an aircraft. What gave *Homo sapiens* an edge over all other animals and turned us into the masters of the planet was not our individual rationality but our unparalleled ability to think together in large groups.[1]

Individual humans know embarrassingly little about the world, and as history has progressed, they have come to know less and less. A hunter-gatherer in the Stone Age knew how to make her own clothes, how to start a fire, how to hunt rabbits, and how to escape lions. We think we know far more today, but as individuals, we actually know far less. We rely on the expertise of others for almost all our needs. In one humbling experiment, people were asked to evaluate how well they understood the workings of an ordinary zipper. Most people confidently replied that they understood zippers very well—after all, they use them all the time. They were then asked to describe in as much detail as possible all the steps involved in the zipper's operation. Most people had no idea.[2] This is what Steven Sloman and Philip Fernbach have termed "the knowledge illusion." We think we know a lot, even though individually we know very little, because we treat knowledge in the minds of others as if it were our own.

This is not necessarily bad. Our reliance on groupthink has made us masters of the world, and the knowledge illusion enables us to go through life without being caught in an impossible effort to understand everything ourselves. From an evolutionary perspective, trusting in the knowledge of others has worked extremely well for *Homo sapiens*.

Yet like many other human traits that made sense in past ages but cause trouble in the modern age, the knowledge illusion has its downside. The world is becoming ever more complex, and people fail to realize just how ignorant they are of what's going on. Consequently, some people who know next to nothing about meteorology or biology nevertheless propose policies regarding climate change and genetically modified crops, while others hold extremely strong views about what should be done in Iraq or Ukraine without being able to locate these countries on a map. People rarely appreciate their ignorance, because they lock themselves inside an echo chamber of like-minded friends and self-confirming news feeds, where their beliefs are constantly reinforced and seldom challenged.[3]

Providing people with more and better information is unlikely to improve matters. Scientists hope to dispel wrong views by better science education, and pundits hope to sway public opinion on issues such as Obamacare or global warming by presenting the public with accurate facts and expert reports. Such hopes are grounded in a misunderstanding of how humans actually think. Most of our views are shaped by communal groupthink rather than individual rationality, and we hold on to these views due to group loyalty. Bombarding people with facts and exposing their individual ignorance is likely to backfire. Most people don't like too many facts, and they certainly don't like to feel stupid. Don't be so sure that you can convince Tea Party supporters of the truth of global warming by presenting them with sheets of statistical data.[4]

The power of groupthink is so pervasive that it is difficult to break its hold even when its views seem to be rather arbitrary. For example, in the United States, right-wing conservatives tend to care far less about things such as pollution and endangered species than left-wing progressives, which is why Louisiana has much weaker environmental regulations than Massachusetts. We are used to this situation, so we take it for granted, but it is really quite surprising. One would think that conservatives would care far more about the conservation of the old ecological order and about protecting their ancestral lands, forests, and rivers. In contrast, progressives would be expected to be far more open to radical changes to the countryside, especially if the aim is to speed up progress and increase the human standard of living. However, once the party line has been set on these issues by various historical quirks, it becomes second nature for conservatives to dismiss concerns about polluted rivers and disappearing birds, while left-wing progressives tend to fear any disruption to the old ecological order.[5]

Even scientists are not immune to the power of groupthink. In fact, scientists who believe that facts can change public opinion may themselves be the victims of scientific groupthink. The scientific community believes in the efficacy of facts, and those loyal to that community continue to believe that they can win public debates by throwing the right facts around, despite much empirical evidence to the contrary.

Similarly, the liberal belief in individual rationality may itself be the product of liberal groupthink. In one of the climactic moments of Monty Python's Life of Brian, a huge crowd of starry-eyed followers mistakes Brian for the Messiah. Brian tells his disciples, "You don't need to follow me, you don't need to follow anybody! You've got to think for yourselves! You're all individuals! You're all different!" The enthusiastic crowd then chants in unison, "Yes! We're all individuals! Yes, we are all different!" Monty Python was parodying the counterculture orthodoxy of the 1960s, but the point may be true of the belief in rational individualism in general. Modern democracies are full of crowds shouting in unison, "Yes, the voter knows best! Yes, the customer is always right!"

THE BLACK HOLE OF POWER

The problem of groupthink and individual ignorance besets not just ordinary voters and customers but also presidents and CEOs. They may have at their disposal plenty of advisers and vast intelligence agencies, but this does not necessarily make things better. It is extremely hard to discover the truth when you are ruling the world. You are just far too busy. Most political chiefs and business moguls are forever on the run. Yet if you want to go deeply into any subject, you need a lot of time, and in particular you need the privilege of wasting time. You need to experiment with unproductive paths, explore dead ends, make space for doubts and boredom, and allow little seeds of insight to slowly grow and blossom. If you cannot afford to waste time, you will never find the truth.

Worse still, great power inevitably distorts the truth. Power is all about changing reality rather than seeing it for what it is. When you have a hammer in your hand, everything looks like a nail; when you have great power in your hand, everything looks like an invitation to meddle. Even if you somehow overcome this urge, the people surrounding you will never forget the giant hammer you are holding. Anybody who talks with you will have a conscious or unconscious agenda, and therefore you can never have full faith in what they say. No sultan can ever trust his courtiers and underlings to tell him the truth.

Great power thus acts like a black hole that warps the very space around it. The closer you get to it, the more twisted everything becomes. Each word is made extra heavy upon entering your orbit, and each person you see tries to flatter you, appease you, or get something from you. They know you cannot spare them more than a minute a two, and they are fearful of saying something improper or muddled, so they end up mouthing either empty slogans or the greatest clichés of all.

A couple of years ago I was invited to dinner with the Israeli prime minister, Benjamin Netanyahu. Friends warned me not to go, but I couldn't resist the temptation. I thought I might finally hear some big secrets that are divulged only to important ears behind closed doors. What a disappointment it was! There were about thirty people there, and everyone tried to get the great man's attention, impress him with their wit, curry favor, or get something out of him. If anyone there knew any big secrets, they did an extremely good job of keeping them to themselves. This was hardly Netanyahu's fault, or indeed anybody's fault. It was the fault of the gravitational pull of power.

If you really want truth, you need to escape the black hole of power and allow yourself to waste a lot of time wandering here and there on the periphery. Revolutionary knowledge rarely makes it to the center, because the center is built on existing knowledge. The guardians of the old order usually determine who gets to reach the centers of power, and they tend to filter out the carriers of disturbing, unconventional ideas. Of course, they filter out an incredible amount of rubbish too. Not being invited to the Davos World Economic Forum is hardly a guarantee of wisdom. That's why you need to waste so much time in the periphery: while it might contain some brilliant revolutionary insights, it is mostly full of uninformed guesses, debunked models, superstitious dogmas, and ridiculous conspiracy theories.

Leaders are thus trapped in a double bind. If they remain at the center of power, they will have an extremely distorted vision of the world. If they venture to the margins, they will waste too much of their precious time. And the problem will only get worse. In the coming decades, the world will become even more complex than it is today. Individual humans—whether pawns or kings—will consequently know even less about the technological gadgets, economic currents, and political dynamics that shape the world. As Socrates observed more than two thousand years ago, the best we can do

under such conditions is to acknowledge our own individual ignorance.

But what then about morality and justice? If we cannot understand the world, how can we hope to tell the difference between
right and wrong, justice and injustice?

16

....

Justice

Our Sense of Justice Might Be Out of Date

Like all our other senses, our sense of justice also has ancient evolutionary roots. Human morality was shaped over the course of millions of years of evolution to deal with the social and ethical dilemmas that cropped up in the lives of small hunter-gatherer bands. If I went hunting with you and I killed a deer while you caught nothing, should I share my booty with you? If you went gathering mushrooms and came back with a full basket, does the fact that I am stronger than you allow me to snatch all these mushrooms for myself? And if I know that you plot to kill me, is it okay for me to act preemptively and slit your throat in the dark of night?[1]

On the face of things, not much has changed since we left the African savannah for the urban jungle. One might think that the questions we face today—the Syrian civil war, global inequality, global warming—are just the same old questions writ large. But that is an illusion. Size matters, and from the standpoint of justice, like many other standpoints, we are barely adapted to the world in which we live.

The problem is not one of values. Whether secular or religious, citizens of the twenty-first century have plenty of values. The problem is with implementing these values in a complex global world. It's all the fault of numbers. The foragers' sense of justice was structured to cope with dilemmas relating to the lives of a few dozen people in an area of a few dozen square miles. When we try to comprehend relationships between millions of people across entire continents, our moral sense is overwhelmed.

Justice demands not just a set of abstract values, but also an understanding of concrete cause-and-effect relations. If you collected a basket of mushrooms to feed your children with and I now take that basket from you by force, so that all your work has been for naught and your children will go to sleep hungry, that is unfair. It's easy to grasp this, because it's easy to see the cause-and-effect relation. Unfortunately, an inherent feature of our modern global world is that its causal relations are highly ramified and complex. I can live at home peacefully, never raising a finger to harm anyone, and yet according to left-wing activists, I am a full partner to the wrongs inflicted by Israeli soldiers and settlers in the West Bank. According to the socialists, my comfortable life is based on child labor in dismal Third World sweatshops. Animal-welfare advocates remind me that my life is interwoven with one of the most appalling crimes in history—the subjugation of billions of farm animals to a brutal regime of exploitation.

Am I really to blame for all that? It's not easy to say. Since I depend for my existence on a mind-boggling network of economic and political ties, and since global causal connections are so tangled, I find it difficult to answer even the simplest questions, such as where my lunch comes from, who made the shoes I'm wearing, and what my pension fund is doing with my money.[2]

STEALING RIVERS

A primeval hunter-gatherer knew very well where her lunch came from (she gathered it herself), who made her moccasins (he slept twenty yards from her), and what her pension fund was doing (it was playing in the mud; back then, people had only one pension fund, called "children"). I am far more ignorant than that hunter-gatherer. Years of research might expose the fact that the government I voted for is secretly selling weapons to a shady dictator halfway across the world. But during the time it takes me to find that out, I might be missing far more important discoveries, such as the fate of the chickens whose eggs I ate for dinner.

The system is structured in such a way that those who make no effort to know can remain in blissful ignorance, and those who do make an effort will find it very difficult to discover the truth. How is it possible to avoid stealing when the global economic system is ceaselessly stealing on my behalf and without my knowledge? It doesn't matter whether you judge actions by their consequences (it is wrong to steal because it makes the victims miserable) or believe in categorical duties that should be followed irrespective of consequences (it is wrong to steal because God said so). The problem is that it has become extremely complicated to grasp what we are actually doing.

The commandment not to steal was formulated in the days when stealing meant physically taking something with your own hand that did not belong to you. Yet today, the really important arguments about theft concern completely different scenarios. Suppose I invest $10,000 in shares of a big petrochemical corporation, which provides me with an annual 5 percent return on my investment. The corporation is highly profitable because it does not pay for externalities. It dumps toxic waste into a nearby river without caring about the damage it causes to the regional water supply, to the public's health, or to the local wildlife. It uses its wealth to enlist a legion of lawyers who protect it against any demand for compensation. It also retains lobbyists who block any attempt to legislate stronger environmental regulations.

Can we accuse the corporation of "stealing a river"? And what about me personally? I have never broken into anyone's house or snatched dollar bills from anyone's purse. I am not aware how this particular corporation is generating its profits. I barely remember that part of my portfolio is invested in it. So am I guilty of theft? How can we act morally when we have no way of knowing all the relevant facts?

One can try to evade the problem by adopting a "morality of intentions." What's important is what I intend, not what I actually do or the outcome of what I do. However, in a world in which everything is interconnected, the supreme moral imperative becomes the imperative to know. The greatest crimes in modern history resulted not just from hatred and greed but even more so from ignorance and indifference. Charming English ladies financed the Atlantic slave trade by buying shares and bonds in the London stock exchange without ever setting foot in either Africa or the Caribbean. They then sweetened their four o'clock tea with snow-white sugar cubes produced in hellish plantations about which they knew nothing.

In Germany in the late 1930s, the local post office manager might have been an upright citizen looking after the welfare of his employees and personally helping people in distress find missing parcels. He was always the first to arrive at work and the last to leave, and even in snowstorms he made sure that the mail was delivered on time. Alas, his efficient and hospitable post office was a vital cell in the nerve system of the Nazi state. It was speeding along racist propaganda, recruitment orders to the Wehrmacht, and stern orders to the local SS branch. There is something amiss with the intentions of those who do not make a sincere effort to know.

But what counts as "a sincere effort to know"? Should postmasters in every country open the mail they are delivering, and resign or revolt if they discover government propaganda? It is easy to look back with absolute moral certainty at Nazi Germany of the 1930s because we know where the chain of causes and effects led. But without the benefit of hindsight, moral certainty might be beyond our reach. The bitter truth is that the world has simply become too complicated for our hunter-gatherer brains.

Most of the injustices in the contemporary world result from large-scale structural biases rather than from individual prejudices, and our hunter-gatherer brains did not evolve to detect structural biases. We are all complicit in at least some such biases, and we just don't have the time and energy to discover them all. Writing this book brought the lesson home to me on a personal level. When discussing global issues, I am always in danger of privileging the viewpoint of the global elite over that of various disadvantaged groups. The global elite commands the conversation, so it is impossible to miss its views. Disadvantaged groups, in contrast, are routinely silenced, so it is easy to forget about them—not out of deliberate malice, but out of sheer ignorance.

For example, I know absolutely nothing about the unique views and problems of aboriginal Tasmanians. Indeed, I know so little that in a previous book I assumed aboriginal Tasmanians didn't exist anymore, because they were all wiped out by European settlers. In fact, there are thousands of people alive today who trace their ancestry back to the aboriginal population of Tasmania, and they struggle with many unique problems—one of which is that their very existence is frequently denied, not least by learned scholars.

Even if you personally belong to a disadvantaged group and therefore have a deep firsthand understanding of its viewpoint, that does not mean you understand the viewpoint of all other such groups. For each group and subgroup faces a different maze of glass ceilings, double standards, coded insults, and institutional discrimination. A thirty-year-old African American man has thirty years' experience of what it means to be an African American man. But he has no experience of what it means to be an African American woman, a Bulgarian Roma, a blind Russian, or a Chinese lesbian.

As he grew up, this African American man was repeatedly stopped and searched by the police for no apparent reason—something the Chinese lesbian never had to undergo. In contrast, being born into an African American family in an African American neighborhood meant that he was surrounded by people like him who taught him what he needed to know in order to survive and flourish as an African American man. The Chinese lesbian was not born into a lesbian family in a lesbian neighborhood, and maybe she had nobody in the world to teach her key lessons. For this reason, growing up black in Baltimore doesn't make it easy to understand the struggle of growing up lesbian in Hangzhou.

In previous eras this mattered less, because you weren't responsible for the plight of people halfway across the world. If you made an effort to sympathize with your less fortunate neighbors, that was usually enough. But today major global debates about things such as climate change and artificial intelligence have an impact on everybody—whether in Tasmania, Hangzhou, or Baltimore—so we need to take into account all viewpoints. Yet how can anyone do that? How can anyone understand the web of relations among thousands of intersecting groups across the world?[3]

DOWNSIZE OR DENY?

Even if we truly want to, most of us are no longer capable of understanding the major moral problems of the world. People can comprehend relations between two foragers, among twenty foragers, or between two neighboring clans. They are ill-equipped, though, to comprehend relations among several million Syrians, among half a billion Europeans, or among all the intersecting groups and subgroups of the planet.

In trying to comprehend and judge moral dilemmas of this scale, people often resort to one of four methods. The first is to downsize the issue. To understand the Syrian civil war as though it were occurring between two foragers, for example, one imagines the Assad regime as a lone person and the rebels as another person; one of them is bad and one of them is good. The historical complexity of the conflict is replaced by a simple, clear plot.[4]

The second method is to focus on a touching human story that ostensibly stands for the whole conflict. When you try to explain to people the true complexity of the conflict by means of statistics and precise data, you lose them, but a personal story about the fate of one child activates the tear ducts, makes the blood boil, and generates false moral certainty.[5] This is something that many charities have understood for a long time. In one noteworthy experiment, people were asked to donate money to help a poor seven-year-old girl from Mali named Rokia. Many were moved by her story and opened their hearts and purses. However, when in addition to Rokia's personal story the researchers also presented people with statistics about the broader problem of poverty in Africa, respondents suddenly became *less* willing to help. In another study, scholars solicited donations to help either one sick child or eight sick children. People gave more money to the single child than to the group of eight.[6]

The third method of dealing with large-scale moral dilemmas is to weave conspiracy theories. How does the global economy function, and is it good or bad? That question is too complicated to grasp. It is far easier to imagine that twenty multibillionaires are pulling the strings behind the scenes, controlling the media and fomenting wars in order to enrich themselves. This is almost always a baseless fantasy. The contemporary world is too complicated, not only for our sense of justice but also for our managerial abilities. No one—including the multibillionaires, the CIA, the Freemasons, and the Elders of Zion—really understands what is going on in the world. So no one is capable of pulling the strings effectively.[7]

These three methods try to deny the true complexity of the world. The fourth and ultimate method is to create a dogma, put our trust in some allegedly all-knowing theory, institution, or chief, and follow it wherever it leads us. Religious and ideological dogmas are still highly attractive in our scientific age precisely because they offer us a safe haven from the frustrating complexity of reality. As noted earlier, secular movements have not been exempt from this danger. Even if you start with a rejection of all religious dogma and with a firm commitment to scientific truth, sooner or later the complexity of reality becomes so vexing that you might be driven to fashion a doctrine that shouldn't be questioned. While such doctrines provide people with intellectual comfort and moral certainty, it is debatable whether they provide justice.

What should we do? Should we adopt the liberal dogma and trust the aggregate of individual voters and customers? Or perhaps we should reject the individualist approach and, like many previous cultures in history, empower communities to make sense of the world *together*? Such a solution, however, only takes us from the frying pan of individual ignorance into the fire of biased groupthink. Hunter-gatherer bands, village communes, and even city neighborhoods could think together about the common problems they faced. But we now suffer from global problems, without having a global community. Neither Facebook, nationalism, nor religion is anywhere near creating such a community. All the existing human tribes are absorbed in advancing their particular interests rather than in understanding the global truth. Neither Americans, Chinese, Muslims, nor Hindus constitute "the global community," so any single group's interpretation of reality is not trustworthy.

Should we call it quits, then, and declare that the human quest to understand the truth and find justice has failed? Have we officially entered the post-truth era?

17

....

Post-Truth

Some Fake News Lasts Forever

We are repeatedly told these days that we are living in a new and frightening era of "post-truth," and that lies and fictions are all around us. Examples are not hard to come by. For example, in late February 2014 Russian special units bearing no army insignia invaded Ukraine and occupied key installations in the Crimea. The Russian government and President Putin in person repeatedly denied that these were Russian troops, describing them instead as spontaneous "self-defense groups" that may have acquired Russian-looking equipment from local shops.[1] As they voiced this rather preposterous claim, Putin and his aides knew perfectly well that they were lying.

Russian nationalists can excuse this lie by arguing that it served a higher truth. Russia was engaged in a just war, and if it is okay to kill for a just cause, surely it is also okay to lie. The higher cause that allegedly justified the invasion of Ukraine was the preservation of the sacred Russian nation. According to Russian national myths, Russia is a sacred entity that has endured for a thousand years despite repeated attempts by vicious enemies to invade and dismember it. Following the Mongols, the Poles, the Swedes, Napoleon's Grande Armée, and Hitler's Wehrmacht, in the 1990s it was NATO, the United States, and the EU that attempted to destroy Russia by detaching parts of its body and forming them into "fake countries" such as Ukraine. For many Russian nationalists, the idea that Ukraine is a separate nation from Russia constitutes a far bigger lie than anything uttered by President Putin during his holy mission to reintegrate the Russian nation.

Ukrainian citizens, outside observers, and professional historians may well be outraged by this explanation and regard it as a kind of "atom bomb lie" in the Russian arsenal of deception. To claim that Ukraine does not exist as a nation and as an independent country disregards a long list of historical facts—for example, that during the thousand years of supposed Russian unity, Kiev and Moscow were part of the same country for only about three hundred years. It also violates numerous international laws and treaties that Russia has accepted and that guarantee the sovereignty and borders of independent Ukraine. Most important, it ignores what millions of Ukrainians think about themselves. Don't they have a say about who they are?

Ukrainian nationalists would certainly agree with Russian nationalists that there are some fake countries around. But Ukraine isn't one of them. Rather, these fake countries are the Luhansk People's Republic and the Donetsk People's Republic, which Russia has set up to mask its unprovoked invasion of Ukraine.[2]

Whichever side you support, it seems that we are indeed living in a terrifying era of post-truth, when not just particular military incidents but entire histories and nations might be faked. But if this is the era of post-truth, when, exactly, was the halcyon age of truth? In the 1980s? The 1950s? The 1930s? And what triggered our transition to the post-truth era? The internet? Social media? The rise of Putin and Trump?

A cursory look at history reveals that propaganda and disinformation are nothing new, and even the habit of denying entire nations and creating fake countries has a long pedigree. In 1931 the

Japanese army staged mock attacks on itself to justify its invasion of China, and then created the fake country of Manchukuo to legitimize its conquests. China itself has long denied that Tibet ever existed as an independent country. British settlement in Australia was justified by the legal doctrine of *terra nullius* ("nobody's land" in Latin), which effectively erased fifty thousand years of Aboriginal history.

In the early twentieth century a favorite Zionist slogan spoke of the return of "a people without a land (the Jews) to a land without a people (Palestine)." The existence of the local Arab population was conveniently ignored. In 1969 Israeli prime minister Golda Meir famously said that there is no Palestinian people and never was. Such views are still very common in Israel even today, despite decades of armed conflicts against something that doesn't exist. For example, in February 2016 Knesset member Anat Berko gave a speech to her fellow parliamentarians in which she doubted the reality of the Palestinian people. Her proof? The letter *p* does not even exist in Arabic, so how can there be a Palestinian people? (In Arabic, *f* stands for what in other languages is pronounced *p*, and the Arabic name for Palestine is Falastin.)

THE POST-TRUTH SPECIES

In fact, humans have always lived in the age of post-truth. *Homo sapiens* is a post-truth species, whose power depends on creating and believing fictions. Ever since the Stone Age, self-reinforcing myths have served to unite human collectives. Indeed, *Homo sapiens* conquered this planet thanks above all to the unique human ability to create and spread fictions. We are the only mammals that can cooperate with numerous strangers because only we can invent fictional stories, spread them around, and convince millions of others to believe in them. As long as everybody believes in the same fictions, we all obey the same laws and can thereby cooperate effectively.

So if you blame Facebook, Trump, or Putin for ushering in a new and frightening era of post-truth, remind yourself that centuries ago millions of Christians locked themselves inside a self-reinforcing mythological bubble, never daring to question the factual veracity of the Bible, while millions of Muslims put their unquestioning faith in the Quran. For millennia, much of what passed for "news" and "facts" in human social networks were stories about miracles, angels, demons, and witches, with bold reporters giving live coverage straight from the deepest pits of the underworld. We have zero scientific evidence that Eve was tempted by the serpent, that the souls of all infidels burn in hell after they die, or that the creator of the universe doesn't like it when a Brahmin marries a Dalit—yet billions of people have believed in these stories for thousands of years. Some fake news lasts forever.

I am aware that many people might be upset by my equating religion with fake news, but that's exactly the point. When a thousand people believe some made-up story for one month, that's fake news. When a billion people believe it for a thousand years, that's a religion, and we are admonished not to call it "fake news" in order not to hurt the feelings of the faithful (or incur their wrath). Note, however, that I am not denying the effectiveness or potential benevolence of religion. Just the opposite. For better or worse, fiction is among the most effective tools in humanity's tool kit. By bringing people together, religious creeds make large-scale human cooperation possible. They inspire people to build hospitals, schools, and bridges in addition to armies and prisons. Adam and Eve never existed, but Chartres Cathedral is still beautiful. Much of the Bible may be fictional, but it can still bring joy to billions and can still encourage humans to be compassionate, courageous, and creative— just like other great works of fiction, such as *Don Quixote, War and Peace,* and the Harry Potter books.

Again, some people might be offended by my comparison of the Bible to Harry Potter. If you are a scientifically minded Christian, you might explain away all the errors, myths, and contradictions in the Bible by arguing that the holy book was never meant to be read as a factual account, but rather as a metaphorical story containing deep wisdom. But isn't that true of the Harry Potter stories too?

If you are a fundamentalist Christian, you are more likely to insist that every word of the Bible is literally true. Let's assume for a moment that you are right, and that the Bible is indeed the infallible word of the one true God. What, then, do you make of the Quran, the Talmud, the Book of Mormon, the Vedas, the Avesta, and the Egyptian Book of the Dead? Aren't you tempted to say that these texts are elaborate fictions created by flesh-and-blood humans (or perhaps by devils)? And how do you view the divinity of Roman emperors such as Augustus and Claudius? The Roman Senate claimed to have the power to turn people into gods, and then expected the empire's subjects to worship these gods. Wasn't that a fiction? In fact, we have at least one example in history of a false god who acknowledged the fiction with his own mouth. As noted earlier, Japanese militarism in the 1930s and early 1940s relied on a fanatical belief in the divinity of Emperor Hirohito. After Japan's defeat Hirohito publicly proclaimed that he wasn't a god after all.

So even if we agree that the Bible is the true word of God, that still leaves us with billions of devout Hindus, Muslims, Jews, Egyptians, Romans, and Japanese who for thousands of years put their trust in fictions. Again, that does not mean that these fictions are necessarily worthless or harmful. They can still be beautiful and inspiring.

Of course, not all religious myths have been equally beneficent. On August 29, 1255, the body of a nine-year-old English boy called Hugh was found in a well in the town of Lincoln. Even in the absence of Facebook and Twitter, rumor quickly spread that Hugh had been ritually murdered by the local Jews. The story only grew with retelling, and one of the most renowned English chroniclers of the day, Matthew Paris, provided a detailed and gory description of how prominent Jews from throughout England gathered in Lincoln to fatten up, torture, and finally crucify the abducted child.

Nineteen Jews were tried and executed for the alleged murder. Similar blood libels became popular in other English towns, leading to a series of pogroms in which whole Jewish communities were massacred. Eventually in 1290 the entire Jewish population of England was expelled.[3]

The story doesn't end there. A century after the expulsion of the Jews from England, Geoffrey Chaucer—the father of English literature—included a blood libel modeled on the story of Hugh of Lincoln in the *Canterbury Tales* ("The Prioress's Tale"). The tale culminates with the hanging of the Jews. Similar blood libels subsequently became a staple of every anti-Semitic movement from late medieval Spain to modern Russia. A distant echo can even be heard in the 2016 "fake news" story that Hillary Clinton headed a child-trafficking network that held children as sex slaves in the basement of a popular pizzeria. Enough Americans believed that story to hurt Clinton's election campaign, and one person even came armed with a gun to said pizzeria and demanded to see the basement (it turned out that the pizzeria had no basement).[4]

As for Hugh of Lincoln himself, nobody knows how he really found his death, but he was buried in Lincoln Cathedral and was venerated as a saint. He was reputed to perform various miracles, and his tomb continued to draw pilgrims even centuries after the expulsion of all Jews from England.[5] Only in 1955—ten years after the Holocaust—did Lincoln Cathedral repudiate the blood libel story, placing a plaque near Hugh's tomb that reads:

Trumped-up stories of "ritual murders" of Christian boys by Jewish communities were common throughout Europe during the Middle Ages and even much later. These fictions cost many innocent Jews their lives. Lincoln had its own legend and the alleged victim was buried in the Cathedral in the year 1255. Such stories do not redound to the credit of Christendom.[6]

Well, some fake news only lasts seven hundred years.

ONCE A LIE, ALWAYS THE TRUTH

Ancient religions have not been the only ones to use fiction to cement cooperation. In more recent times, each nation has created its own national mythology, while movements such as communism, fascism, and liberalism fashioned elaborate self-reinforcing credos. Joseph Goebbels, the Nazi propaganda maestro and perhaps the most accomplished media-wizard of the modern age, allegedly explained his method succinctly: "A lie told once remains a lie, but a lie told a thousand times becomes the truth."[7] In *Mein Kampf* Hitler wrote, "The most brilliant propagandist technique will yield no success unless one fundamental principle is borne in mind constantly—it must confine itself to a few points and repeat them over and over."[8] Can any present-day fake-news peddler improve on that?

The Soviet propaganda machine was equally agile with the truth, rewriting the history of everything from entire wars to individual photographs. On June 29, 1936, the official newspaper *Pravda* (the name means "truth") carried on its front page a photo of a smiling Joseph Stalin embracing Gelya Markizova, a seven-year-old girl. The image became a Stalinist icon, enshrining Stalin as the "Father of the Nation" and idealizing the "happy Soviet childhood." Printing presses and factories all over the country began churning out millions of posters, sculptures, and mosaics of the scene, which were displayed in public institutions from one end of the Soviet Union to the other. Just as no Russian Orthodox church was complete without an icon of the Virgin Mary holding baby Jesus, so no Soviet school could do without an icon of Papa Stalin holding little Gelya.

Alas, in Stalin's empire fame was often an invitation to disaster. Within a year, Gelya's father was arrested on the bogus charges that he was a Japanese spy and a Trotskyite terrorist. In 1938 he was executed, one of millions of victims of the Stalinist terror. Gelya and her mother were exiled to Kazakhstan, where the mother soon died under mysterious circumstances. What to do now with the count-less icons depicting the Father of the Nation with a daughter of a convicted "enemy of the people"? No problem. From that moment onward, Gelya Markizova vanished, and the "happy Soviet child" in the ubiquitous image was identified as Mamlakat Nakhangova, a thirteen-year-old Tajik girl who had earned the Order of Lenin by diligently picking lots of cotton in the fields. (If anyone thought that the girl in the picture didn't look like a thirteen-year-old, they knew better than to voice such counterrevolutionary heresy.)[9]

The Soviet propaganda machine was so efficient that it managed to hide monstrous atrocities at home while projecting a utopian vi-sion abroad. Today Ukrainians complain that Putin has successfully deceived many Western media outlets about Russia's actions in the Crimea and Donbas. Yet in the art of deception he can hardly hold a candle to Stalin. In the early 1930s left-wing Western journalists and intellectuals were praising the USSR as an ideal society at a time when Ukrainians and other Soviet citizens were dying in the mil-lions from the man-made famine that Stalin orchestrated. Whereas in the age of Facebook and Twitter it is sometimes hard to decide which version of events to believe, at least it is no longer possible for a regime to kill millions without the world knowing about it.

In addition to religions and ideologies, commercial firms also rely on fiction and fake news. Branding often involves retelling the same fictional story again and again, until people become convinced it is the truth. What images come to mind when you think about Coca-Cola? Do you think about healthy young people engaging in sports and having fun together? Or do you think about overweight diabetes patients lying in a hospital bed? Drinking lots of Coca-Cola will not make you young, will not make you healthy, and will not make you athletic—rather, it will increase your chances of suffering from obesity and diabetes. Yet for decades Coca-Cola has invested billions of dollars in linking itself to youth, health, and sports—and billions of humans subconsciously believe in this linkage.

The truth is that truth was never high on the agenda of *Homo sapiens.* Many people assume that if a particular religion or ideology misrepresents reality, its adherents are bound to discover it sooner or later, because they will not be able to compete with clearer-sighted rivals. Well, that's just another comforting myth. In practice, the power of human cooperation depends on a delicate balance between truth and fiction.

If you distort reality too much, it will indeed weaken you by making you act in unrealistic ways. For example, in 1905 an East African medium called Kinjikitile Ngwale claimed to be possessed by the snake spirit Hongo. The new prophet had a revolutionary message to the people of the German colony of East Africa: unite and drive out the Germans. To make the message more appealing, Ngwale provided his followers with magic medicine that would allegedly turn German bullets into water (*maji* in Swahili). Thus began the Maji Rebellion. It failed. For on the battlefield, German bullets didn't turn into water. Rather, they tore mercilessly into the bodies of the ill-armed rebels.[10] Two thousand years earlier, the Jewish Great Revolt against the Romans was similarly inspired by an ardent belief that God would fight for the Jews and help them defeat the seemingly invincible Roman Empire. It too failed, leading to the destruction of Jerusalem and the exile of the Jews.

On the other hand, you cannot organize masses of people effectively without relying on some mythology. If you stick to unalloyed reality, few people will follow you. Without myths, it would have been impossible to organize not just the failed Maji and Jewish revolts but also the far more successful rebellions of the Mahdi and the Maccabees.

In fact, false stories have an intrinsic advantage over the truth when it comes to uniting people. If you want to gauge group loyalty, requiring people to believe an absurdity is a far better test than asking them to believe the truth. If a big chief says that the sun rises in the east and sets in the west, loyalty to the chief is not required in order to applaud him. But if the chief says the sun rises in the west and sets in the east, only true loyalists will clap their hands. Similarly, if all your neighbors believe the same outrageous tale, you can count on them to stand together in times of crisis. If they are willing to believe only accredited facts, what does that prove?

You might argue that at least in some cases it is possible to organize people effectively through consensual agreement rather than through fictions and myths. In the economic sphere, for example, money and corporations bind people together far more effectively than any god or holy book, even though everyone knows that they are just a human convention. In the case of a holy book, a true believer would say, "I believe that the book is sacred," while in the case of the dollar, a true believer would say only, "I believe that *other people* believe that the dollar is valuable." It is obvious that the dollar is just a human creation, yet people all over the world respect it. If so, why can't humans abandon all myths and fictions and organize themselves on the basis of consensual conventions such as the dollar?

Such conventions, however, are not clearly distinct from fiction. The difference between holy books and money, for example, is far smaller than it might at first seem. When most people see a dollar bill, they forget that it is just a human convention. As they see the green piece of paper with the picture of the dead white man, they see it as something valuable in and of itself. They hardly ever remind themselves, "Actually, this is a worthless piece of paper, but because other people view it as valuable, I can make use of it." If you observed a human brain in an fMRI scanner, you would see that as someone is presented with a suitcase full of hundred-dollar bills, the parts of the brain that start buzzing with excitement are not the skeptical parts ("Other people believe this is valuable") but rather the greedy parts ("Holy shit! I want this!"). Conversely, in the vast majority of cases people begin to sanctify the Bible or the Vedas or the Book of Mormon only after long and repeated exposure to other people who view it as sacred. We learn to respect holy books in exactly the same way we learn to respect paper currency.

For this reason there is no strict division in practice between knowing that something is just a human convention and believing that something is inherently valuable. In many cases, people are ambiguous or forgetful about this division. To give another example, in a deep philosophical discussion about it, almost everybody would agree that corporations are fictional stories created by human beings. Microsoft isn't the buildings it owns, the people it employs, or the shareholders it serves—rather, it is an intricate legal fiction woven by lawmakers and lawyers. Yet 99 percent of the time, we aren't engaged in deep philosophical discussions, and we treat corporations as if they are real entities in the world, just like tigers or humans.

Blurring the line between fiction and reality can be done for many purposes, starting with "having fun" and going all the way to "survival." You cannot play games or read novels unless you suspend disbelief at least for a little while. To really enjoy soccer, you have to accept the rules of the game and forget for at least ninety minutes that they are merely human inventions. If you don't, you will think it utterly ridiculous for twenty-two people to go running after a ball. Soccer might begin with just having fun, but it can become far more serious stuff, as any English soccer hooligan or Argentinian soccer nationalist will attest. Soccer can help formulate personal identities, it can cement large-scale communities, and it can even provide reasons for violence. The conflicts between nations and religions are something like the rivalries between soccer fans.

Humans have a remarkable ability to know and not know at the same time. Or, more correctly, they can know something when they really think about it, but most of the time they don't think about it, so they don't know it. If you really focus, you realize that money is fiction. But you usually don't think about it. If you are asked about it, you know that soccer is a human invention. But in the heat of a match, nobody asks about it. If you devote the time and energy, you can discover that nations are elaborate yarns. But in the midst of a war, you don't have the time and energy. If you demand the ultimate truth, you realize that the story of Adam and Eve is a myth. But how often do you demand the ultimate truth?

Truth and power can travel together only so far. Sooner or later they go their separate paths. If you want power, at some point you will have to spread fictions. If you want to know the truth about the world, at some point you will have to renounce power. You will have to admit things—for example, about the sources of your own power—that will anger allies, dishearten followers, or undermine social harmony. Scholars throughout history have faced this dilemma: Do they serve power or truth? Should they aim to unite people by making sure everyone believes in the same story, or should they let people know the truth even at the price of disunity? The most powerful scholarly establishments—whether of Christian priests, Confucian mandarins, or Communist ideologues—placed unity above truth. That's why they were so powerful.

As a species, humans prefer power to truth. We spend far more time and effort on trying to control the world than on trying to understand it—and even when we try to understand it, we usually do so in the hope that understanding the world will make it easier to control it. Therefore, if you dream of a society in which truth reigns supreme and myths are ignored, you have little to expect from *Homo sapiens*. Better to try your luck with chimps.

GETTING OUT OF THE BRAINWASHING MACHINE

All this does not mean that fake news is not a serious problem, or that politicians and priests have license to lie through their teeth. It would also be totally wrong to conclude that everything is just fake news, that any attempt to discover the truth is doomed to failure, and that there is no difference whatsoever between serious journalism and propaganda. Underneath all the fake news, there are real facts and real suffering. In Ukraine, for example, Russian soldiers are really fighting, thousands have really died, and hundreds of thousands have really lost their homes. Human suffering is often caused by belief in fiction, but the suffering itself is still real.

Instead of accepting fake news as the norm, we should recognize it is a far more difficult problem than we tend to assume, and we should strive even harder to distinguish reality from fiction. Don't expect perfection. One of the greatest fictions of all is to deny the complexity of the world and think in absolute terms: pristine purity versus satanic evil. No politician tells the whole truth and nothing but the truth, but some politicians are still far better than others. Given the choice, I would trust Churchill much more than Stalin, even though the British prime minister was not above embellishing the truth when it suited him. Similarly, no newspaper is free of biases and mistakes, but some newspapers make an honest effort to find out the truth, whereas others are a brainwashing machine. If I'd lived in the 1930s, I hope I would have had the sense to believe the *New York Times* more than *Pravda* and *Der Stürmer*.

It is the responsibility of all of us to invest time and effort in uncovering our biases and in verifying our sources of information. As noted in earlier chapters, we cannot investigate everything ourselves. But precisely because of that, we need to at least carefully investigate our favorite sources of information—be they a newspaper, a website, a TV network, or a person. In Chapter 20 we will explore in far greater depth how to avoid brainwashing and how to distinguish reality from fiction. Here I would like to offer two simple rules of thumb.

First, if you want reliable information, pay good money for it. If you get your news for free, you might well be the product. Suppose a shady billionaire offered you the following deal: "I will pay you $30 a month, and in exchange you will allow me to brainwash you for an hour every day, installing in your mind whichever political and commercial biases I want." Would you take the deal? Few sane people would. So the shady billionaire offers a slightly different deal: "You will allow me to brainwash you for one hour every day, and in exchange, I will not charge you anything for this service." Now the deal suddenly sounds tempting to hundreds of millions of people. Don't follow their example.

The second rule of thumb is that if some issue seems exceptionally important to you, make the effort to read the relevant scientific literature. And by scientific literature I mean peer-reviewed articles, books published by well-known academic publishers, and the writings of professors from reputable institutions. Science obviously has its limitations, and it has gotten many things wrong in the past. Nevertheless, the scientific community has been our most reliable source of knowledge for centuries. If you think the scientific community is wrong about something, that's certainly possible, but at least know the scientific theories you are rejecting, and provide some empirical evidence to support your claim.

Scientists, for their part, need to be far more engaged with current public debates. Scientists should not be afraid of making their voices heard when the debate wanders into their field of expertise, be it medicine or history. Of course, it is extremely important to go on doing academic research and to publish the results in scientific journals that only a few experts read. But it is equally important to communicate the latest scientific theories to the general public through popular science books, and even through the skillful use of art and fiction.

Does that mean scientists should start writing science fiction? That is actually not such a bad idea. Art plays a key role in shaping people's views of the world, and in the twenty-first century science fiction is arguably the most important genre of all, for it shapes how most people understand things such as AI, bioengineering, and climate change. We certainly need good science, but from a political perspective, a good science-fiction movie is worth far more than an article in *Science* or *Nature*.

18

....

Science Fiction

The Future Is Not What You See in the Movies

Humans control the world because they can cooperate better than any other animal, and they can cooperate so well because they believe in fictions. Poets, painters, and playwrights are therefore at least as important as soldiers and engineers. People go to war and build cathedrals because they believe in God, and they believe in God because they have read poems about God, because they have seen pictures of God, and because they have been mesmerized by theatrical plays about God. Similarly, our belief in the modern mythology of capitalism is underpinned by the artistic creations of Hollywood and the pop industry. We believe that buying more stuff will make us happy, because we saw the capitalist paradise with our own eyes on television.

In the early twenty-first century, perhaps the most important artistic genre is science fiction. Very few people read the latest articles in the fields of machine learning or genetic engineering. Instead, movies such as *The Matrix* and *Her* and TV series such as *Westworld* and *Black Mirror* shape how people understand the most important technological, social, and economic developments of our time. This also means that science fiction needs to be far more responsible in the way it depicts scientific realities; otherwise it might imbue people with the wrong ideas or focus their attention on the wrong problems.

As noted in an earlier chapter, perhaps the worst sin of present-day science fiction is that it tends to confuse intelligence with consciousness. As a result, it is overly concerned about a potential war between robots and humans, when in fact we need to fear a conflict between a small superhuman elite empowered by algorithms and a vast underclass of disempowered *Homo sapiens*. In thinking about the future of AI, Karl Marx is still a better guide than Steven Spielberg.

Indeed, many movies about artificial intelligence are so divorced from scientific reality that one suspects they are just allegories of completely different concerns. For example, the 2015 movie *Ex Machina* seems to be about an AI expert who falls in love with a female robot only to be duped and manipulated by her. But in reality, this is not a movie about the human fear of intelligent robots. It is a movie about the male fear of intelligent women, and in particular the fear that female liberation might lead to female domination. Whenever you see a movie about an AI in which the AI is female and the scientist is male, it's probably a movie about feminism rather than cybernetics. For why on earth would an AI have a sexual or gender identity? Sex is a characteristic of organic multicellular beings. What can it possibly mean for a nonorganic cybernetic being?

LIVING IN A BOX

One theme that science fiction has explored with far greater insight concerns the danger of technology being used to manipulate and control human beings. *The Matrix* depicts a world in which almost all humans are imprisoned in cyberspace, and everything they experience is shaped by a master algorithm. *The Truman Show* focuses on a single individual who is the unwitting star of a reality TV show. Unbeknownst to him, all his friends and acquaintances—including his mother, his wife, and his best friend—are actors, everything that happens to him follows a well-crafted script, and everything he says and does is recorded by hidden cameras and avidly followed by millions of fans.

However, both movies—despite their brilliance—in the end recoil from the full implications of their scenarios. They assume that the humans trapped within the matrix have an authentic self that remains untouched by all the technological manipulations, and that beyond the matrix awaits an authentic reality that the heroes can access if they only try hard enough. The matrix is just an artificial barrier separating your inner authentic self from the outer authentic world. After many trials and tribulations both heroes— Neo in *The Matrix* and Truman in *The Truman Show*—manage to transcend and escape the web of manipulations, discover their authentic selves, and reach the authentic promised land.

Curiously enough, this authentic promised land is identical in all important respects to the fabricated matrix. When Truman breaks out of the TV studio, he seeks to reunite with his high-school sweetheart, whom the director of the TV show had eliminated from the show. Yet if Truman fulfills that romantic fantasy, his life would look exactly like the perfect Hollywood dream that *The Truman Show* sold to millions of viewers across the globe—plus vacations in Fiji. The movie does not give us even a hint about what kind of alternative life Truman can find in the real world.

Similarly, when Neo breaks out of the matrix by swallowing the famous red pill, he discovers that the world outside is no different from the world inside. Both outside and inside there are violent conflicts and people driven by fear, lust, love, and envy. The movie should have ended with Neo being told that the reality he has accessed is just a bigger matrix, and that if he wants to escape into the "true real world," he must again choose between the blue pill and the red pill.

The current technological and scientific revolution implies not that authentic individuals and authentic realities can be manipulated by algorithms and TV cameras but rather that authenticity is a myth. People are afraid of being trapped inside a box, but they don't realize that they are already trapped inside a box—their brain—which is locked within the bigger box of human society with its myriad fictions. When you escape the matrix the only thing you discover is a bigger matrix. When the peasants and workers revolted against the tsar in 1917, they ended up with Stalin; when you begin to explore the manifold ways the world manipulates you, in the end you realize that your core identity is a complex illusion created by neural networks.

People fear that if they are trapped inside a box, they will miss out on all the wonders of the world. As long as Neo is stuck inside the matrix and Truman is stuck inside the TV studio, they will never visit Fiji, Paris, or Machu Picchu. But in truth, everything you will ever experience in life is within your own body and your own mind. Breaking out of the matrix or traveling to Fiji won't make any difference. It's not that somewhere in your mind there is an iron chest with a big red warning sign that reads OPEN ONLY IN FIJI! and when you finally travel to the South Pacific you get to open the chest, and out come all kinds of special emotions and feelings that you can have only in Fiji. And if you never visit Fiji in your life, then you missed these special feelings forever. No. Whatever you can feel in Fiji, you can feel anywhere in the world, even inside the matrix.

Perhaps we are all living inside a giant computer simulation, *Matrix*-style. That would contradict all our national, religious, and ideological stories. But our mental experiences would still be real. If it turns out that human history is an elaborate simulation run on a supercomputer by rat scientists from the planet Zircon, that would be rather embarrassing for Karl Marx and the Islamic State. But these rat scientists would still have to answer for the Armenian genocide and for Auschwitz. How did they get that one past Zircon University's ethics committee? Even if the gas chambers were just electric signals in silicon chips, the experiences of pain, fear, and despair were not one iota less excruciating for that.

Pain is pain, fear is fear, and love is love—even in the matrix. It doesn't matter if the fear you feel is inspired by a collection of atoms in the outside world or by electrical signals manipulated by a computer. The fear is still real. So if you want to explore the reality of your mind, you can do that inside the matrix as well as outside it.

Most science-fiction movies actually tell a very old story: the victory of mind over matter. Thirty thousand years ago, the story went like this: "Mind imagines a stone knife; hand creates a knife; human kills mammoth." But the truth is that humans gained control of the world not so much by inventing knives and killing mammoths as by manipulating human minds. The mind is not the subject that freely shapes historical actions and biological realities; the mind is an object that is being shaped by history and biology. Even our most cherished ideals—freedom, love, creativity—are like a stone knife that somebody else shaped in order to kill some mammoth. According to the best scientific theories and the most up-to-date technological tools, the mind is never free of manipulation. There is no authentic self waiting to be liberated from the manipulative shell.

Do you have any idea how many movies, novels, and poems you have consumed over the years, and how these artifacts have shaped and sharpened your idea of love? Romantic comedies are to love as porn is to sex and Rambo is to war. And if you think you can press some delete button and wipe out all trace of Hollywood from your subconscious and your limbic system, you are deluding yourself.

We like the idea of shaping stone knives, but we don't like the idea of being stone knives ourselves. So the matrix variation of the old mammoth story goes something like this: "Mind imagines a robot; hand creates a robot; robot kills terrorists but also tries to control the mind; mind kills robot." Yet this story is false. The problem is not that the mind will not be able to kill the robot. The problem is that the mind that imagined the robot in the first place was already the product of much earlier manipulations. Therefore killing the robot will not free us.

DISNEY LOSES FAITH IN FREE WILL

In 2015 Pixar Studios and Walt Disney Pictures released a far more realistic and troubling animation saga about the human condition, which quickly became a blockbuster among children and adults alike. *Inside Out* tells the story of an eleven-year-old girl, Riley Andersen, who moves with her parents from Minnesota to San Francisco. Missing her friends and hometown, she has difficulties adjusting to her new life, and she tries to run away back to Minnesota. Yet unbeknownst to Riley, there is a far greater drama going on. Riley is not the unwitting star of a TV reality show, and she isn't trapped in the matrix. Rather, Riley herself is the matrix, and there is something trapped inside her.

Disney has built its empire by retelling one myth over and over. In countless Disney movies, the heroes face difficulties and dangers, but they eventually triumph by finding their authentic self and following their free choices. *Inside Out* brutally dismantles this myth. It adopts the latest neurobiological view of humans and takes viewers on a journey into Riley's brain only to discover that she has no authentic self and that she never makes any free choices. Riley is in fact a huge robot managed by a collection of conflicting biochemical mechanisms, which the movie personifies as cute cartoon characters: the yellow and cheerful Joy, the blue and morose Sadness, the red and short-tempered Anger, and so on. By manipulating a set of buttons and levers in Headquarters while watching Riley's every move on a huge TV screen, these characters control all of Riley's moods, decisions, and actions.

Riley's failure to adjust to her new life in San Francisco results from a fuck-up in Headquarters that has knocked her brain out of balance. To make things right, Joy and Sadness go on an epic journey through Riley's brain, riding on the train of thought, exploring the subconscious prison, and visiting the inner studio where a team of artistic neurons are busy producing dreams. As we follow these personified biochemical mechanisms into the depths of Riley's brain, we never encounter a soul, an authentic self, or a free will. Indeed, the moment of revelation on which the entire plot hinges happens not when Riley discovers her single authentic self but rather when it becomes evident that Riley cannot be identified with any single core and that her well-being depends on the interaction of many different mechanisms.

At first, viewers are led to identify Riley with the lead character—the yellow cheerful Joy. Yet eventually it turns out that this identification was the critical mistake that threatened to ruin Riley's life. By thinking that she alone is the authentic essence of Riley, Joy browbeats all the other inner characters, thereby disrupting the delicate equilibrium of Riley's brain. Catharsis comes when Joy understands her mistake and she—along with the viewers—realizes that Riley isn't Joy, or Sadness, or any of the other characters. Riley is a complex story produced by the conflicts and collaborations of all the biochemical characters together.

The truly amazing thing is not only that Disney dared to market a movie with such a radical message but that it became a worldwide hit. Perhaps it succeeded so well because *Inside Out* is a comedy with a happy ending, and most viewers could easily have missed both its neurological meaning and its sinister implications.

The same cannot be said about the most prophetic science-fiction book of the twentieth century. You cannot miss its sinister nature. Written almost a century ago, in 1931, it becomes more relevant with each passing year. When Aldous Huxley wrote *Brave New World,* communism and fascism were entrenched in Russia and Italy, Nazism was on the rise in Germany, militaristic Japan was embarking on its war of conquest in China, and the entire world was gripped by the Great Depression. Yet Huxley managed to see through all these dark clouds and envision a future society without wars, famines, and plagues, enjoying uninterrupted peace, prosperity, and health. It is a consumerist world that gives complete free rein to sex, drugs, and rock 'n' roll and whose supreme value is happiness. The underlying assumption of the book is that humans are biochemical algorithms, science can hack the human algorithm, and technology can then be used to manipulate it.

In this brave new world, the World Government uses advanced biotechnology and social engineering to make sure that everyone is always content and no one has any reason to rebel. It is as if Joy, Sadness, and the other characters in Riley's brain have been turned into loyal government agents. There is therefore no need for a secret police, concentration camps, or a Ministry of Love à la Orwell's *1984*. Indeed, Huxley's genius consists in showing that you can control people far more securely through love and pleasure than through fear and violence.

It is clear that Orwell is describing a frightening nightmare world in *1984*, and the only unanswered question is "How do we avoid such a terrible fate?" Reading *Brave New World* is a disconcerting and challenging experience in large part because you are hard-pressed to put your finger on what exactly makes it dystopian. The world is peaceful and prosperous, and everyone is supremely satisfied all the time. What could possibly be wrong with that?

Huxley addresses this question directly in the novel's climactic moment: the dialogue between Mustapha Mond, the World Controller for Western Europe, and John the Savage, who has lived all his life on a native reservation in New Mexico, and who is the only other man in London who still knows anything about Shakespeare or God.

When John the Savage tries to incite the people of London to rebel against the system that controls them, they react with utter apathy to his call, but the police arrest him and bring him before Mustapha Mond. The World Controller has a pleasant chat with

John, explaining that if he insists on being antisocial, he should just remove himself to some secluded place and live as a hermit. John then questions the views that underlie the global order, and accuses the World Government of eliminating not just truth and beauty in its pursuit of happiness, but all that is noble and heroic in life.

Mustapha Mond explains to the savage that "civilization has absolutely no need of nobility or heroism. These things are symptoms of political inefficiency. In a properly organized society like ours, nobody has any opportunities for being noble or heroic. Conditions have got to be thoroughly unstable before the occasion can arise." Since there are no more wars, revolutions, or social conflicts, there is just no need for nobility or heroism.

Similarly, in the past people had to exert great effort and undergo years of hard moral training in order to overcome their anger, their hatred, and their dangerous passions. But now, if your anger or passion threatens to overwhelm you, all you need to do is swallow a few pills. "Anybody can be virtuous now," concludes Mustapha. "You can carry at least half your morality about in a bottle."

Exasperated, the Savage insists that effort and struggle have their merits, and asks Mustapha, "Isn't there something in living dangerously?" The World Controller agrees wholeheartedly that there is a great deal in living dangerously. Humans need strong stimulations, which is why the World Government decreed that every citizen must undergo a Violent Passion Surrogate treatment each month. These treatments mimic the physiological effects of extreme fear and rage so that people can enjoy all the effects of murdering someone—or being murdered—without suffering any of the inconveniences.

"But I like the inconveniences," says the Savage.

"We don't," said the Controller. "We prefer to do things comfortably."

"But I don't want comfort. I want God, I want poetry, I want real danger, I want freedom, I want goodness. I want sin."

"In fact," said Mustapha Mond, "you're claiming the right to be unhappy."

"All right then," said the Savage defiantly, "I'm claiming the right to be unhappy."

"Not to mention the right to grow old and ugly and impotent; the right to have syphilis and cancer; the right to have too little to eat; the right to be lousy; the right to live in constant apprehension of what may happen tomorrow; the right to catch typhoid; the right to be tortured by unspeakable pains of every kind."

There was a long silence.

"I claim them all," said the Savage at last.

Mustapha Mond shrugged his shoulders. "You're welcome," he said.[1]

John the Savage retires to an uninhabited wilderness and there lives as a hermit. Years of living on an Indian reservation and of being brainwashed by Shakespeare and religion have conditioned him to reject all the blessings of modernity. But word of such an unusual and exciting fellow quickly spreads, people flock to watch him and record all his doings, and soon enough he becomes a celebrity. Sick at heart of all the unwanted attention, the Savage escapes the civilized matrix not by swallowing a red pill but by hanging himself.

Unlike the creators of *The Matrix* and *The Truman Show,* Huxley doubted the possibility of escape, because he questioned whether there was anybody to make the escape. Since your brain and your "self" are part of the matrix, to escape the matrix you must escape your self. That, however, is a possibility worth exploring. Escaping the narrow definition of self might well become a necessary survival skill in the twenty-first century.

PART V

....

Resilience

How do you live in an age of bewilderment, when the old stories have collapsed and no new story has yet emerged to replace them?

19

....

Education

Change Is the Only Constant

Humankind is facing unprecedented revolutions, all our old stories are crumbling, and no new story has so far emerged to replace them. How can we prepare ourselves and our children for a world of such unprecedented transformations and radical uncertainties? A baby born today will be thirtysomething in 2050. If all goes well, that baby will still be around in 2100, and might even be an active citizen of the twenty-second century. What should we teach that baby that will help him or her survive and flourish in the world of 2050 or of the twenty-second century? What kind of skills will he or she need in order to get a job, understand what is happening around him or her, and navigate the maze of life?

Unfortunately, since nobody knows what the world will look like in 2050—not to mention 2100—we don't know the answer to these questions. Of course, humans have never been able to predict the future with accuracy. But today it is more difficult than ever before, because once technology enables us to engineer bodies, brains, and minds, we will no longer be able to be certain about anything—including things that previously seemed fixed and eternal.

A thousand years ago, in 1018, there were many things people didn't know about the future, but they were nevertheless convinced that the basic features of human society were not going to change. If you lived in China in 1018, you knew that by 1050 the Song Empire might collapse, the Khitans might invade from the north, and plagues might kill millions. However, it was clear to you that even in 1050 most people would still work as farmers and weavers, rulers would still rely on humans to staff their armies and bureaucracies, men would still dominate women, life expectancy would still be about forty, and the human body would remain exactly the same. For that reason, in 1018 poor Chinese parents taught their children how to plant rice or weave silk; wealthier parents taught their boys how to read the Confucian classics, write calligraphy, or fight on horseback, and they taught their girls to be modest and obedient housewives. It was obvious that these skills would still be needed in 1050.

In contrast, today we have no idea how China or the rest of the world will look in 2050. We don't know what people will do for a living, we don't know how armies or bureaucracies will function, and we don't know what gender relations will be like. Some people will probably live much longer than today, and the human body itself might undergo an unprecedented revolution thanks to bioengineering and direct brain-to-computer interfaces. Much of what kids learn today will likely be irrelevant by 2050.

At present, too many schools focus on cramming information into kids' brains. In the past this made sense, because information was scarce, and even the slow trickle of existing information was repeatedly blocked by censorship. If you lived, say, in a small provincial town in Mexico in 1800, it was difficult for you to know much about the wider world. There was no radio, television, daily newspaper, or public library.[1] Even if you were literate and had access to a private library, there was not much to read other than novels and religious tracts. The Spanish Empire heavily censored all texts printed locally and allowed only a dribble of vetted publications to be imported from the outside.[2] Much the same was true if you lived in some provincial town in Russia, India, Turkey, or China. When modern schools came along, teaching every child to read and write and imparting the basic facts of geography, history, and biology, they represented an immense improvement.

In contrast, in the twenty-first century we are flooded by enormous amounts of information, and the censors don't even try to block it. Instead, they are busy spreading misinformation or distracting us with irrelevancies. If you live in some provincial Mexican town and you have a smartphone, you can spend many lifetimes just reading Wikipedia, watching TED Talks, and taking free online courses. No government can hope to conceal all the information it doesn't like. On the other hand, it is alarmingly easy to inundate the public with conflicting reports and red herrings. People all over the world are but a click away from the latest accounts of the bombardment of Aleppo or of melting ice caps in the Arctic, but there are so many contradictory accounts that it is hard to know what to believe. Besides, countless other things are just a click away as well, making it difficult to focus, and when politics or science look too complicated it is tempting to switch to some funny cat videos, celebrity gossip, or porn.

In such a world, the last thing a teacher needs to give her pupils is more information. They already have far too much of it. Instead, people need the ability to make sense of information, to tell the difference between what is important and what is unimportant, and above all to combine many bits of information into a broad picture of the world.

In truth, this has been the ideal of Western liberal education for centuries, but up till now even many Western schools have been rather slack in fulfilling it. Teachers allowed themselves to focus on imparting data while encouraging students "to think for themselves." Due to their fear of authoritarianism, liberal schools have had a particular horror of grand narratives. They've assumed that as long as we give students lots of data and a modicum of freedom, the students will create their own picture of the world, and even if this generation fails to synthesize all the data into a coherent and meaningful story about the world, there will be plenty of time to construct a better synthesis in the future. We have now run out of time. The decisions we will make in the next few decades will shape the future of life itself, and we can make these decisions based only on our present worldview. If this generation lacks a comprehensive view of the cosmos, the future of life will be decided at random.

THE HEAT IS ON

Besides information, most schools also focus too much on providing students with a set of predetermined skills, such as solving differential equations, writing computer code in C++, identifying chemicals in a test tube, or conversing in Chinese. Yet since we have no idea what the world and the job market will look like in 2050, we don't really know what particular skills people will need. We might invest a lot of effort teaching kids how to write in C++ or speak Chinese, only to discover that by 2050 AI can code software far better than humans, and a new Google Translate app will enable you to conduct a conversation in almost flawless Mandarin, Cantonese, or Hakka, even though you only know how to say *"Ni hao."*

So what should we be teaching? Many pedagogical experts argue that schools should switch to teaching "the four Cs"—critical thinking, communication, collaboration, and creativity.[3] More broadly, they believe, schools should downplay technical skills and emphasize general-purpose life skills. Most important of all will be the ability to deal with change, learn new things, and preserve your mental balance in unfamiliar situations. In order to keep up with the world of 2050, you will need not merely to invent new ideas and products but above all to reinvent yourself again and again.

For as the pace of change increases, not just the economy but the very meaning of "being human" is likely to mutate. Already in 1848 the *Communist Manifesto* declared that "all that is solid melts into air." Marx and Engels, however, were thinking mainly about social and economic structures. By 2048, physical and cognitive structures will also melt into air, or into a cloud of data bits.

In 1848 millions of people were losing their jobs on village farms and were going to the big cities to work in factories. But upon reaching the big city, they were unlikely to change their gender or to add a sixth sense. And if they found a job in some textile factory, they could expect to remain in that profession for the rest of their working lives.

By 2048, people might have to cope with migrations to cyberspace, with fluid gender identities, and with new sensory experiences generated by computer implants. If they find both work and meaning in designing up-to-the-minute fashions for a 3-D virtual reality game, within a decade not just this particular profession but all jobs demanding this level of artistic creation might be taken over by AI. So at twenty-five you might introduce yourself on a dating site as "a twenty-five-year-old heterosexual woman who lives in London and works in a fashion shop." At thirty-five you might say you are "a gender-nonspecific person undergoing age adjustment, whose neocortical activity takes place mainly in the NewCosmos virtual world, and whose life mission is to go where no fashion designer has gone before." At forty-five both dating and self-definitions are so passé. You just wait for an algorithm to find (or create) the perfect match for you. As for drawing meaning from the art of fashion design, you are so irrevocably outclassed by the algorithms that looking at your crowning achievements from the previous decade fills you with embarrassment rather than pride. And at forty-five you still have many decades of radical change ahead of you.

Please don't take this scenario literally. Nobody can predict the specific changes we will witness in the future. Any particular scenario is likely to be far from the truth. If somebody describes the world of the mid-twenty-first century to you and it sounds like science fiction, it is probably false. But then again, if somebody describes the world of the mid-twenty-first century to you and it *doesn't* sound like science fiction, it is certainly false. We cannot be sure of the specifics; change itself is the only certainty.

Such profound change may well transform the basic structure of life, making discontinuity its most salient feature. From time immemorial life was divided into two complementary parts: a period of learning followed by a period of working. In the first part of life you accumulated information, developed skills, constructed a worldview, and built a stable identity. Even if at fifteen you spent most of your day working in your family's rice field (rather than in a formal school), the most important thing you were doing was learning: how to cultivate rice, how to conduct negotiations with the greedy rice merchants from the big city, and how to resolve conflicts over land and water with the other villagers. In the second part of life you relied on your accumulated skills to navigate the world, earn a living, and contribute to society. Of course even at fifty you continued to learn new things about rice, merchants, and conflicts, but these were just small tweaks to your well-honed abilities.

By the middle of the twenty-first century, accelerating change plus longer life spans will make this traditional model obsolete. Life will come apart at the seams, and there will be less and less continuity between different periods of life. "Who am I?" will be a more urgent and complicated question than ever before.[4]

This is likely to involve immense levels of stress. For change is almost always stressful, and after a certain age most people just don't like to change. When you are fifteen, your entire life is change. Your body is growing, your mind is developing, your relationships are deepening. Everything is in flux, and everything is new. You are busy inventing yourself. Most teenagers find it frightening, but at the same time, it is also exciting. New vistas are opening before you, and you have an entire world to conquer.

By the time you are fifty, you don't want change, and most people have given up on conquering the world. Been there, done that, got the T-shirt. You prefer stability. You have invested so much in your skills, your career, your identity, and your worldview that you don't want to start all over again. The harder you've worked on building something, the more difficult it is to let go of it and make room for something new. You might still cherish new experiences and minor adjustments, but most people in their fifties aren't ready to overhaul the deep structures of their identity and personality.

There are neurological reasons for this. Though the adult brain is more flexible and volatile than was once thought, it is still less malleable than the teenage brain. Reconnecting neurons and rewiring synapses is hard work.[5] But in the twenty-first century, you can't afford stability. If you try to hold on to some stable identity, job, or worldview, you risk being left behind as the world flies by you with a whoosh. Given that life expectancy is likely to increase, you might subsequently have to spend many decades as a clueless fossil. To stay relevant—not just economically but above all socially—you will need the ability to constantly learn and to reinvent yourself, certainly at a young age like fifty.

As strangeness becomes the new normal, your past experiences, as well as the past experiences of the whole of humanity, will become less reliable guides. Humans as individuals and humankind as a whole will increasingly have to deal with things nobody ever encountered before, such as superintelligent machines, engineered bodies, algorithms that can manipulate your emotions with uncanny precision, rapid man-made climate cataclysms, and the need to change your profession every decade. What is the right thing to do when confronting a completely unprecedented situation? How should you act when you are flooded by enormous amounts of information and there is absolutely no way you can absorb and analyze it all? How do you live in a world where profound uncertainty is not a bug but a feature?

To survive and flourish in such a world, you will need a lot of mental flexibility and great reserves of emotional balance. You will have to repeatedly let go of some of what you know best, and learn to feel at home with the unknown. Unfortunately, teaching kids to embrace the unknown while maintaining their mental balance is far more difficult than teaching them an equation in physics or the causes of the First World War. You cannot learn resilience by reading a book or listening to a lecture. Teachers themselves usually lack the mental flexibility that the twenty-first century demands, since they themselves are the product of the old educational system.

The Industrial Revolution has bequeathed us the production-line theory of education. In the middle of town there is a large concrete building divided into many identical rooms, each room equipped with rows of desks and chairs. At the sound of a bell, you go to one of these rooms together with thirty other kids who were all born the same year as you. Every hour a different grown-up walks in and starts talking. The grown-ups are all paid to do so by the government. One of them tells you about the shape of the earth, another tells you about the human past, and a third tells you about the human body. It is easy to laugh at this model, and almost everybody agrees that no matter its past achievements, it is now bankrupt. But so far we haven't created a viable alternative. Certainly not a scalable alternative that can be implemented in rural Mexico rather than just in wealthy California suburbs.

HACKING HUMANS

So the best advice I can give a fifteen-year-old stuck in an outdated school somewhere in Mexico, India, or Alabama is: don't rely on the adults too much. Most of them mean well, but they just don't understand the world. In the past, it was a relatively safe bet to follow the adults, because they knew the world quite well, and the world changed slowly. But the twenty-first century is going to be different. Because of the increasing pace of change, you can never be certain whether what the adults are telling you is timeless wisdom or out-dated bias.

So on what can you rely instead? Perhaps on technology? That's an even riskier gamble. Technology can help you a lot, but if technology gains too much power over your life, you might become a hostage to its agenda. Thousands of years ago humans invented agriculture, but this technology enriched just a tiny elite while enslaving the majority of humans. Most people found themselves working from sunrise till sunset plucking weeds, carrying water buckets, and harvesting corn under a blazing sun. It could happen to you too.

Technology isn't bad. If you know what you want in life, technology can help you get it. But if you don't know what you want in life, it will be all too easy for technology to shape your aims for you and take control of your life. Especially as technology gets better at understanding humans, you might increasingly find yourself serving it, instead of it serving you. Have you seen those zombies who roam the streets with their faces glued to their smartphones? Do you think they control the technology, or does the technology control them?

Should you rely on yourself, then? That sounds great on *Sesame Street* or in an old-fashioned Disney film, but in real life it doesn't work so well. Even Disney is coming to realize it. Just like Riley Andersen, most people barely know themselves, and when they try to "listen to themselves" they easily become prey to external manipulations. The voice we hear inside our heads is never trustworthy, because it always reflects state propaganda, ideological brainwashing, and commercial advertisements, not to mention biochemical bugs.

As biotechnology and machine learning improve, it will become easier to manipulate people's deepest emotions and desires, and it will become more dangerous than ever to just follow your heart. When Coca-Cola, Amazon, Baidu, or the government knows how to pull the strings of your heart and press the buttons of your brain, will you still be able to tell the difference between your self and their marketing experts?

To succeed at such a daunting task, you will need to work very hard at getting to know your operating system better—to know what you are and what you want from life. This is, of course, the oldest advice in the book: know thyself. For thousands of years philosophers and prophets have urged people to know themselves. But this advice was never more urgent than in the twenty-first century, because unlike in the days of Laozi or Socrates, now you have serious competition. Coca-Cola, Amazon, Baidu, and the government are all racing to hack you. Not your smartphone, not your computer, and not your bank account; they are in a race to hack *you* and your organic operating system. You might have heard that we are living in the era of hacking computers, but that's not even half the truth. In fact, we are living in the era of hacking humans.

The algorithms are watching you right now. They are watching where you go, what you buy, whom you meet. Soon they will monitor all your steps, all your breaths, all your heartbeats. They are relying on Big Data and machine learning to get to know you better and better. And once these algorithms know you better than you know yourself, they can control and manipulate you, and you won't be able to do much about it. You will live in the matrix, or in *The Truman Show*. In the end, it's a simple empirical matter: if the algorithms indeed understand what's happening within you better than you understand it yourself, authority will shift to them.

Of course, you might be perfectly happy ceding all authority to the algorithms and trusting them to decide things for you and for the rest of the world. If so, just relax and enjoy the ride. You don't need to do anything about it. The algorithms will take care of everything. If, however, you want to retain some control over your personal existence and the future of life, you have to run faster than the algorithms, faster than Amazon and the government, and get to know yourself before they do. To run fast, don't take much baggage with you. Leave all your illusions behind. They are very heavy.

20

....

Meaning

Life Is Not a Story

W ho am I? What should I do in life? What is the meaning of
life? Humans have been asking these questions from time
immemorial. Every generation needs a new answer, because what
we know and don't know keeps changing. Given everything we
know and don't know about science, about God, about politics,
and about religion, what is the best answer we can give today?

What kind of an answer do people expect? In almost all cases,
when people ask about the meaning of life, they expect to be told a
story. *Homo sapiens* is a storytelling animal that thinks in stories
rather than in numbers or graphs, and believes that the universe itself works like a story, replete with heroes and villains, conflicts and
resolutions, climaxes and happy endings. When we look for the
meaning of life, we want a story that will explain what reality is all
about and what my particular role is in the cosmic drama. This role
makes me a part of something bigger than myself, and gives meaning to all my experiences and choices.

One popular story, told for thousands of years to billions of anxious humans, explains that we are all part of an eternal cycle that

encompasses and connects all beings. Each being has a distinctive function to fulfill in the cycle. To understand the meaning of life means to understand your unique function, and to live a good life means to accomplish that function.

The Hindu epic the Bhagavad Gita relates how in the midst of a murderous civil war, the great warrior prince Arjuna is consumed with doubt. Seeing his friends and relatives in the opposing army, he hesitates over whether to fight and kill them. He begins to wonder what good and evil are, who decided it, and what the purpose of human life is. The god Krishna then explains to him that within the great cosmic cycle each being possesses a unique "dharma," the path you must follow and the duties you must fulfill. If you realize your dharma, no matter how hard the path may be, you enjoy peace of mind and liberation from doubt. If you refuse to follow your dharma and try to adopt somebody else's path—or wander about with no path at all—you will disturb the cosmic balance and will never be able to find either peace or joy. It makes no difference what your particular path is, as long as you follow it. A washerwoman who devotedly follows the way of the washerwoman is far superior to a prince who strays off the way of the prince. Having understood the meaning of life, Arjuna duly proceeds to follow *his* dharma as a warrior. He kills his friends and relatives, leads his army to victory, and becomes one of the most esteemed and beloved heroes of the Hindu world.

The 1994 Disney epic *The Lion King* repackaged this ancient story for modern audiences, with the young lion Simba standing in for Arjuna. When Simba wants to know the meaning of existence, his father, the lion king Mufasa, tells him about the great Circle of Life. Mufasa explains that the antelopes eat the grass, the lions eat the antelopes, and when the lions die their bodies decompose and feed the grass. This is how life continues from generation to generation, provided each animal plays its part in the drama. Everything is connected, and everyone depends on everyone else, so if even a blade of grass fails to fulfill its vocation, the entire Circle of Life might unravel. Simba's vocation, says Mufasa, is to rule the lion kingdom after Mufasa's death and keep the other animals in order.

However, when Mufasa is prematurely murdered by his evil brother Scar, young Simba blames himself for the catastrophe. Racked with guilt, he leaves the lion kingdom, shuns his royal destiny, and wanders off into the wilderness. There he meets two other outcasts, a meerkat and a warthog, and together they spend a few carefree years off the beaten path. Their antisocial philosophy means that they answer every problem by chanting "Hakuna matata"—no worries.

But Simba cannot escape his dharma. As he matures, he becomes increasingly troubled, not knowing who he is and what he should do in life. At the climactic moment of the movie, the spirit of Mufasa reveals himself to Simba in a vision and reminds Simba of the Circle of Life and of his royal identity. Simba also learns that in his absence, the evil Scar has assumed the throne and mismanaged the kingdom, which now suffers greatly from disharmony and famine. Simba finally understands who he is and what he must do. He returns to the lion kingdom, kills his uncle, becomes king, and reestablishes harmony and prosperity. The movie ends with a proud Simba presenting his newly born heir to the assembled animals, ensuring the continuation of the great Circle of Life.

The Circle of Life presents the cosmic drama as a circular story. For all Simba and Arjuna know, lions have been eating antelopes and warriors have been fighting battles for countless eons and will continue to do so forever and ever. The eternal repetition gives power to the story, implying that this is the natural course of things, and that if Arjuna shuns combat or if Simba refuses to become king, they will be rebelling against the very laws of nature.

If I believe in some version of the Circle of Life story, it means that I have a fixed and true identity that determines my duties in life. For many years I may be doubtful or ignorant of this identity, but one day, in some great climactic moment, it will be revealed, and I will understand my role in the cosmic drama. Though I may subsequently encounter many trials and tribulations, I will be free of doubts and despair.

Other religions and ideologies believe in a linear cosmic drama, which has a definitive beginning, a not-too-long middle, and a once-and-for-all ending. For example, the Muslim story says that in the beginning Allah created the entire universe and laid down its laws. He then revealed those laws to humans in the Quran. Unfortunately, ignorant and wicked people rebelled against Allah and tried to break or hide these laws, and it is up to virtuous and loyal Muslims to uphold the laws and spread knowledge of them to others. Eventually, on Judgment Day, Allah will pass judgment on the conduct of each and every individual. He will reward the righteous with everlasting bliss in paradise, and toss the wicked into the burning pits of hell.

This grand narrative implies that my small but important role in life is to follow Allah's commands, spread knowledge of His laws, and ensure obedience to His wishes. If I believe the Muslim story, I find meaning in praying five times a day, donating money to build a new mosque, and struggling against apostates and infidels. Even the most mundane activities—washing hands, drinking wine, having sex—are imbued with cosmic meaning.

Nationalism too upholds a linear story. The Zionist story begins with the biblical adventures and achievements of the Jewish people, recounts two thousand years of exile and persecution, reaches a climax with the Holocaust and the establishment of the state of Israel, and looks forward to the day when Israel will enjoy peace and prosperity and become a moral and spiritual beacon to the world. If I believe in the Zionist story, I will conclude that my life's mission is to advance the interests of the Jewish nation by protecting the purity of the Hebrew language, by fighting to regain lost Jewish territory, or perhaps by having and raising a new generation of loyal Israeli children.

In this case too, even humdrum undertakings are infused with meaning. On Independence Day, Israeli schoolchildren often sing a popular Hebrew song together praising any action done for the sake of the motherland. One kid sings, "I've built a house in the land of Israel," another kid chants, "I've planted a tree in the land of Israel," a third chimes in with "I've written a poem in the land of Israel," and so it goes, on and on, until finally they all join together in a chorus singing "So we have a house, and a tree, and a poem [and whatever else you would like to add] in the land of Israel."

Communism tells an analogous story, but focuses on class rather than ethnicity. The *Communist Manifesto* opens with this proclamation:

The history of all hitherto existing society is the history of class struggles. Freeman and slave, patrician and plebeian, lord and serf, guild-master and journeyman, in a word, oppressor and oppressed, stood in constant opposition to one another, carried on an uninterrupted, now hidden, now open fight, a fight that each time ended, either in a revolutionary reconstitution of society at large, or in the common ruin of the contending classes.[1]

The manifesto goes on to explain that in modern times, "society as a whole is more and more splitting up into two great hostile camps, into two great classes directly facing each other: Bourgeoisie and Proletariat."[2] Their struggle will end with the victory of the proletariat, which will signal the end of history and the establishment of the communist paradise on earth, in which nobody will own anything and everyone will be completely free and happy.

If I believe in this communist story, I will conclude that my life's mission is to speed up the global revolution by writing fiery pamphlets to raise class consciousness, organizing strikes and demonstrations, or perhaps assassinating greedy capitalists and fighting against their lackeys. The story gives meaning to even the smallest of gestures, such as boycotting a brand that exploits textile workers in Bangladesh or arguing with my capitalist-pig father-in-law over Christmas dinner.

When I look at the entire range of stories that seek to define my true identity and give meaning to my actions, I am struck by the realization that scale matters very little. Some stories, such as Simba's Circle of Life, seem to stretch on for eternity: it is only against the backdrop of the entire universe that I can know who I am. Other stories, such as most nationalist and tribal myths, are puny by comparison. Zionism holds sacred the adventures of about 0.2 percent of humankind and 0.005 percent of the earth's surface during a tiny fraction of human history. The Zionist story fails to ascribe any meaning to the Chinese empires, to the tribes of New Guinea, and to the Andromeda galaxy, as well as to the countless eons that passed before the existence of Moses, Abraham, and the evolution of apes.

Such myopia can have serious repercussions. For example, one of the major obstacles for any peace treaty between Israelis and Palestinians is that Israelis are unwilling to divide the city of Jerusalem. They argue that this city is "the eternal capital of the Jewish people"—and surely you cannot compromise on something eternal.[3] What are a few dead people compared to eternity? This is of course utter nonsense. Eternity is at the very least 13.8 billion years—the current age of the universe. Planet Earth was formed about 4.5 billion years ago, and humans have existed for at least 2 million years. In contrast, the city of Jerusalem was established just 5,000 years ago and the Jewish people are at most 3,000 years old. This hardly qualifies as eternity.

As for the future, physics tells us that planet Earth will be absorbed by an expanding sun about 7.5 billion years from now and that our universe will continue to exist for at least 13 billion years more.[4] Does anyone seriously believe that the Jewish people, the state of Israel, or the city of Jerusalem will still exist 13,000 years from now, let alone in 13 billion years? Looking to the future, Zionism has a horizon of no more than a few centuries, yet it is enough to exhaust the imagination of most Israelis and somehow qualify as "eternity." And people are willing to make sacrifices for the sake of "the eternal city," which they would probably refuse to make for an ephemeral collection of houses.

As a teenager in Israel, I too was initially captivated by the nation-alist promise to become part of something bigger than myself. I wanted to believe that if I gave my life to the nation, I would live forever in the nation. But I couldn't fathom what it meant "to live forever in the nation." The phrase sounded very profound, but what did it actually mean? I remember one particular Memorial Day cer-emony when I was about thirteen or fourteen. Whereas in the United States Memorial Day is marked mainly by bargain shopping, in Israel Memorial Day is an extremely solemn and important event. Schools hold ceremonies to remember the fallen soldiers in Israel's many wars. The kids dress in white, recite poems, sing songs, place wreaths, and wave flags. So there I was at my school's ceremony, dressed in white, and in between flag waving and poem recitations, I naturally thought that when I grew up I too wanted to be a fallen soldier. After all, if I was a heroic fallen soldier who had sacrificed his life for Israel, then I would have all these kids reciting poems and waving flags in my honor.

But then I thought, "Wait a minute. If I am dead, how will I know that these kids are really reciting poems in my honor?" So I tried to imagine myself dead. And I imagined myself lying under some white tombstone in a neat military cemetery, listening to the poems coming from above the ground. But then I thought, "If I am dead, then I cannot hear any poems, because I don't have ears, and I don't have a brain, and I cannot hear or feel anything. So what's the point?"

Even worse, by the time I was thirteen I knew that the universe was a couple of billion years old and would probably go on existing for billions of years more. Could I realistically expect Israel to exist for such a long time? Would *Homo sapiens* kids dressed in white still recite poems in my honor after two hundred million years? There was something fishy about the whole business.

If you happen to be Palestinian, don't feel smug. It is just as unlikely that there will be any Palestinians around two hundred million years from now. In all probability by then there won't be any mammals whatsoever. Other national movements are just as narrow-minded. Serbian nationalism cares little about events in the Jurassic era, whereas Korean nationalists believe that a small peninsula on the east coast of Asia is the only part of the cosmos that really matters in the grand scheme of things.

Of course, even Simba—for all his devotion to the everlasting Circle of Life—never contemplates the fact that lions, antelopes, and grass aren't really eternal. Simba does not consider what the universe was like before the evolution of mammals, nor what the fate of his beloved African savannah will be once humans kill all the lions and cover the grasslands with asphalt and concrete. Would this render Simba's life utterly meaningless?

All stories are incomplete. Yet in order to construct a viable identity for myself and give meaning to my life, I don't really need a complete story devoid of blind spots and internal contradictions. To give meaning to my life, a story needs to satisfy just two conditions. First, it must give *me* some role to play. A New Guinean tribesman is unlikely to believe in Zionism or in Serbian nationalism, because these stories don't care at all about New Guinea and its people. Like movie stars, humans like only those scripts that reserve an important role for them.

Second, whereas a good story need not extend to infinity, it must extend beyond my horizons. The story must provide me with an identity and give meaning to my life by embedding me within something bigger than myself. But there is always a danger that I might start wondering what gives meaning to that "something bigger." If the meaning of my life is to help the proletariat or the Polish nation, what exactly gives meaning to the proletariat or to the Polish nation? There is a story of a man who claimed that the world was kept in place by resting on the back of a huge elephant. When asked what the elephant stood on, he replied that it stood on the back of a large turtle. And the turtle? On the back of an even bigger turtle. And that bigger turtle? The man snapped, "Don't worry about it. From there it's turtles all the way down."

Most successful stories remain open-ended. They never need to explain where meaning ultimately comes from, because they are so good at capturing people's attention and keeping it inside a safe zone. For instance when explaining that the world rests on the back of a huge elephant, you should preempt any difficult questions by describing in great detail the way that the flapping of the elephant's gigantic ears causes hurricanes, and how when the elephant quivers with anger earthquakes shake the surface of the earth. If you weave a good enough yarn, it won't occur to anyone to ask what the elephant is standing on. Similarly, nationalism enchants us with tales of heroism, moves us to tears by recounting past disasters, and ignites our fury by dwelling on the injustices our nation suffered. We get so absorbed in this national epic that we start evaluating everything that happens in the world by its impact on our nation, and hardly think of asking what makes our nation so important in the first place.

When you believe a particular story, it makes you extremely interested in its minutest details, while keeping you blind to anything that falls outside its scope. Devout communists may spend countless hours debating whether it is permissible to make an alliance with social democrats in the early stages of revolution, but they seldom stop to ponder the place of the proletariat in the evolution of mammalian life on planet Earth or in the spread of organic life in the cosmos. Such idle talk is considered a counterrevolutionary waste of breath.

Though some stories go to the trouble of encompassing the entirety of space and time, the ability to control attention allows many other successful stories to remain far more modest in scope. A crucial law of storytelling is that once a story manages to extend beyond the audience's horizon, its ultimate scope matters little. People may display the same murderous fanaticism for the sake of a thousand-year-old nation as for the sake of a billion-year-old god. People are just not good with large numbers. In most cases, it takes surprisingly little to exhaust our imagination.

Given everything we know about the universe, it would seem utterly impossible for any sane person to believe that the ultimate truth about the universe and human existence is the story of Israeli, German, or Russian nationalism—or indeed of nationalism in general. A story that ignores almost the whole of time, the whole of space, the Big Bang, quantum physics, and the evolution of life is at most just a tiny part of the truth. Yet people somehow manage not to see beyond it.

Indeed, billions of people throughout history believed that for their lives to have meaning, they didn't even need to be absorbed into a nation or a great ideological movement. It was enough for them to just "leave something behind," thereby ensuring that their personal story would continue beyond their death. The "something" I leave behind is ideally my soul or my personal essence. If I am reborn in a new body after the death of my present body, then death is not the end. It is merely the space between two chapters, and the plot that began in one chapter will carry on into the next. Many people have at least a vague faith in such a theory, even if they do not base it on any specific theology. They don't need an elaborate dogma—they just need the reassuring feeling that their story will continue beyond the horizon of death.

This theory of life as a never-ending epic is extremely attractive and common, but it suffers from two main problems. First, by lengthening my personal story I don't really make it more meaningful. I just make it longer. Indeed, the two great religions that embrace the idea of a never-ending cycle of births and deaths, Hinduism and Buddhism, share a horror of the futility of it all. Millions upon millions of times I learn how to walk, I grow up, I fight with my mother-in-law, I get sick, I die—and then I do it all over again. What's the point? If I could accumulate all the tears I have shed in all my previous lives, they would fill the Pacific Ocean; if I gathered together all the teeth and hair I have lost, they would make a mound higher than the Himalayas. And what do I have to show for all that? No wonder that Hindu and Buddhist sages have focused much of their efforts on finding a way to get off this merry-go-round rather than to perpetuate it.

The second problem with this theory is the paucity of supporting evidence. What proof do I have that in a past life I was a medieval peasant, a Neanderthal hunter, a *Tyrannosaurus rex*, or an amoeba? (If I really lived millions of lives, I must have been a dinosaur and an amoeba at some point, for humans have existed for only the last 2.5 million years.) And in the future, will I be reborn as a cyborg, an intergalactic explorer, or even a frog? Basing my life on this promise is a bit like selling my house in exchange for a postdated check drawn on a bank above the clouds.

People who doubt that some kind of soul or spirit really survives their death therefore strive to leave behind something a bit more tangible. That "something tangible" could take one of two forms: cultural or biological. I might leave behind a poem, say, or some of my precious genes. My life has meaning because people will still read my poem a hundred years from now, or because my kids and grandchildren will still be around. And what is the meaning of their lives? Well, that's their problem, not mine. The meaning of life is thus a bit like playing with a live hand grenade. Once you pass it on to somebody else, you are safe.

Alas, this modest hope of "leaving something behind" is rarely fulfilled. Most organisms that ever existed became extinct without leaving any genetic inheritance. Almost all the dinosaurs, for example. Or a Neanderthal family that became extinct as *Homo sapiens* took over. Or my grandmother's Polish clan. In 1934 my grandma Fanny immigrated to Jerusalem with her parents and two sisters, but most of their relatives stayed behind in the Polish towns of Chmielnik and Czestochowa. A few years later the Nazis came along and wiped them out to the very last child.

Attempts at leaving behind some cultural legacy are seldom more successful. Nothing has remained of my grandmother's Polish clan except for a few faded faces in the family album, and at the age of ninety-six, even my grandmother cannot match names to the faces any longer. To the best of my knowledge, they haven't left behind any cultural creation—not a poem, not a diary, not even a grocery list. You might argue that they have a share in the collective inheritance of the Jewish people or of the Zionist movement, but that hardly gives meaning to their individual lives. Moreover, how do you know that all of them cherished their Jewish identity or agreed with the Zionist movement? Maybe one of them was a committed communist and sacrificed his life spying for the Soviets. Maybe another wanted nothing more than to assimilate into Polish society, served as an officer in the Polish army, and was killed by the Soviets in the Katyn massacre. Maybe a third was a radical feminist, rejecting all traditional religious and nationalist identities. Since they left nothing behind, it is all too easy to recruit them posthumously to this or that cause, and they cannot even protest.

If we cannot leave something tangible behind, such as a gene or a poem, might it be enough if we just make the world a little better? You can help somebody, and that somebody will subsequently help somebody else, and you thereby contribute to the overall improvement of the world, and constitute a small link in the great chain of kindness. Maybe you serve as a mentor for a difficult but brilliant child, who goes on to be a doctor who saves the lives of hundreds. Maybe you help an old lady cross the street, brightening up an hour of her life. Though it has its merits, the great chain of kindness is a bit like the great chain of turtles—it is far from clear where its meaning comes from. A wise old man was asked what he learned about the meaning of life. "Well," he answered, "I have learned that I am here on earth in order to help other people. What I still haven't figured out is why the other people are here."

For those who don't trust great chains, future legacies, or collective epics, perhaps the safest and most parsimonious story they can turn to is romance. It doesn't seek to go beyond the here and now. As countless love poems testify, when you are in love, the entire universe is reduced to the earlobe, the eyelash, or the nipple of your beloved. When gazing at Juliet leaning her cheek upon her hand,

Romeo exclaims "O, that I were a glove upon that hand, / That I might touch that cheek!" By connecting with a single body here and now, you feel connected with the entire cosmos.

In truth, your beloved is just another human being, no different in essence from the multitudes you ignore every day on the train and in the supermarket. But to you, he or she seems infinite, and you are happy to lose yourself in that infinity. Mystic poets of all traditions have often conflated romantic love with cosmic union, writing about God as a lover. Romantic poets have repaid the compliment by writing about their lovers as gods. If you are really in love with someone, you never worry about the meaning of life.

And what if you are not in love? Well, if you believe in the romantic story but you are not in love, you at least know what the aim of your life is: to find true love. You have seen it in countless movies and read about it in innumerable books. You know that one day you will meet that special someone, you will see infinity inside two sparkling eyes, your entire life will suddenly make sense, and all the questions you ever had will be answered by repeating one name over and over again, just like Tony in *West Side Story* or Romeo upon seeing Juliet looking down at him from the balcony.

THE WEIGHT OF THE ROOF

While a good story must give me a role and must extend beyond my horizons, it need not be true. A story can be pure fiction, yet provide me with an identity and make me feel that my life has meaning. To the best of our scientific understanding, none of the thousands of stories that different cultures, religions, and tribes have invented throughout history is true. They are all just human inventions. If you ask for the true meaning of life and get a story in reply, know that this is the wrong answer. The exact details don't really matter. *Any* story is wrong, simply for being a story. The universe just does not work like a story.

So why do people believe in these fictions? One reason is that their personal identity is built on the story. People are taught to believe in the story from early childhood. They hear it from their parents, their teachers, their neighbors, and the general culture long before they develop the intellectual and emotional independence necessary to question and verify such stories. By the time their intellect matures, they are so heavily invested in the story that they are far more likely to use their intellect to rationalize it than to doubt it. Most people who go on identity quests are like children going on a treasure hunt: they find only what their parents have hidden for them in advance.

Second, not only are our personal identities built on the story, but so are our collective institutions. Consequently, it is extremely frightening to doubt the story. In many societies, anyone who tries to do so is ostracized or persecuted. Even if not, it takes strong nerves to question the very fabric of society. For if indeed the story is false, then the entire world as we know it makes no sense. State laws, social norms, economic institutions—they might all collapse.

Most stories are held together by the weight of their roof rather than by the strength of their foundations. Consider the Christian story. It has the flimsiest of foundations. What evidence do we have that the son of the Creator of the entire universe was born as a carbon-based life-form somewhere in the Milky Way about two thousand years ago? What evidence do we have that it happened in the Galilee area, and that His mother was a virgin? Yet enormous global institutions have been built on top of that story, and their weight presses down with such overwhelming force that they keep the story in place. Entire wars have been waged over changing a single word of the story. The thousand-year schism between Western Christians and Eastern Orthodox Christians, which has manifested itself recently in the mutual butchery of Croats by Serbs and Serbs by Croats, began over the lone word *filioque* ("and from the son" in Latin). The Western Christians wanted to insert this word into the Christian profession of faith, while the Eastern Christians vehemently objected. (The theological implications of adding that word are so arcane that it would be impossible to explain them here in any meaningful way. If you are curious, ask Google.)

Once personal identities and entire social systems are built on top of a story, it becomes unthinkable to doubt it, not because of the evidence supporting it, but because its collapse will trigger a personal and social cataclysm. In history, the roof is sometimes more important than the foundations.

HOCUS-POCUS AND THE INDUSTRY OF BELIEF

The stories that provide us with meaning and identity are all fictional, but humans need to believe in them. It's obvious *why* humans want to believe the story, but *how* do they actually believe? How do we make the story *feel* real? Priests and shamans discovered the answer to this question thousands of years ago: rituals. A ritual is a magical act that makes the abstract concrete and the fictional real. The essence of ritual is the magical spell "Hocus-pocus, X is Y!"[5]

How to make Christ real to his devotees? In the ceremony of Mass, the priest takes a piece of bread and a glass of wine and proclaims that the bread is Christ's flesh, the wine is Christ's blood, and by eating and drinking them the faithful attain communion with Christ. What could be more real than actually tasting Christ in your mouth? Traditionally, the priest made these bold proclamations in Latin, the ancient language of religion, law, and the secrets of life. In front of the amazed eyes of the assembled peasants the priest held high a piece of bread and exclaimed *"Hoc est corpus!"*—"This is the body!"—and the bread supposedly became the flesh of Christ. In the minds of the illiterate peasants, who did not speak Latin, *"Hoc est corpus!"* got garbled into "Hocus-pocus!" Thus was born the powerful spell that can transform a frog into a prince and a pumpkin into a carriage.[6]

A thousand years before the birth of Christianity, the ancient Hindus used the same trick. The Brihadaranyaka Upanishad interprets the ritual sacrifice of a horse as a realization of the entire story of the cosmos. The text follows the "Hocus-pocus, X is Y!" structure: "The head of the sacrificial horse is the dawn, its eye the sun, its vital force the air, its open mouth the fire called Vaisvanara, and the body of the sacrificial horse is the year . . . its members are the seasons, its joints the months and fortnights, its feet the days and nights, its bones the stars, and its flesh the clouds . . . its yawning is lightning, its shaking the body is thundering, its making water is raining, and its neighing is voice."[7]

Almost anything can be turned into a ritual by imbuing deep religious meaning in mundane gestures such as lighting candles, ringing bells, or counting beads. The same is true of physical gestures such as bowing the head, prostrating the whole body, or bringing both palms together. Various forms of headgear, from the Sikh turban to the Muslim hijab, are so laden with meaning that they have been the cause of fierce political struggles and even bloodshed.

Food too can be loaded with spiritual significance far beyond its nutritional value, be it Easter eggs that symbolize new life and Christ's resurrection or the bitter herbs and unleavened bread that Jews eat at Passover to remember their slavery in Egypt and their miraculous escape. There is hardly a dish in the world that hasn't been interpreted to symbolize something. On New Year's Day Jews eat honey so that the coming year will be sweet, they eat fish heads so that they will be fruitful like fish and will move forward rather than back, and they eat pomegranates so that their good deeds will multiply like the many seeds of the pomegranate.

Similar rituals have been used for political purposes. For thousands of years crowns, thrones, and staffs represented kingdoms and entire empires, and millions of people died in brutal wars waged over the possession of "the throne" or "the crown." Royal courts cultivated protocols that were so elaborate in nature that they matched the most intricate of religious ceremonies. In the military, discipline and ritual are inseparable, and soldiers from ancient Rome to the present day spend countless hours marching in formation, saluting superiors, and shining boots. Napoleon famously observed that he could make men sacrifice their lives for a colorful ribbon.

Perhaps nobody understood the political importance of rituals better than Confucius, who saw the strict observance of rites (li) as the key to social harmony and political stability. Confucian classics such as *The Book of Rites, The Rites of Zhou,* and *The Book of Etiquette and Rites* recorded in the minutest details which ritual should be performed at which state occasion, down to the number of ritual vessels used in the ceremony, the type of musical instruments played, and the colors of the robes to be worn. Whenever China was hit by some crisis, Confucian scholars were quick to blame it on the neglect of rites, like a sergeant major who blames military defeat on slack soldiers not shining their boots.[8]

In the modern West, the Confucian obsession with rituals has often been seen as a sign of shallowness and archaism. In fact, it probably testifies to Confucius's profound and timeless appreciation of human nature. It is perhaps no coincidence that Confucian cultures—first and foremost in China, but also in neighboring Korea, Vietnam, and Japan—produced extremely long-lasting social and political structures. If you want to know the ultimate truth of life, rites and rituals are a huge obstacle. But if you are interested in social stability and harmony, as Confucius was, truth is often a liability, whereas rites and rituals are among your best allies.

This principle is as relevant in the twenty-first century as it was in ancient China. The power of hocus-pocus is alive and well in our modern industrial world. For many people in 2018, two wooden sticks nailed together are God, a colorful poster on the wall is the revolution, and a piece of cloth flapping in the wind is the nation. You cannot see or hear France, because it exists only in your imagination, but you can certainly see the tricolor and hear "La Marseillaise." By waving a colorful flag and singing an anthem you transform the nation from an abstract story into a tangible reality.

Thousands of years ago devout Hindus sacrificed precious horses; today they invest in producing costly flags. The national flag of India is known as the *tiranga* (literally, "tricolor"), because it consists of three stripes of saffron, white, and green. The 2002 Flag Code of India proclaims that the flag "represents the hopes and aspirations of the people of India. It is the symbol of our national pride. Over the last five decades, several people including members of the armed forces have ungrudgingly laid down their lives to keep the tricolor flying in its full glory."[9] The Flag Code then quotes Sarvepalli Radhakrishnan, India's second president, who explained:

> The saffron color denotes renunciation or disinterestedness. Our leaders must be indifferent to material gains and dedicate themselves to their work. The white in the center is light, the path of truth to guide our conduct. The green shows our relation to the soil, our relation to the plant life here on which all other life depends. The Ashoka wheel in the center of the white is the wheel of the law of dharma. Truth or Satya, dharma or virtue ought to be the controlling principles of all those who work under this flag.[10]

In 2017 India's nationalist government hoisted one of the largest flags in the world at Attari on the Indo-Pakistan border, in a gesture calculated to inspire neither renunciation nor disinterestedness but rather Pakistani envy. That particular *tiranga* was 115 feet long and 78 feet wide, and was hoisted on a 360-foot-high flagpole (what would Freud have said about that?). The flag could be seen as far as the Pakistani metropolis of Lahore. Unfortunately, strong winds kept tearing the flag, and national pride required that it be stitched together again and again, at great cost to Indian taxpayers.[11] Why does the Indian government invest scarce resources in weaving enormous flags instead of building sewage systems in Delhi's slums?

Because the flag makes India real in a way that sewage systems do not.

Indeed, the very cost of the flag makes the ritual more effective. Of all rituals, sacrifice is the most potent, because of all the things in the world, suffering is the most real. You can never ignore it or doubt it. If you want to make people really believe in some fiction, entice them to make a sacrifice on its behalf. Once you suffer for a story, it is usually enough to convince you that the story is real. If you fast because God commanded you to do so, the tangible feeling of hunger makes God present more than any statue or icon. If you lose your legs in a patriotic war, your stumps and wheelchair make the nation more real than any poem or anthem. On a less grandiose level, by preferring to buy inferior local pasta to imported high-quality Italian pasta you might make a small daily sacrifice that makes the nation feel real even in the supermarket.

This is of course a logical fallacy. If you suffer because of your belief in God or in the nation, that does not prove that your beliefs are true. Maybe you are just paying the price of your gullibility. However, most people don't like to admit that they are fools. Consequently, the more they sacrifice for a particular belief, the stronger their faith becomes. This is the mysterious alchemy of sacrifice. In order to bring us under his power, the sacrificing priest need not give us anything at all—not rain, or money, or victory in war. Rather, he needs to take away something. Once he convinces us to make some painful sacrifice, we are trapped.

It works in the commercial world too. If you buy a secondhand Fiat for $2,000, you are likely to complain about it to anyone willing to listen to you. But if you buy a brand-new Ferrari for $200,000, you will sing its praises far and wide, not because it is such a good car but because you have paid so much money for it that you have to believe it is the most wonderful thing in the world. Even in romance, any aspiring Romeo or Werther knows that without sacrifice, there is no true love. The sacrifice is not just a way to convince your lover that you are serious; it is also a way to convince yourself that you are really in love. Why do you think women ask their lovers for diamond rings? Once the lover makes such a huge financial sacrifice, he must convince himself that it was for a worthy cause.

Self-sacrifice is extremely persuasive not just for the martyrs themselves but also for their bystanders. Few gods, nations, or revolutions can sustain themselves without martyrs. If you presume to question the divine drama, the nationalist myth, or the revolutionary saga, you are immediately chastised: "But the blessed martyrs died for this! Do you dare say that they died for nothing? Do you think these heroes were fools?"

For Shiite Muslims, the drama of the cosmos reached its climactic moment on the day of Ashura, which was the tenth day of the month of Muharram, sixty-one years after the Hijrah (October 10, 680, according to the Christian calendar). On that day, at Karbala in Iraq, soldiers of the evil usurper Yazid massacred Husayn ibn Ali, the grandson of the Prophet Muhammad, along with a small group of followers. For Shiites, Husayn's martyrdom has come to symbolize the eternal struggle of good against evil and of the oppressed against injustice. Just as Christians repeatedly reenact the drama of the crucifixion and imitate the Passion of Christ, so Shiites reenact the drama of Ashura and imitate the Passion of Husayn. Millions of Shiites flock yearly to the holy shrine in Karbala, established where Husayn was martyred, and on the day of Ashura Shiites throughout the world stage mourning rituals, in some cases flagellating themselves with chains and cutting themselves with knives.

Yet the importance of Ashura is not limited to one place and one day. Ayatollah Ruhollah Khomeini and numerous other Shiite leaders have repeatedly told their followers that "every day is Ashura and every place is Karbala."[12] The martyrdom of Husayn at Karbala in this way gives meaning to every event, anywhere, anytime, and even the most mundane decisions are seen as having an impact on the great cosmic struggle between good and evil. If you dare doubt this story, you will immediately be reminded of Karbala—and to doubt or mock the martyrdom of Husayn is just about the worst offense you can possibly commit.

Alternatively, if martyrs are scarce and people are unwilling to sacrifice themselves, the sacrificing priest might get them to sacrifice somebody else instead. You might sacrifice a human to the vengeful god Ba'al, burn a heretic at the stake for the greater glory of Jesus Christ, execute adulterous women because Allah said so, or send class enemies to the gulag. Once you do this, a slightly different alchemy of sacrifice begins to work its magic on you. When you inflict suffering on yourself in the name of some story, it gives you a choice: "Either the story is true or I am a gullible fool." When you inflict suffering on others, you are also given a choice: "Either the story is true or I am a cruel villain." And just as we don't want to admit we are fools, we also don't want to admit we are villains. We prefer to believe that the story is true.

In March 1839, in the Iranian city of Mashhad, a Jewish woman who suffered from some skin disease was told by a local quack that if she killed a dog and washed her hands in its blood, she would be cured. Mashhad is a holy Shiite city, and it so happened that the woman undertook the grisly therapy on the sacred day of Ashura. She was observed by some Shiites, who believed—or claimed to believe—that the woman killed the dog in mockery of the Karbala martyrdom. Word of this unthinkable sacrilege quickly spread through the streets of Mashhad. Egged on by the local imam, an angry mob stormed the Jewish quarter, torched the synagogue, and murdered thirty-six Jews on the spot. All the surviving Jews of Mashhad were then given a stark choice: convert to Islam immediately or be killed. The sordid episode did no harm to Mashhad's reputation as "Iran's spiritual capital."[13]

When we think of human sacrifice we usually have in mind gruesome rituals in Canaanite or Aztec temples, and it is common to argue that monotheism brought an end to this terrible practice. In fact, monotheists practiced human sacrifice on a much larger scale than most polytheistic cults. Christianity and Islam have killed far more people in the name of God than did the followers of Ba'al or Huitzilopochtli. At a time when the Spanish conquistadores put an end to human sacrifices to the Aztec and Inca gods, back home in Spain the Inquisition was burning heretics by the cartload.

Sacrifices can come in all shapes and sizes. They don't always involve knife-wielding priests or bloody pogroms. Judaism, for example, forbids working or traveling on the holy day of Sabbath (the literal meaning of the word "sabbath" is "to stand still" or "to rest"). The Sabbath starts at sunset on Friday and lasts until sunset on Saturday, and in between Orthodox Jews refrain from almost any kind of work, including even tearing toilet paper from a roll in the lavatory. (There has been some discussion of this among the most learned rabbis, who concluded that tearing toilet paper would break the Sabbath taboo; consequently, devout Jews who want to wipe their bottoms on the Sabbath have to prepare a stash of pre-torn toilet paper in advance.)[14]

In Israel, religious Jews often try to force secular Jews and even complete atheists to keep these taboos. Since Orthodox parties usually hold the balance of power in Israeli politics, over the years they have succeeded in passing many laws that banned all kinds of activities on the Sabbath. Though they were unable to outlaw the use of private vehicles on the Sabbath, they have been successful in banning public transportation. This nationwide religious sacrifice affects mainly the weakest sectors of society, especially as Saturday is the only day of the week when working-class people are free to travel and visit distant relatives, friends, and tourist attractions. A rich grandmother has no problem driving to visit her grandchildren in another town, but a poor grandmother who has no car cannot visit her grandchildren, because there are no buses or trains running on the Sabbath.

By inflicting such difficulties on hundreds of thousands of citizens, the religious parties confirm and establish their unwavering faith in Judaism. Though no blood is shed, the well-being of many people is still being sacrificed. If Judaism is just a fictional story, then it is cruel and heartless to prevent a grandmother from visiting her grandchildren or an impoverished student from going to the beach to have some fun. By nevertheless doing so, the religious parties tell the world—and themselves—that they really believe in the Jewish story. What, do you think they enjoy harming people for no good reason whatsoever?

Sacrifice not only strengthens your faith in the story but also often substitutes for all your other obligations toward it. Most of the great stories of humankind have set up ideals that most people cannot fulfill. How many Christians really follow the Ten Commandments to the letter, never lying or coveting? How many Buddhists have reached the stage of egolessness? How many socialists work to the utmost of their ability while taking no more than they really need?

Unable to live up to the ideal, people turn to sacrifice as a solution. A Hindu may engage in tax fraud, visit the occasional prostitute, and mistreat his elderly parents, but he convinces himself that he is a very pious person because he supports the destruction of the Babri Mosque at Ayodhya and has even donated money to build a Hindu temple in its stead. Just as in ancient times, so also in the twenty-first century the human quest for meaning all too often ends with a succession of sacrifices.

THE IDENTITY PORTFOLIO

The ancient Egyptians, Canaanites, and Greeks hedged their bets when it came to sacrifices. They had many gods, and if one failed, they hoped that another would still come through. So they sacrificed to the sun god in the morning, to the earth goddess at noon, and to a mixed lot of fairies and demons in the evening. That too hasn't changed much. All the stories and gods in which people believe today—be they Yahweh, Mammon, the nation, or the revolution—are incomplete, full of holes, and riddled with contradictions. Therefore people rarely put their entire faith in a single story. Instead, they keep a portfolio of several stories and several identities, switching from one to the other as the need arises. Such cognitive dissonances are inherent in almost all societies and movements.

Consider a typical Tea Party supporter who somehow squares ardent faith in Jesus Christ with firm objection to government welfare policies and staunch support for the National Rifle Association. Wasn't Jesus's message focused on helping the poor rather than arming yourself to the teeth? The viewpoints might seem incompatible, but the human brain has a lot of drawers and compartments, and some neurons just don't talk to one another. Similarly, you can find plenty of Bernie Sanders supporters who have a vague belief in some future revolution while also believing in the importance of investing their money wisely. They can easily switch from discussing the unjust distribution of wealth in the world to talking about the performance of their Wall Street portfolios.

Hardly anyone has just one identity. Nobody is just a Muslim, or just an Italian, or just a capitalist. But every now and then a fanatical creed comes along and insists that people should believe in only one story and have only one identity. In recent generations the most fanatical such creed was fascism. Fascism insisted that people should not believe any story except the nationalist story and should have no identity except their national identity.

Not all nationalists are fascists. Most nationalists have great faith in the story of their nation and emphasize its unique merits and the unique obligations they have toward it—but they nevertheless acknowledge that there is more to the world than just their nation. I can be a loyal Italian with special obligations toward the Italian nation and still have other identities. I can also be a socialist, a Catholic, a husband, a father, a scientist, and a vegetarian, and each of these identities entails additional obligations. Sometimes several of my identities pull me in different directions, and some of my obligations come into conflict with one another. But who said life was easy?

Fascism is what happens when nationalism wants to make life too easy for itself, by denying all other identities and obligations. There has been a lot of confusion lately about the exact meaning of fascism. People call almost anyone they don't like a "fascist." The term is in danger of degenerating into an all-purpose term of abuse. So what does it really mean? In brief, while nationalism teaches me that my nation is unique and that I have special obligations toward it, fascism says that my nation is supreme, and that I owe my nation exclusive obligations. I should never prefer the interests of any group or individual over the interests of my nation, no matter what the circumstances are. Even if my nation stands to make but a paltry profit from inflicting much misery on millions of strangers in a far-off land, I should have no qualms about supporting my nation. Otherwise, I am a despicable traitor. If my nation demands that I kill millions of people—I should kill millions. If my nation demands that I betray truth and beauty—I should betray truth and beauty.

How does a fascist evaluate art? How does a fascist know whether a movie is a good movie? Very simple. There is just one yardstick. If the movie serves the national interests—it is a good movie. If the movie does not serve the national interests—it is a bad movie. And how does a fascist decide what to teach kids in school? He uses the same yardstick. Teach the kids whatever serves the interests of the nation; the truth does not matter.[15]

This worship of the nation is extremely attractive, not only because it simplifies many difficult dilemmas, but also because it causes people to think that they belong to the most important and most beautiful thing in the world—their nation. The horrors of the Second World War and the Holocaust indicate the terrible consequences of this line of thinking. Unfortunately, when people talk of the ills of fascism they often do a poor job, because they tend to depict fascism as a hideous monster while failing to explain what is so seductive about it. This is why people today sometimes adopt fascist ideas without realizing it. People think, "I was taught that fascism is ugly, and when I look in the mirror I see something very beautiful, so I cannot be a fascist."

It is a bit like the mistake Hollywood movies make when they depict the bad guys—Voldemort, Lord Sauron, Darth Vader—as ugly and mean. They are usually cruel and nasty even to their most loyal supporters. What I never understand when watching such movies is why anyone would be tempted to follow a disgusting creep like Voldemort?

The problem with evil is that in real life it is not necessarily ugly. It can look very beautiful. Christianity knew this better than Hollywood, which is why traditional Christian art tended to depict Satan as a gorgeous hunk. That is why it is so difficult to resist Satan's temptations. That is also why it is difficult to deal with fascism. When you look in the fascist mirror, what you see there isn't ugly at all. When Germans looked in the fascist mirror in the 1930s, they saw Germany as the most beautiful thing in the world. If today Russians look in the fascist mirror, they will see Russia as the most beautiful thing in the world. And if Israelis look in the fascist mirror, they will see Israel as the most beautiful thing in the world. They will then want to lose themselves inside that beautiful collective.

The word "fascism" comes from the Latin *fascis,* meaning "a bundle of rods." That sounds like a rather unglamorous symbol for one of the most ferocious and deadly ideologies in world history, but it has a deep and sinister meaning. A single rod is very weak, and you can easily snap it in two. However, once you bundle many rods together into a *fascis,* it becomes almost impossible to break them. This implies that the individual is a thing of no consequence, but as long as the collective sticks together, it is very powerful.[16] Fascists therefore believe in privileging the interests of the collective over those of any individual, and demand that no single rod ever dare break the unity of the bundle.

Of course, it is never clear where one human "bundle of rods" ends and another begins. Why should I view Italy as the bundle of rods to which I belong? Why not my family, or the city of Florence, or the province of Tuscany, or the continent of Europe, or the entire human species? The milder forms of nationalism will tell me that I can indeed have obligations toward my family, Florence, Europe, and the whole of humankind as well as having special obligations to Italy. In contrast, Italian fascists demand absolute loyalty to Italy alone.

Despite the best efforts of Mussolini and his Fascist Party, most Italians remained rather lukewarm about putting Italy before their *famiglia*. In Germany the Nazi propaganda machine did a much more thorough job, but even Hitler didn't manage to make people forget all their alternative stories. Even in the darkest days of the Nazi era, people held on to some backup stories in addition to the official one. This became patently clear in 1945. You might have thought that after twelve years of Nazi brainwashing many Germans would be utterly incapable of making sense of their postwar lives. They had put all their faith in one great story; what to do when that story exploded? Yet most Germans recovered with amazing speed. Somewhere in their minds they maintained other stories about the world, and no sooner had Hitler shot a bullet through his brain than people in Berlin, Hamburg, and Munich adopted new identities and found new meaning in their lives.

True, about 20 percent of the Nazi gauleiters—the regional party leaders—committed suicide, as did about 10 percent of the generals.[17] But that means that 80 percent of the gauleiters and 90 percent of the generals were quite happy to continue living. The vast majority of card-carrying Nazis and even rank-and-file SS members neither went insane nor killed themselves. They went on to become productive farmers, teachers, doctors, and insurance agents.

Yet even suicide doesn't prove an absolute commitment to a single story. On November 13, 2015, the Islamic State orchestrated several suicide attacks in Paris that killed 130 people. The extremist group explained that it did so in order to take revenge for the French air force's bombing of Islamic State activists in Syria and Iraq, and in the hope that France would be deterred from carrying out such bombardments in the future.[18] In the same breath, the Islamic State also declared that all the Muslims killed by the French air force were martyrs who now enjoyed eternal bliss in heaven.

Something here doesn't make sense. If the martyrs killed by the French air force are indeed now in heaven, why should anyone seek revenge for their deaths? Revenge for what, exactly? For sending people to heaven? If you've just learned that your beloved brother won a million dollars in the lottery, would you start blowing up lottery outlets in revenge? So why go rampaging in Paris just because the French air force gave a few of your brothers a one-way ticket to paradise? It would be even worse if you did manage to deter the French from carrying out further bombings in Syria, for in that case fewer Muslims would get to heaven.

We might be tempted to conclude that Islamic State activists don't really believe that martyrs go to heaven. That's why they are angry when they are bombed and killed. But if so, why do some of them strap on explosive belts and willingly blow themselves to smithereens? In all likelihood, the answer is that they hold on to two contradictory stories without thinking too much about the inconsistencies. As noted earlier, some neurons are just not on speaking terms with one another.

Eight centuries before the French air force bombed Islamic State strongholds in Syria and Iraq, another French army invaded the Middle East, in what is known to posterity as the Seventh Crusade. Led by the saintly King Louis IX, the Crusaders hoped to conquer the Nile Valley and turn Egypt into a Christian bulwark. However, they were defeated at the Battle of Mansoura and most of the Crusaders were taken captive. A Crusader knight, Jean de Joinville, later wrote in his memoirs that when the battle was lost and they decided to surrender, one of his men said, "I cannot agree with this decision. What I advise is that we should all let ourselves be slain, for thus we shall go to paradise." Joinville comments dryly that "none of us heeded his advice."[19]

Joinville does not explain why they refused. After all, these were men who had left their comfortable chateaux in France for a long and perilous adventure in the Middle East largely because they believed in the promise of eternal salvation. Why, then, when they were but a moment away from the everlasting bliss of paradise, did they prefer Muslim captivity instead? Apparently, though the Crusaders fervently believed in salvation and paradise, at the moment of truth they opted to hedge their bets.

THE SUPERMARKET AT ELSINORE

Throughout history almost all humans believed in several stories at the same time and were never absolutely convinced of the truth of any one of them. This uncertainty rattled most religions, which therefore considered faith to be a cardinal virtue and doubt to be among the worst sins possible—as if there were something intrinsically good about believing things without evidence. With the rise of modern culture, however, the tables were turned. Faith began to look increasingly like mental slavery, while doubt came to be seen as a precondition for freedom.

Sometime between 1599 and 1602, William Shakespeare wrote his version of *The Lion King*, better known as *Hamlet*. Yet unlike Simba, Hamlet doesn't complete the Circle of Life. He remains skeptical and ambivalent to the very end, never discovering what life is all about and never making up his mind whether it is better to be or not to be. In this, Hamlet is the paradigmatic modern hero. Modernity didn't reject the plethora of stories it inherited from the past. Instead, it opened a supermarket for them. The modern human is free to sample them all, choosing and combining whatever fits his or her taste.

Some people cannot stand so much freedom and uncertainty. Modern totalitarian movements such as fascism reacted violently to the supermarket of doubtful ideas and outdid even traditional religions in demanding absolute faith in a single story. Most modern people, however, took a liking to the supermarket. What do you do when you don't know what life is all about and which story to believe? You sanctify the very ability to choose. You stand in the supermarket aisle, with the power and freedom to choose whatever you like, examining the products laid out before you, and . . . Freeze that frame, cut, the end. Run the credits.

According to liberal mythology, if you spend a long enough time in that big supermarket, sooner or later you will experience the liberal epiphany and realize the true meaning of life: all the stories on the supermarket shelves are fakes. The meaning of life isn't a ready-made product. There is no divine script, and nothing outside me can give meaning to my life. It is I who imbue everything with meaning through my free choices and through my own feelings.

In the fantasy film *Willow*—a run-of-the-mill George Lucas fairy tale—the eponymous hero is an ordinary dwarf who dreams of becoming a great sorcerer and mastering the secrets of existence. One day such a sorcerer passes through the dwarf village in search of an apprentice. Willow and two other hopeful dwarves present themselves, and the sorcerer gives the aspirants a simple test. He extends his right hand, spreads his fingers, and asks in a Yoda-like voice: "The power to control the world is in which finger?" Each of the three dwarves picks a finger—but they all pick the wrong one. Nevertheless, the sorcerer notices something about Willow and later asks him, "When I held up my fingers, what was your first impulse?" Says Willow in embarrassment, "Well, it was stupid—to pick my own finger." "Aha!" the sorcerer exclaims in triumph. "That was the correct answer! You lack faith in yourself." Liberal mythology never tires of repeating this lesson.

It is our own human fingers that wrote the Bible, the Quran, and the Vedas, and it is our minds that give these stories power. They are no doubt beautiful stories, but their beauty is strictly in the eyes of the beholder. Jerusalem, Mecca, Varanasi, and Bodh Gaya are sacred places, but only because of the feelings humans experience when they go there. In itself, the universe is only a meaningless hodge-podge of atoms. Nothing is inherently beautiful, sacred, or sexy; human feelings make it so. It is only human feelings that make a red apple seductive and a piece of turd disgusting. Take away human feelings, and you are left with a bunch of molecules.

We hope to find meaning by fitting ourselves into some ready-made story about the universe, but according to the liberal interpretation of the world, the truth is exactly the opposite. The universe does not give me meaning. *I* give meaning to the universe. This is my cosmic vocation. I have no fixed destiny or dharma. If I find myself in Simba's or Arjuna's shoes, I can choose to fight for the crown of a kingdom, but I don't have to. I can just as well join a wandering circus, go to Broadway to sing in a musical, or move to Silicon Valley to launch a start-up. I am free to create my own dharma.

Like all cosmic stories, the liberal story too starts with a creation narrative. It says that the creation occurs every moment, and that I am the creator. What then is the aim of my life? To create meaning by feeling, by thinking, by desiring, and by inventing. Anything that limits the human liberty to feel, think, desire, and invent limits the meaning of the universe. Therefore liberty from such limitations is the supreme ideal.

In practical terms, those who believe in the liberal story live by the light of two commandments: create, and fight for liberty. Creativity can manifest itself in writing a poem, exploring your sexuality, inventing a new app, or discovering a previously unknown chemical. Fighting for liberty includes anything that frees people from social, biological, or physical constraints, be it demonstrating against brutal dictators, teaching girls to read, finding a cure for cancer, or building a spaceship. The liberal pantheon of heroes houses Rosa Parks and Pablo Picasso alongside Louis Pasteur and the Wright brothers.

This sounds extremely exciting and profound in theory. Unfortunately, human freedom and human creativity are not what the liberal story imagines them to be. To the best of our scientific understanding, there is no magic behind our choices and creations. They are the product of billions of neurons exchanging biochemical signals, and even if you liberate humans from the yoke of the Catholic Church and the Soviet Union, their choices will still be dictated by biochemical algorithms as ruthless as the Inquisition and the KGB.

The liberal story instructs me to seek freedom to express and realize myself. But both the "self" and freedom are mythological chimeras borrowed from the fairy tales of ancient times. Liberalism has a particularly confused notion of "free will." Humans obviously have a will, they have desires, and they are sometimes free to fulfill their desires. If by "free will" you mean the freedom to do what you desire, then yes, humans have free will. But if by "free will" you mean the freedom to choose what to desire, then no, humans have no free will.

If I am sexually attracted to men, I may be free to realize my fantasies, but I am not free to feel an attraction to women instead. In some cases I might decide to restrain my sexual urges or even try "sexual conversion therapy," but the very desire to change my sexual orientation is something forced upon me by my neurons, egged on perhaps by cultural and religious biases. Why does one person feel ashamed of his sexuality and strive to alter it, while another person celebrates the same sexual desires without a trace of guilt? You can say that the former might have stronger religious feelings than the latter. But do people freely choose whether to have strong or weak religious feelings? Again, a person might decide to go to church every Sunday in a conscious effort to strengthen his weak religious feelings—but why does one person aspire to be more religious, while another is perfectly happy to remain an atheist? This may result from any number of cultural and genetic dispositions, but it is never the result of "free will."

What's true of sexual desire is true of all desire, and indeed of all feelings and thoughts. Just consider the next thought that pops into your mind. Where did it come from? Did you freely choose to think it, and only then did you think it? Certainly not. The process of self-exploration begins with simple things, and becomes progressively harder. At first, we realize that we do not control the world outside us. I don't decide when it rains. Then we realize that we do not control what's happening inside our own body. I don't control my blood pressure. Next, we understand that we don't even govern our brain. I don't tell the neurons when to fire. That's more difficult. Ultimately we should realize that we do not control our desires, or even our reactions to these desires.

Realizing this can help us become less obsessive about our opinions, about our feelings, and about our desires. We don't have free will, but we can be a bit more free from the tyranny of our will. Humans usually place so much importance on their desires that they try to control and shape the entire world according to these desires. In pursuit of their cravings, humans fly to the moon, wage world wars, and destabilize the entire ecosystem. If we understand that our desires are not the magical manifestations of free choice but are rather the product of biochemical processes (influenced by cultural factors that are also beyond our control), we might be less preoccupied with them. It is better to understand ourselves, our minds, and our desires than to try to realize whatever fantasy pops into our heads.

And in order to understand ourselves, a crucial step is to acknowledge that the "self" is a fictional story that the intricate mechanisms of our mind constantly manufacture, update, and rewrite. There is a storyteller in my mind that explains who I am, where I come from, where I am heading, and what is happening to me right now. Like the government spin doctors who explain the latest political upheavals, my inner narrator repeatedly gets things wrong but rarely, if ever, admits it. And just as the government builds a national myth with flags, icons, and parades, so my inner propaganda machine creates a personal myth with prized memories and cherished traumas that often bear little resemblance to the truth.

In the age of Facebook and Instagram you can observe this myth-making process more clearly than ever before, because some of it has been outsourced from the mind to the computer. It is fascinating and terrifying to behold people spending countless hours constructing and embellishing a perfect self online, becoming attached to their own creation, and mistaking it for the truth about themselves.[20] That's how a family holiday fraught with traffic jams, petty squabbles, and tense silences becomes a collection of beautiful panoramas, perfect dinners, and smiling faces; 99 percent of what we experience never becomes part of the story of the self.

It is particularly noteworthy that our fantasy self tends to be very visual, whereas our actual experiences are corporeal. In the fantasy, you observe a scene in your mind's eye or on the computer screen. You see yourself standing on a tropical beach, the blue sea behind you, a big smile on your face, one hand holding a cocktail, the other arm around your lover's waist. Paradise. What the picture does not show is the annoying fly that bites your leg, the cramping in your stomach from eating fish that had gone slightly off, the tension in your jaw as you fake a big smile, and the ugly fight the happy couple had five minutes ago. If we could only feel what the people in the photos felt while taking them!

If you really want to understand yourself, you should not identify with your Facebook account or with the inner story of the self. Instead, you should observe the actual flow of body and mind. You will see thoughts, emotions, and desires appear and disappear without much reason and without any command from you, just as different winds blow from this or that direction and mess up your hair. And just as you are not the winds, so also you are not the jumble of thoughts, emotions, and desires you experience, and you are certainly not the sanitized story you tell about them with hindsight. You experience all of them, but you don't control them, you don't own them, and you are not them. People ask "Who am I?" and expect to be told a story. The first thing you need to know about yourself is that you are not a story.

NO STORY

Liberalism took a radical step in denying all cosmic dramas, but then it recreated the drama within the human being: the universe has no plot, so it is up to us humans to create a plot, and this is our vocation and the meaning of our life. Thousands of years before our liberal age, ancient Buddhism went further by denying not just all cosmic dramas but even the inner drama of human creation. The universe has no meaning, it claimed, and human feelings too carry no meaning. They are just ephemeral vibrations, appearing and disappearing for no particular purpose. That's the truth. Get over it.

As noted earlier, the Brihadaranyaka Upanishad tells us, "The head of the sacrificial horse is the dawn, its eye the sun . . . its members the seasons, its joints the months and fortnights, its feet the days and nights, its bones the stars and its flesh the clouds." In contrast, the Mahasatipatthana Sutta, a key Buddhist text, explains that when a human meditates, he or she observes the body carefully, noting, "In this body, there are hairs of the head, hairs of the skin, nails, teeth, skin, flesh, sinews, bones, marrow, kidney, heart . . . saliva, nasal mucus, synovial fluid and urine. Thus he dwells, observing body . . . Now his understanding is established: 'This is body!' "[21] The hairs, bones, or urine stand for nothing else. They are just what they are.

In passage after passage the text goes on to explain that no matter what the mediator observes in the body or in the mind, he or she just understands it as it is. When the mediator breathes, "breathing in a deep breath, he understands properly 'I am breathing in a deep breath.' Breathing in a shallow breath, he understands properly 'I am breathing in a shallow breath.' "[22] The long breath does not represent the seasons and the short breath does not represent the days. They are just vibrations in the body.

The Buddha taught that the three basic realities of the universe are that everything is constantly changing, nothing has any enduring essence, and nothing is completely satisfying. You can explore the furthest reaches of the galaxy, of your body, or of your mind, but you will never encounter something that does not change, that has an eternal essence, and that completely satisfies you.

Suffering emerges because people fail to appreciate this. They believe that there is some eternal essence somewhere, and if only they can find it and connect to it, they will be completely satisfied. This eternal essence is sometimes called God, sometimes the nation, sometimes the soul, sometimes the authentic self, and sometimes true love—and the more people are attached to it, the more disappointed and miserable they become when they fail to find it. Worse yet, the greater the attachment, the greater the hatred such people develop toward any person, group, or institution that seems to stand between them and their cherished goal.

According to the Buddha, then, life has no meaning, and people don't need to create any meaning. They just need to realize that there is no meaning, and therefore be liberated from the suffering caused by our attachments and our identification with empty phenomena. "What should I do?" ask people, and the Buddha advises: "Do nothing. Absolutely nothing." The whole problem is that we constantly do something. Not necessarily on the physical level—we can sit immobile for hours with closed eyes—yet on the mental level we are extremely busy creating stories and identities, fighting battles, and winning victories. To really do nothing means that the mind also does nothing and creates nothing.

Unfortunately, this too very easily turns into a heroic epic. Even as you sit with closed eyes and observe the breath coming in and out of the nostrils, you might well start constructing stories about it: "My breath is a bit forced, and if I breathe more calmly, I will become healthier," or "If I just keep observing my breath and do nothing, I will become enlightened, and be the wisest and happiest person in the world." Then the epic starts expanding, and people embark on a quest not just to liberate themselves from their own attachments but also to convince others to do so. Having accepted that life has no meaning, I find meaning in explaining this truth to others, arguing with the unbelievers, giving lectures to the skeptics, donating money to build monasteries, and so on. "No story" can all too easily become just another story.

The history of Buddhism provides a thousand examples of how people who believe in the transience and emptiness of all phenomena and in the importance of having no attachments can squabble and fight over the government of a country, the possession of a building, or even the meaning of a word. Fighting other people because you believe in the glory of an eternal God is unfortunate but understandable; fighting other people because you believe in the emptiness of all phenomena is truly bizarre—but so very human.

In the eighteenth century, the royal dynasties of both Burma and neighboring Siam prided themselves on their devotion to the Buddha, and gained legitimacy by protecting the Buddhist faith. The kings endowed monasteries, built pagodas, and listened every week to learned monks who preached eloquent sermons on the five basic moral commitments of every human being: to abstain from killing, stealing, sexual abuse, deception, and intoxication. The two kingdoms nevertheless fought each other relentlessly. On April 7, 1767, the army of the Burmese king Hsinbyushin stormed the capital of Siam after a long siege. The victorious troops killed, looted, raped, and probably also got intoxicated here and there. They then burned down much of the city, with its palaces, monasteries, and pagodas, and carried home thousands of slaves and cartloads of gold and jewels.

King Hsinbyushin did not take his Buddhism lightly. Seven years after his great victory, the king made a royal progression down the great Irrawaddy River, worshipping at the important pagodas on the way, and asking Buddha to bless his armies with more victories. When Hsinbyushin reached Rangoon, he rebuilt and expanded the most sacred structure in all of Burma: the Shwedagon Pagoda. He then gilded the enlarged edifice with his own weight in gold, erected a gold spire on top of the pagoda, and studded it with precious gems (perhaps looted from Siam). He also used the occasion to execute the captive king of Pegu, his brother, and his son.[23]

In 1930s Japan, people even found imaginative ways to combine Buddhist doctrines with nationalism, militarism, and fascism. Radical Buddhist thinkers such as Nissho Inoue, Ikki Kita, and Tanaka Chigaku argued that in order to dissolve one's egoistic attachments, people should completely give themselves up to the emperor, excise all personal thinking, and observe total loyalty to the nation. Various ultranationalist organizations were inspired by such ideas, including a fanatical military group that sought to overthrow Japan's conservative political system by a campaign of assassination. They murdered the former finance minister, the director general of the Mitsui corporation, and eventually the prime minister, Inukai Tsuyoshi. They thereby speeded up the transformation of Japan into a military dictatorship. When the military then embarked on war, Buddhist priests and Zen meditation masters preached selfless obedience to state authority and recommended self-sacrifice for the war effort. In contrast, Buddhist teachings on compassion and nonviolence were somehow forgotten and had no perceptible influence on the behavior of Japanese troops in Nanjing, Manila, or Seoul.[24]

Today, the human rights record of Buddhist Myanmar is among the worst in the world, and a Buddhist monk, Ashin Wirathu, leads the anti-Muslim movement in the country. He claims that he only wants to protect Myanmar and Buddhism against Muslim jihadi conspiracies, but his sermons and articles are so inflammatory that in February 2018 Facebook removed his page, citing the company's prohibition on hate speech. During a 2017 interview with the *Guardian* the monk preached compassion for a passing mosquito, but when confronted with allegations that Muslim women have been raped by the Myanmar military he laughed and said, "Impossible. Their bodies are too disgusting."[25]

There is very little chance that world peace and global harmony will arrive once seven billion human beings start meditating regularly. Observing the truth about yourself is just so difficult! Even if you somehow manage to get most humans to try it, many of us will quickly distort the truth we encounter into some story with heroes, villains, and enemies, and in that story find really good excuses to go to war.

THE TEST OF REALITY

Even though all these big stories are fictions generated by our own minds, there is no reason for despair. Reality still exists. You cannot play a part in any make-believe drama, but why would you want to do that in the first place? The big question facing humans isn't "what is the meaning of life?" but rather "how do we stop suffering?" When you give up all the fictional stories, you can observe reality with far greater clarity than before, and if you really know the truth about yourself and about the world, nothing can make you miserable. But that is of course much easier said than done.

We humans have conquered the world thanks to our ability to create and believe fictional stories. We are therefore particularly bad at knowing the difference between fiction and reality. Overlooking this difference has been a matter of survival for us. If you nevertheless want to know the difference, the place to start is with suffering. Because as noted earlier, the realest thing in the world is suffering.

When you are confronted by some great story and you wish to know whether it is real or imaginary, one of the key questions to ask is whether the central hero of the story can suffer. For example, if somebody tells you the story of the Polish nation, take a moment to reflect on whether Poland can suffer. Adam Mickiewicz, the great Romantic poet and the father of modern Polish nationalism, famously called Poland "the Christ of nations." Writing in 1832, decades after Poland was partitioned between Russia, Prussia, and Austria and shortly after the Polish uprising of 1830 was brutally crushed by the Russians, Mickiewicz explained that the horrendous suffering of Poland was a sacrifice on behalf of the whole of humanity, comparable to the sacrifice of Christ, and that just like Christ, Poland would rise from the dead.

In a famous passage Mickiewicz wrote:

Poland said [to the people of Europe], "Whosoever will come to me shall be free and equal for I am FREEDOM." But the kings, when they heard it, were frightened in their hearts, and they crucified the Polish nation and laid it in its grave, crying out "We have slain and buried Freedom." But they cried out foolishly . . . For the Polish Nation did not die . . . On the Third Day, the Soul shall return to the Body; and the Nation shall arise and free all the peoples of Europe from Slavery.[26]

Can a nation really suffer? Has a nation eyes, hands, senses, affections, and passions? If you prick it, can it bleed? Obviously not. If it is defeated in war, loses a province, or even forfeits its independence, it still cannot experience pain, sadness, or any other kind of misery, for it has no body, no mind, and no feelings whatsoever. In truth, it is just a metaphor. Only in the imagination of certain humans is Poland a real entity capable of suffering. Poland endures because these humans lend it their bodies—not just by serving as soldiers in the Polish army but by incarnating in flesh the joys and sorrows of the nation. When in May 1831 news reached Warsaw of the Polish defeat at the Battle of Ostrołęka, human stomachs twisted in distress, human chests heaved with pain, human eyes filled with tears.

All that does not justify the Russian invasion, of course, nor does it undermine the right of Poles to establish an independent country and decide on their own laws and customs. Yet it does mean that, ultimately, reality cannot be the story of the Polish nation, for the very existence of Poland depends on images in human minds.

In contrast, consider the fate of a Warsaw woman who was robbed and raped by the invading Russian troops. Unlike the metaphorical suffering of the Polish nation, the suffering of that woman was very real. It may well have been caused by human beliefs in various fictions, such as Russian nationalism, Orthodox Christianity, and macho heroism, all of which inspired many of the Russian statesmen and soldiers. However, the resulting suffering was still 100 percent real.

Whenever politicians start talking in mystical terms, beware. They might be trying to disguise and excuse real suffering by wrapping it up in big, incomprehensible words. Be particularly careful about the following four words: "sacrifice," "eternity," "purity," "redemption." If you hear any of these four, sound the alarm. And if you happen to live in a country whose leader routinely says things like "Their sacrifice will redeem the purity of our eternal nation," know that you are in deep trouble. To preserve your sanity, always try to translate such hogwash into real terms: a soldier crying out in agony, a woman beaten and brutalized, a child shaking in fear.

So if you want to know the truth about the universe, about the meaning of life, and about your own identity, the best place to start is by observing suffering and exploring what it is.

The answer isn't a story.

21

....

Meditation

Just Observe

Now that I have criticized so many stories, religions, and ideologies, it is only fair that I put myself in the firing line too, and explain how somebody so skeptical can still manage to wake up cheerful in the morning. I hesitate to do so, partly for fear of self-indulgence and partly because I don't want to give the wrong impression that what works for me will work for everybody. I am very aware that the quirks of my genes, neurons, personal history, and dharma are not shared by everyone. But readers should probably know which hues color the glasses through which I see the world, thereby distorting my vision and my writing.

As a teenager I was restless and troubled. The world made no sense to me, and I got no answers to the big questions I had about life. In particular, I didn't understand why there was so much suffering in the world and in my own life, and what could be done about it. All I got from the people around me and from the books I read were elaborate fictions: religious myths about gods and heavens, nationalist myths about the motherland and its historical mission, romantic myths about love and adventure, or capitalist myths about economic growth and how buying and consuming stuff would make me happy. I had enough sense to realize that these were probably all fictions, but I had no idea how to find truth.

When I began studying at university, I thought it would be the ideal place to find answers. But I was disappointed. The academic world provided me with powerful tools with which to deconstruct all the myths humans ever created, but it didn't offer satisfying answers to the big questions of life. On the contrary, it encouraged me to focus on narrower and narrower questions. I eventually found myself writing a doctorate at the University of Oxford about the autobiographical texts of medieval soldiers. As a side hobby I read a lot of books about philosophy and had lots of philosophical debates, but though this provided endless intellectual entertainment, it hardly provided real insight. I felt extremely frustrated.

Eventually my good friend Ron suggested that I try putting aside all the books and intellectual discussions for a few days and take a Vipassana meditation course. ("Vipassana" means "introspection" in the Pali language of ancient India.) I thought it was some New Age mumbo-jumbo, and since I had no interest in hearing yet another mythology, I declined to go. But after a year of patient nudging, in April 2000 he convinced me to go to a ten-day Vipassana retreat.[1]

Before this I knew very little about meditation and presumed it involved all kinds of complicated mystical theories. I was therefore amazed by how practical the teaching turned out to be. The teacher at the course, S. N. Goenka, instructed the students to sit with crossed legs and closed eyes, and to focus all their attention on the breath coming in and out of their nostrils. "Don't do anything," he kept saying. "Don't try to control the breath or to breathe in any particular way. Just observe the reality of the present moment, whatever it may be. When the breath comes in, you are just aware— now the breath is coming in. When the breath goes out, you are just aware—now the breath is going out. And when you lose your focus and your mind starts wandering in memories and fantasies, just re-

main aware—now my mind has wandered away from the breath."
It was the most important thing anybody had ever told me.

When people ask the big questions of life, they usually have absolutely no interest in knowing when their breath is coming into their nostrils and when it is going out. Rather, they want to know things like what happens after you die. Yet the real enigma of life is not what happens after you die but what happens before you die. If you want to understand death, you need to understand life.

People ask, "When I die, will I just vanish completely? Will I go to heaven? Will I be reborn in a new body?" These questions are based on the assumption that there is an "I" that endures from birth to death, and the question is "What will happen to this 'I' at death?" But what is there that endures from birth to death? The body keeps changing every moment, the brain keeps changing every moment, the mind keeps changing every moment. The more closely you observe yourself, the more obvious it becomes that nothing endures even from one moment to the next. So what holds together an entire life? If you don't know the answer to that question, you don't understand life, and you certainly have no chance of understanding death. If and when you ever discover what holds life together, the answer to the big question of death will also become apparent.

People say, "The soul endures from birth to death and thereby holds life together"—but that is just a story. Have you ever observed a soul? You can explore this at any moment, not just at the moment of death. If you can understand what happens to you as one moment ends and another moment begins, you will also understand what will happen to you at the moment of death. If you can really observe yourself for the duration of a single breath, you will understand it all.

The first thing I learned by observing my breath was that notwithstanding all the books I had read and all the classes I had attended at university, I knew almost nothing about my mind, and I had very little control over it. Despite my best efforts, I couldn't observe the reality of my breath coming in and out of my nostrils for more than ten seconds before my mind wandered away. For years I had lived under the impression that I was the master of my life, the CEO of my own personal brand. But a few hours of meditation were enough to show me that I had hardly any control over myself. I was not the CEO; I was barely the gatekeeper. I was asked to stand at the gateway of my body—the nostrils—and just observe whatever comes in or goes out, yet after a few moments I lost my focus and abandoned my post. It was an eye-opening experience.

As the course progressed, students were taught to observe not just their breath but sensations throughout their body. Not special sensations of bliss and ecstasy, but rather the most mundane and ordinary sensations: heat, pressure, pain, and so on. The technique of Vipassana is based on the insight that the flow of mind is closely interlinked with sensations of the body. Between me and the world there are always bodily sensations. I never react to events in the outside world; I always react to the sensations in my own body. When the sensation is unpleasant, I react with aversion. When the sensation is pleasant, I react with a craving for more. Even when we think we react to what another person has done, to President Trump's latest tweet, or to a distant childhood memory, the truth is that we always react to our immediate bodily sensations. If we are outraged that somebody insulted our nation or our god, what makes the insult unbearable is the burning sensation in the pit of our stomach and the band of pain that grips our heart. Our nation feels nothing, but our body really hurts.

You want to know what anger is? Well, just observe the sensations that arise and pass through your body while you are angry. I was twenty-four years old when I went to this retreat, and had experienced anger probably ten thousand times, yet I had never bothered to observe how anger actually feels. Whenever I had been angry, I had focused on the object of my anger—something somebody did or said—rather than on the sensory reality of the anger.

I think I learned more about myself and about humans in general by observing my sensations for those ten days than I had learned in my whole life up to that point. And to do so I didn't have to accept any story, theory, or mythology. I just had to observe reality as it is. The most important thing I realized was that the deepest source of my suffering is in the patterns of my own mind. When I want something and it doesn't happen, my mind reacts by generating suffering. Suffering is not an objective condition in the outside world. It is a mental reaction generated by my own mind. Learning this is the first step toward ceasing to generate more suffering.

Since that first course in 2000, I began meditating for two hours every day, and each year I take a long meditation retreat of a month or two. It is not an escape from reality. It is getting in touch with reality. For at least two hours a day I actually observe reality as it is, while for the other twenty-two hours I get overwhelmed by emails and tweets and cute-puppy videos. Without the focus and clarity provided by this practice, I could not have written *Sapiens* or *Homo Deus*. At least for me, meditation never came into conflict with scientific research. Rather, it has been another valuable tool in the scientific tool kit, especially when trying to understand the human mind.

DIGGING FROM BOTH ENDS

Science finds it hard to decipher the mysteries of the mind largely because we lack efficient tools. Many people, including many scientists, tend to confuse the mind with the brain, but they are really very different things. The brain is a material network of neurons, synapses, and biochemicals. The mind is a flow of subjective experiences, such as pain, pleasure, anger, and love. Biologists assume that the brain somehow produces the mind and that biochemical reactions in billions of neurons somehow produce experiences such as pain and love. However, so far we have absolutely no explanation for how the mind emerges from the brain. Why is it that when billions of neurons are firing electrical signals in a particular pattern, I feel pain, and when the neurons fire in a different pattern, I feel love? We haven't got a clue. Therefore, even if the mind indeed emerges from the brain, studying the mind is a different undertaking from studying the brain, at least for now.

Brain research is progressing in leaps and bounds thanks to the help of microscopes, brain scanners, and powerful computers. But we cannot see the mind in a microscope or brain scanner. These devices enable us to detect biochemical and electrical activities in the brain, but they do not give us any access to the subjective experiences associated with these activities. As of 2018, the only mind I can access directly is my own. If I want to know what other sentient beings are experiencing, I can do so only on the basis of secondhand accounts, which naturally suffer from numerous distortions and limitations.

We could no doubt collect many secondhand accounts and use statistics to identify recurring patterns. Such methods have enabled psychologists and brain scientists not only to gain a much better understanding of the mind but also to improve and even save the lives of millions. However, it is hard to go beyond a certain point using only secondhand reports. In science, when you investigate a particular phenomenon, it is best to observe it directly. Anthropologists, for example, make extensive use of secondary sources, but if you really want to understand Samoan culture, sooner or later you will have to pack your bags and visit Samoa.

Of course, merely visiting isn't enough. A blog written by a backpacker traveling through Samoa would not be considered a scientific anthropological study, because most backpackers lack the necessary tools and training. Their observations are too random and biased. To become trustworthy anthropologists, we must learn how to observe human cultures in a methodical and objective manner, free from preconceptions and prejudices. That's what you study in the department of anthropology, and that's what enables anthropologists to play such a vital role in bridging gaps between different cultures.

The scientific study of mind seldom follows this anthropological model. Whereas anthropologists often report their visits to distant islands and mysterious countries, scholars of consciousness rarely undertake such personal journeys to the realms of the mind. For the only mind I can directly observe is my own, and no matter how difficult it is to observe Samoan culture without bias and prejudice, it is even harder to observe my own mind objectively. After more than a century of hard work, anthropologists today have at their disposal powerful procedures for objective observation. In contrast, whereas mind scholars have developed many tools for collecting and analyzing secondhand accounts, when it comes to observing our own minds we have barely scratched the surface.

In the absence of modern methods for direct mind observation, we might try out some of the tools developed by premodern cultures. Several ancient cultures devoted a lot of attention to the study of the mind, and they relied not on collecting secondhand accounts but on training people to observe their own minds systematically. The methods they developed are bunched together under the generic term "meditation." Today this term is often associated with religion and mysticism, but in principle meditation is any method for the direct observation of one's own mind. Though many religions have made extensive use of various meditation techniques, this doesn't mean meditation is necessarily religious. Many religions have also made extensive use of books, yet that doesn't mean reading books is a religious practice.

Over the millennia humans have developed hundreds of meditation techniques, which differ in their principles and effectiveness. I have had personal experience with only one technique, Vipassana, so it is the only one about which I can talk with any authority. Like a number of other meditation techniques, Vipassana is said to have been discovered in ancient India by the Buddha. Over the centuries numerous theories and stories have been ascribed to the Buddha, often without any supporting evidence. But you need not believe any of them in order to meditate. The teacher from whom I learned

Vipassana, Goenka, was a very practical kind of guide. He repeatedly instructed students that when they observe the mind they must put aside all secondhand descriptions, religious dogmas, and philosophical conjectures, focusing instead on their own experience and on whatever reality they actually encounter. Every day numerous students would come to his room to seek guidance and ask questions. At the entrance to the room a sign said: "Please avoid theoretical and philosophical discussions, and focus your questions on matters related to your actual practice."

The actual practice is to observe body sensations and mental reactions to sensations in a methodical, continuous, and objective manner, thereby uncovering the basic patterns of the mind. People sometimes turn meditation into a pursuit of special experiences of bliss and ecstasy. Yet in truth, consciousness is the greatest mystery in the universe, and mundane feelings of heat and itching are every bit as mysterious as feelings of rapture or cosmic oneness. Vipassana meditators are cautioned never to embark on a search for special experiences; instead they are encouraged to concentrate on understanding the reality of their mind, whatever this reality might be.

In recent years scholars of both mind and brain have shown increasing interest in such meditation techniques, but most researchers have so far used this tool only indirectly.[2] The typical scientist doesn't actually practice meditation herself. Rather, she invites experienced meditators to her laboratory, covers their heads with electrodes, asks them to meditate, and observes the resulting brain activity. That can teach us many interesting things about the brain, but if the aim is to understand the mind, we are missing some of the most important insights. It's like someone who is trying to understand the structure of matter by observing a stone through a magnifying glass. You hand this person a microscope and say: "Try this. You will see much better." He takes the microscope, picks up his trusted magnifying glass, and carefully observes through the magnifying glass the matter from which the microscope is made. The point is that meditation is a tool for observing the mind directly. You miss most of its potential if, instead of meditating yourself, you monitor electrical activities in the brain of some other meditator.

I am certainly not suggesting abandoning the present tools and practices of brain research. Meditation doesn't replace them, but it might complement them. It's a bit like when engineers excavate a tunnel through a huge mountain. Why dig from only one side? Better to dig simultaneously from both. If the brain and the mind are indeed one and the same, the two tunnels are bound to meet. And if the brain and the mind aren't the same? Then it is all the more important to dig into the mind and not just into the brain.

Some universities and laboratories have indeed begun using meditation as a research tool rather than as a mere object for brain studies. Yet this process is still in its infancy, partly because it requires an extraordinary investment on the part of the researchers. Serious meditation demands a tremendous amount of discipline. If you try to objectively observe your sensations, the first thing you'll notice is how wild and impatient the mind is, and how difficult it is to focus it even on a relatively distinct sensation such as breath.

When a microscope goes out of focus, we just need to turn a small handle. If the handle is broken, we can call a technician to repair it. But when the mind loses focus we cannot repair it so easily. It usually takes a lot of training to calm the mind and make it concentrate so it can start observing itself methodically and objectively. Perhaps in the future we will be able to pop a pill to achieve instant focus. Yet since meditation aims to explore the mind rather than just focus it, such a shortcut might prove counterproductive. The pill might make us very alert and focused, but at the same time it might also prevent us from exploring the entire spectrum of the mind. After all, we can easily focus the mind today by watching a good thriller on TV—but the mind is so concentrated on the movie that it cannot observe its own dynamics.

Yet even if we cannot rely on such technological gadgets, we shouldn't give up. We can be inspired by anthropologists, zoologists, and astronauts. Anthropologists and zoologists spend years on faraway islands, exposed to a plethora of ailments and dangers. Astronauts devote many years to difficult training regimes, preparing for their hazardous excursions to outer space. If we are willing to make such efforts in order to understand foreign cultures, unknown species, and distant planets, it might be worth working just as hard in order to understand our own minds. And we had better understand our minds before the algorithms make our minds up for us.

Self-observation has never been easy, but it might get harder with time. As history unfolded, humans created more and more complex stories about themselves, which made it increasingly difficult to know who we really are. These stories were intended to unite large numbers of people, accumulate power, and preserve social harmony. They were vital for feeding billions of hungry people and making sure those people didn't cut each other's throats. When people tried to observe themselves, what they usually discovered were these ready-made stories. An open-ended exploration was too dangerous. It threatened to undermine the social order.

As technology improved, two things happened. First, as flint knives gradually evolved into nuclear missiles, destabilizing the social order became more dangerous. Second, as cave paintings gradually evolved into television broadcasts, it became easier to delude people. In the near future, algorithms might bring this process to completion, making it well-nigh impossible for people to observe the reality about themselves. It will be the algorithms that will decide for us who we are and what we should know about ourselves.

For a few more years or decades, we still have a choice. If we make the effort, we can still investigate who we really are. But if we want to make use of this opportunity, we had better do it now.

ACKNOWLEDGMENTS

I would like to thank all those who helped me to write—and also to delete.

To Michal Shavit, my publisher at Penguin Random House in the UK, who first came up with the idea for this book, and who guided me through the long process of writing; and also to the entire Penguin Random House team, for all their hard work and support.

To David Milner, who as usual did a terrific job editing the manuscript. Sometimes I just needed to think what David might say, to work extra hard on the text.

To Suzanne Dean, my creative director at Penguin Random House, who is the genius behind the book jacket.

To Preena Gadher and her colleagues at Riot Communications, for orchestrating a brilliant PR campaign.

To Cindy Spiegel from Spiegel & Grau, for her feedback and for taking care of things across the Atlantic.

To all my other publishers in all the world's continents (except Antarctica), for their trust, dedication, and professional work.

To my research assistant, Idan Sherer, for checking up on everything from ancient synagogues to artificial intelligence.

To Shmuel Rosner, for his continual support and good advice.

To Yigal Borochovsky and Sarai Aharoni, who read the manuscript and devoted much time and effort to correcting my mistakes and enabling me to see things from new perspectives.

To Danny Orbach, Uri Sabach, Yoram Yovell, and Ron Merom, for their insights on kamikaze, surveillance, psychology, and algorithms.

To my devoted team—Ido Ayal, Maya Orbach, Naama Wartenburg, and Eilona Ariel—who have spent many days in email hell on my account.

To all my friends and family members, for their patience and love.

To my mother, Pnina, and my mother-in-law, Hannah, for donating their time and experience.

To my spouse and manager, Itzik, without whom none of this would have happened. I only know how to write books. He does everything else.

And finally, to all my readers, for their interest, time, and comments. If a book sits on a shelf and no one reads it, does it make a sound?

As noted in the introduction, this book has been written in conversation with the public. Many of the chapters were composed in response to questions I was asked by readers, journalists, and colleagues. Earlier versions of some segments were previously published as essays and articles, which gave me the opportunity to receive feedback and hone my arguments. These earlier versions include the following essays and articles:

"If We Know Meat Is Murder, Why Is It So Hard for Us to Change and Become Moral?," *Haaretz*, June 21, 2012.

"The Theatre of Terror," *Guardian*, January 31, 2015.

"Judaism Is Not a Major Player in the History of Humankind," *Haaretz*, July 31, 2016.

"Yuval Noah Harari on Big Data, Google and the End of Free Will," FT.com, August 26, 2016.

"Isis Is as Much an Offshoot of Our Global Civilization as Google," *Guardian*, September 9, 2016.

"Salvation by Algorithm: God, Technology and New 21st Century Religion," *New Statesman*, September 9, 2016.

"Does Trump's Rise Mean Liberalism's End?," *New Yorker*, October 7, 2016.

"Yuval Noah Harari Challenges the Future According to Facebook," *Financial Times*, March 23, 2017.

"Humankind: The Post-Truth Species," Bloomberg.com, April 13, 2017.

"People Have Limited Knowledge. What's the Remedy? Nobody Knows," *New York Times*, April 18, 2017.

"The Meaning of Life in a World Without Work," *Guardian*, May 8, 2017.

"In Big Data vs. Bach, Computers Might Win," *Bloomberg View*, May 13, 2017.

"Are We About to Witness the Most Unequal Societies in History?," *Guardian*, May 24, 2017.

"Universal Basic Income Is Neither Universal nor Basic," *Bloomberg View*, June 4, 2017.

"Why It's No Longer Possible for Any Country to Win a War," Time.com, June 23, 2017.

"The Age of Disorder: Why Technology Is the Greatest Threat to Humankind," *New Statesman*, July 25, 2017.

"Reboot for the AI Revolution," *Nature News*, October 17, 2017.

NOTES

....

CHAPTER 1: DISILLUSIONMENT

1. See, for example, George W. Bush's inaugural speech in 2005, where he said: "We are led, by events and common sense, to one conclusion: the survival of liberty in our land increasingly depends on the success of liberty in other lands. The best hope for peace in our world is the expansion of freedom in all the world." "Bush Pledges to Spread Democracy," CNN, January 20, 2005. For Obama, see, for example, Katie Reilly, "Read Barack Obama's Final Speech to the United Nations as President," *Time,* September 20, 2016.

2. William Neikirk and David S. Cloud, "Clinton: Abuses Put China 'On Wrong Side of History,'" *Chicago Tribune,* October 30, 1997.

3. Eric Bradner, "Hillary Clinton's Email Controversy, Explained," CNN, October 28, 2016.

4. Chris Graham and Robert Midgley, "Mexico Border Wall: What Is Donald Trump Planning, How Much Will It Cost and Who Will Pay for It?," *Telegraph,* August 23, 2017; Michael Schuman, "Is China Stealing Jobs? It May Be Losing Them, Instead," *New York Times,* July 22, 2016.

5. For several examples from the nineteenth and early twentieth centu-

ries, see Evgeny Dobrenko and Eric Naiman, eds., *The Landscape of Stalinism: The Art and Ideology of Soviet Space* (Seattle: University of Washington Press, 2003); W. L. Guttsman, *Art for the Workers: Ideology and the Visual Arts in Weimar Germany* (New York: Manchester University Press, 1997). For a general discussion see, for example, Nicholas John Cull, *Propaganda and Mass Persuasion: A Historical Encyclopedia, 1500 to the Present* (Santa Barbara, CA: ABC-CLIO, 2003).

6. For this interpretation, see Ishaan Tharoor, "Brexit: A Modern-Day Peasants' Revolt?," *Washington Post,* June 25, 2016; John Curtice, "US Election 2016: The Trump–Brexit Voter Revolt," BBC, November 11, 2016.

7. The most famous of these remains, of course, Francis Fukuyama, *The End of History and the Last Man* (London: Penguin, 1992).

8. Karen Dawisha, *Putin's Kleptocracy* (New York: Simon & Schuster, 2014); Timothy Snyder, *The Road to Unfreedom: Russia, Europe, America* (New York: Tim Duggan Books, 2018); Anne Garrels, *Putin Country: A Journey into the Real Russia* (New York: Farrar, Straus and Giroux, 2016); Steven Lee Myers, *The New Tsar: The Rise and Reign of Vladimir Putin* (New York: Knopf Doubleday, 2016).

9. Credit Suisse, *Global Wealth Report 2015,* 53; Filip Novokmet, Thomas Piketty, and Gabriel Zucman, "From Soviets to Oligarchs: Inequality and Property in Russia 1905–2016," World Wealth and Income Database, WID.world Working Paper Series no. 2017/09, July 2017; Shaun Walker, "Unequal Russia," *Guardian,* April 25, 2017.

10. Ayelet Shani, "The Israelis Who Take Rebuilding the Third Temple Very Seriously," *Haaretz,* August 10, 2017; "Israeli Minister: We Should Rebuild Jerusalem Temple," *Israel Today,* July 7, 2013; Yuri Yanover, "Dep. Minister Hotovely: The Solution Is Greater Israel Without Gaza," *Jewish Press,* August 25, 2013; "Israeli Minister: The Bible Says West Bank Is Ours," Al Jazeera, February 24, 2017.

11. Reilly, "Read Barack Obama's Final Speech to the United Nations as President."

CHAPTER 2: WORK

1. Gregory R. Woirol, *The Technological Unemployment and Structural Unemployment Debates* (Westport, CT: Greenwood Press, 1996), 18–20; Amy Sue Bix, *Inventing Ourselves Out of Jobs? America's Debate over*

Technological Unemployment, 1929–1981 (Baltimore: Johns Hopkins University Press, 2000), 1–8; Joel Mokyr, Chris Vickers, and Nicolas L. Ziebarth, "The History of Technological Anxiety and the Future of Economic Growth: Is This Time Different?," *Journal of Economic Perspectives* 29, no. 3 (2015): 33–42; Joe Mokyr, *The Gifts of Athena: Historical Origins of the Knowledge Economy* (Princeton, NJ: Princeton University Press, 2002), 255–57; David H. Autor, "Why Are There Still So Many Jobs? The History and the Future of Workplace Automation," *Journal of Economic Perspectives* 29, no. 3 (2015): 3–30; Melanie Arntz, Terry Gregory, and Ulrich Zierahn, "The Risk of Automation for Jobs in OECD Countries," *OECD Social, Employment and Migration Working Papers* 89 (2016); Mariacristina Piva and Marco Vivarelli, "Technological Change and Employment: Were Ricardo and Marx Right?," IZA Institute of Labor Economics, Discussion Paper no. 10471 (2017).

2. See, for example, on AI outperforming humans in flight, and especially combat flight simulation: Nicholas Ernest et al., "Genetic Fuzzy Based Artificial Intelligence for Unmanned Combat Aerial Vehicle Control in Simulated Air Combat Missions," *Journal of Defense Management* 6, no. 1 (2016): 1–7; intelligent tutoring and teaching systems: Kurt VanLehn, "The Relative Effectiveness of Human Tutoring, Intelligent Tutoring Systems, and Other Tutoring Systems," *Educational Psychologist* 46, no. 4 (2011): 197–221; algorithmic trading: Giuseppe Nuti et al., "Algorithmic Trading," *Computer* 44, no. 11 (2011): 61–69; financial planning, portfolio management, etc.: Arash Baharammirzaee, "A Comparative Survey of Artificial Intelligence Applications in Finance: Artificial Neural Networks, Expert System and Hybrid Intelligent Systems," *Neural Computing and Applications* 19, no. 8 (2010): 1165–95; analysis of complex data in medical systems and production of diagnosis and treatment: Marjorie Glass Zauderer et al., "Piloting IBM Watson Oncology Within Memorial Sloan Kettering's Regional Network," *Journal of Clinical Oncology* 32, no. 15 (2014): e17653; creation of original texts in natural language from massive amount of data: Jean-Sébastien Vayre et al., "Communication Mediated Through Natural Language Generation in Big Data Environments: The Case of Nomao," *Journal of Computer and Communication* 5 (2017): 125–48; facial recognition: Florian Schroff, Dmitry Kalenichenko, and James Philbin, "FaceNet: A Unified Em-

bedding for Face Recognition and Clustering," *IEEE Conference on Computer Vision and Pattern Recognition (CVPR)* (2015): 815–23; and driving: Cristiano Premebida, "A Lidar and Vision-Based Approach for Pedestrian and Vehicle Detection and Tracking," *2007 IEEE Intelligent Transportation Systems Conference* (2007).

3. Daniel Kahneman, *Thinking, Fast and Slow* (New York: Farrar, Straus and Giroux, 2011); Dan Ariely, *Predictably Irrational* (New York: Harper, 2009); Brian D. Ripley, *Pattern Recognition and Neural Networks* (Cambridge: Cambridge University Press, 2007); Christopher M. Bishop, *Pattern Recognition and Machine Learning* (New York: Springer, 2007).

4. Seyed Azimi et al., "Vehicular Networks for Collision Avoidance at Intersections," *SAE International Journal of Passenger Cars—Mechanical Systems* 4 (2011): 406–16; Swarun Kumar et al., "CarSpeak: A Content-Centric Network for Autonomous Driving," *SIGCOM Computer Communication Review* 42 (2012): 259–70; Mihail L. Sichitiu and Maria Kihl, "Inter-Vehicle Communication Systems: A Survey," *IEEE Communications Surveys and Tutorials* (2008): 10; Mario Gerla, Eun-Kyu Lee, and Giovanni Pau, "Internet of Vehicles: From Intelligent Grid to Autonomous Cars and Vehicular Clouds," *2014 IEEE World Forum on Internet of Things (WF-IoT)* (Piscataway, NJ: IEEE, 2014), 241–46.

5. David D. Luxton et al., "mHealth for Mental Health: Integrating Smartphone Technology in Behavioral Healthcare," *Professional Psychology: Research and Practice* 42, no. 6 (2011): 505–12; Abu Saleh Mohammad Mosa, Illhoi Yoo, and Lincoln Sheets, "A Systematic Review of Healthcare Applications for Smartphones," *BMC Medical Informatics and Decision Making* 12, no. 1 (2012): 67; Karl Frederick Braekkan Payne, Heather Wharrad, and Kim Watts, "Smartphone and Medical Related App Use Among Medical Students and Junior Doctors in the United Kingdom (UK): A Regional Survey," *BMC Medical Informatics and Decision Making* 12, no. 1 (2012): 121; Sandeep Kumar Vashist, E. Marion Schneider, and John H. T. Loung, "Commercial Smartphone-Based Devices and Smart Applications for Personalized Healthcare Monitoring and Management," *Diagnostics* 4, no. 3 (2014): 104–28; Maged N. Kamel Bouls et al., "How Smartphones Are Changing the Face of Mobile and Participatory Healthcare: An Overview, with Example from eCAALYX," *BioMedical Engineering*

Online 10, no. 24 (2011); Paul J. F. White, Blake W. Podaima, and Marcia R. Friesen, "Algorithms for Smartphone and Tablet Image Analysis for Healthcare Applications," *IEEE Access* 2 (2014): 831–40.

6. World Health Organization, *Global Status Report on Road Safety 2015* (Geneva: WHO, 2016); World Health Organization, "Estimates for 2000–2015, Cause-Specific Mortality," http://www.who.int/health info/global_burden_disease/estimates/en/index1.html, accessed September 6, 2017.

7. For a survey of the causes of car accidents in the United States, see Daniel J. Fagnant and Kara Kockelman, "Preparing a Nation for Autonomous Vehicles: Opportunities, Barriers and Policy Recommendations," *Transportation Research Part A: Policy and Practice* 77 (2015): 167–81; for a general worldwide survey, see, for example, *OECD/ITF, Road Safety Annual Report 2016* (Paris: OECD, 2016).

8. Kristofer D. Kusano and Hampton C. Gabler, "Safety Benefits of Forward Collision Warning, Brake Assist, and Autonomous Braking Systems in Rear-End Collisions," *IEEE Transactions on Intelligent Transportation Systems* 13, no. 4 (2012): 1546–55; James M. Anderson et al., *Autonomous Vehicle Technology: A Guide for Policymakers* (Santa Monica, CA: RAND Corporation, 2014), esp. 13–15; Daniel J. Fagnant and Kara Kockelman, "Preparing a Nation for Autonomous Vehicles: Opportunities, Barriers and Policy Recommendations," *Transportation Research Part A: Policy and Practice* 77 (2015): 167–81; Jean-François Bonnefon, Azim Shariff, and Iyad Rahwan, "Autonomous Vehicles Need Experimental Ethics: Are We Ready for Utilitarian Cars?," 2015, arXiv, https://arxiv.org/abs/1510.03346. For suggestions for intervehicle networks to prevent collision, see Seyed R. Azimi et al., "Vehicular Networks for Collision Avoidance at Intersections," *SAE International Journal of Passenger Cars—Mechanical Systems* 4, no. 1 (2011): 406–16; Swarun Kumar et al., "CarSpeak: A Content-Centric Network for Autonomous Driving," *SIGCOM Computer Communication Review* 42, no. 4 (2012): 259–70; Mihail L. Sichitiu and Maria Kihl, "Inter-Vehicle Communication Systems: A Survey," *IEEE Communications Surveys and Tutorials* 10, no. 2 (2008); Mario Gerla et al., "Internet of Vehicles: From Intelligent Grid to Autonomous Cars and Vehicular Clouds," *2014 IEEE World Forum on Internet of Things (WF-IoT)* (Piscataway, NJ: IEEE, 2014), 241–46.

9. Michael Chui, James Manyika, and Mehdi Miremadi, "Where Ma-

chines Could Replace Humans—and Where They Can't (Yet)," *McKinsey Quarterly*, July 2016.

10. Wu Youyou, Michal Kosinski, and David Stillwell, "Computer-Based Personality Judgments Are More Accurate than Those Made by Humans," *PANS* 112 (2014): 1036–38.

11. Stuart Dredge, "AI and Music: Will We Be Slaves to the Algorithm?," *Guardian*, August 6, 2017. For a general survey of methods, see Jose David Fernández and Francisco Vico, "AI Methods in Algorithmic Composition: A Comprehensive Survey," *Journal of Artificial Intelligence Research* 48 (2013): 513–82.

12. Eric Topol, *The Patient Will See You Now: The Future of Medicine Is in Your Hands* (New York: Basic Books, 2015); Robert Wachter, *The Digital Doctor: Hope, Hype and Harm at the Dawn of Medicine's Computer Age* (New York: McGraw-Hill Education, 2015); Simon Parkin, "The Artificially Intelligent Doctor Will Hear You Now," *MIT Technology Review*, March 9, 2016; James Gallagher, "Artificial Intelligence 'As Good as Cancer Doctors,'" BBC, January 26, 2017.

13. Kate Brannen, "Air Force's Lack of Drone Pilots Reaching 'Crisis' Levels," *Foreign Policy*, January 15, 2015.

14. Tyler Cowen, *Average Is Over: Powering America Beyond the Age of the Great Stagnation* (New York: Dutton, 2013); Brad Bush, "How Combined Human and Computer Intelligence Will Redefine Jobs," TechCrunch, November 1, 2016.

15. Ulrich Raulff, *Farewell to the Horse: The Final Century of Our Relationship* (London: Allen Lane, 2017); Gregory Clark, *A Farewell to Alms: A Brief Economic History of the World* (Princeton, NJ: Princeton University Press, 2008), 286; Margo DeMello, *Animals and Society: An Introduction to Human-Animal Studies* (New York: Columbia University Press, 2012), 197; Clay McShane and Joel Tarr, "The Decline of the Urban Horse in American Cities," *Journal of Transport History* 24, no. 2 (2003): 177–98.

16. Lawrence F. Katz and Alan B. Krueger, "The Rise and Nature of Alternative Work Arrangements in the United States, 1995–2015," *National Bureau of Economic Research* (2016); Peter H. Cappelli and J. R. Keller, "A Study of the Extent and Potential Causes of Alternative Employment Arrangements," *ILR Review* 66, no. 4 (2013): 874–901; Gretchen M. Spreitzer, Lindsey Cameron, and Lyndon Garrett, "Alternative Work Arrangements: Two Images of the New World of

Work," *Annual Review of Organizational Psychology and Organizational Behavior* 4 (2017): 473–99; Sarah A. Donovan, David H. Bradley, and Jon O. Shimabukuru, "What Does the Gig Economy Mean for Workers?," Congressional Research Service, Washington, DC, 2016; "More Workers Are in Alternative Employment Arrangements," Pew Research Center, September 28, 2016.

17. David Ferrucci et al., "Watson: Beyond *Jeopardy!*," *Artificial Intelligence* 199–200 (2013): 93–105.

18. "Google's AlphaZero Destroys Stockfish in 100-Game Match," Chess.com, December 6, 2017; David Silver et al., "Mastering Chess and Shogi by Self-Play with a General Reinforcement Learning Algorithm," 2017, arXiv, https://arxiv.org/pdf/1712:01815.pdf; see also Sarah Knapton, "Entire Human Chess Knowledge Learned and Surpassed by DeepMind's AlphaZero in Four Hours," *Telegraph*, December 6, 2017.

19. Cowen, *Average Is Over;* Tyler Cowen, "What Are Humans Still Good For? The Turning Point in Freestyle Chess May Be Approaching," *Marginal Revolution,* November 5, 2013.

20. Maddalaine Ansell, "Jobs for Life Are a Thing of the Past. Bring on Lifelong Learning," *Guardian,* May 31, 2016.

21. Alex Williams, "Prozac Nation Is Now the United States of Xanax," *New York Times,* June 10, 2017.

22. Simon Rippon, "Imposing Options on People in Poverty: The Harm of a Live Donor Organ Market," *Journal of Medical Ethics* 40 (2014): 145–50; I. Glenn Cohen, "Regulating the Organ Market: Normative Foundations for Market Regulation," *Law and Contemporary Problems* 77 (2014); Alexandra K. Glazier, "The Principles of Gift Law and the Regulation of Organ Donation," *Transplant International* 24 (2011): 368–72; Megan McAndrews and Walter E. Block, "Legalizing Saving Lives: A Proposition for the Organ Market," *Insights to a Changing World Journal,* 2015, 1–17.

23. James J. Hughes, "A Strategic Opening for a Basic Income Guarantee in the Global Crisis Being Created by AI, Robots, Desktop Manufacturing and Biomedicine," *Journal of Evolution and Technology* 24 (2014): 45–61; Alan Cottey, "Technologies, Culture, Work, Basic Income and Maximum Income," *AI and Society* 29 (2014): 249–57.

24. Jon Henley, "Finland Trials Basic Income for Unemployed," *Guardian,* January 3, 2017.

25. "Swiss Voters Reject Proposal to Give Basic Income to Every Adult and Child," *Guardian*, June 5, 2017.

26. Isabel Hunter, "Crammed into Squalid Factories to Produce Clothes for the West on Just 20p a Day, the Children Forced to Work in Horrific Unregulated Workshops of Bangladesh," *Daily Mail*, December 1, 2015; Chris Walker and Morgan Hartley, "The Culture Shock of India's Call Centers," *Forbes*, December 16, 2012.

27. Klaus Schwab and Nicholas Savis, *Shaping the Fourth Industrial Revolution* (Geneva: World Economic Forum, 2018), 54. On long-term development strategies, see Ha-Joon Chang, *Kicking Away the Ladder: Development Strategy in Historical Perspective* (London: Anthem Press, 2003).

28. Lauren Gambini, "Trump Pans Immigration Proposal as Bringing People from 'Shithole Countries,'" *Guardian*, January 12, 2018.

29. For the idea that an absolute improvement in conditions might be coupled with a rise in relative inequality, see in particular Thomas Pikkety, *Capital in the Twenty-First Century* (Cambridge, MA: Harvard University Press, 2013).

30. "2017 Statistical Report on Ultra-Orthodox Society in Israel," Israel Democracy Institute and Jerusalem Institute for Israel Studies, 2017, https://en.idi.org.il/articles/20439; Melanie Lidman, "As Ultra-Orthodox Women Bring Home the Bacon, Don't Say the F-Word," *Times of Israel*, January 1, 2016.

31. Lidman, "As Ultra-Orthodox Women Bring Home the Bacon"; Israel Democracy Institute and Jerusalem Institute for Israel Studies, "Statistical Report on Ultra-Orthodox Society in Israel." As for happiness, Israel was recently ranked eleventh out of thirty-eight in life satisfaction by the OECD: "Life Satisfaction," OECD Better Life Index, http://www.oecdbetterlifeindex.org/topics/life-satisfaction, accessed October 15, 2017.

32. "2017 Statistical Report on Ultra-Orthodox Society in Israel," Israel Democracy Institute and Jerusalem Institute for Israel Studies, 2017, https://en.idi.org.il/articles/20439.

CHAPTER 3: LIBERTY

1. Margaret Thatcher, "Interview for *Woman's Own* ('No Such Thing as Society')," Margaret Thatcher Foundation, September 23, 1987.

2. Keith Stanovich, *Who Is Rational? Studies of Individual Differences in Reasoning* (New York: Psychology Press, 1999).

3. Richard Dawkins, "Richard Dawkins: We Need a New Party—the European Party," *New Statesman*, March 29, 2017.

4. Steven Swinford, "Boris Johnson's Allies Accuse Michael Gove of 'Systematic and Calculated Plot' to Destroy His Leadership Hopes," *Telegraph*, June 30, 2016; Rowena Mason and Heather Stewart, "Gove's Thunderbolt and Boris's Breaking Point: A Shocking Tory Morning," *Guardian*, June 30, 2016.

5. James Tapsfield, "Gove Presents Himself as the Integrity Candidate for Downing Street Job but Sticks the Knife into Boris Again," *Daily Mail*, July 1, 2016.

6. In 2017 a Stanford team produced an algorithm that can purportedly detect whether you are gay or straight with an accuracy of 91 percent, based solely on analyzing a few of your facial pictures (https://osf.io/zn79k). However, since the algorithm was developed on the basis of pictures that people self-selected to upload to dating sites, the algorithm might actually identify differences in cultural ideals. It is not that the facial features of gay people are necessarily different from those of straight people. Rather, gay men uploading photos to a gay dating site try to conform to different cultural ideals than straight men uploading photos to straight dating sites.

7. David Chan, "So Why Ask Me? Are Self-Report Data Really That Bad?," in *Statistical and Methodological Myths and Urban Legends*, ed. Charles E. Lance and Robert J. Vandenberg (New York: Routledge, 2009), 309–36; Delroy L. Paulhus and Simine Vazire, "The Self-Report Method," in *Handbook of Research Methods in Personality Psychology*, ed. Richard W. Robins, R. Chris Farley, and Robert F. Krueger (London: Guilford Press, 2007), 228–33.

8. Elizabeth Dwoskin and Evelyn M. Rusli, "The Technology That Unmasks Your Hidden Emotions," *Wall Street Journal*, January 28, 2015.

9. Norberto Andrade, "Computers Are Getting Better than Humans at Facial Recognition," *Atlantic*, June 9, 2014; Dwoskin and Rusli, "The Technology That Unmasks Your Hidden Emotions"; Sophie K. Scott, Nadine Lavan, Sinead Chen, and Carolyn McGettigan, "The Social Life of Laughter," *Trends in Cognitive Sciences* 18, no. 12 (2014): 618–20.

10. Daniel First, "Will Big Data Algorithms Dismantle the Foundations of Liberalism?," *AI and Society*, June 2017.

11. Carole Cadwalladr, "Google, Democracy and the Truth About Internet Search," *Guardian*, December 4, 2016.

12. Jeff Freak and Shannon Holloway, "How Not to Get to Straddie," *Red Land City Bulletin*, March 15, 2012.

13. Michelle McQuigge, "Woman Follows GPS; Ends Up in Ontario Lake," *Toronto Sun*, May 13, 2016; "Woman Follows GPS into Lake," News.com.au, May 16, 2016.

14. Henry Grabar, "Navigation Apps Are Killing Our Sense of Direction. What If They Could Help Us Remember Places Instead?," *Slate*, July 10, 2017.

15. Joel Delman, "Are Amazon, Netflix, Google Making Too Many Decisions for Us?," *Forbes*, November 24, 2010; Cecilia Mazanec, "Will Algorithms Erode Our Decision-Making Skills?," NPR, February 8, 2017.

16. Bonnefon, Shariff, and Rawhan, "The Social Dilemma of Autonomous Vehicles."

17. Christopher W. Bauman et al., "Revisiting External Validity: Concerns About Trolley Problems and Other Sacrificial Dilemmas in Moral Psychology," *Social and Personality Psychology Compass* 8, no. 9 (2014): 536–54.

18. John M. Darley and Daniel C. Batson, " 'From Jerusalem to Jericho': A Study of Situational and Dispositional Variables in Helping Behavior," *Journal of Personality and Social Psychology* 27, no. 1 (1973): 100–108.

19. Kristofer D. Kusano and Hampton C. Gabler, "Safety Benefits of Forward Collision Warning, Brake Assist, and Autonomous Braking Systems in Rear-End Collisions," *IEEE Transactions on Intelligent Transportation Systems* 13, no. 4 (2012): 1546–55; James M. Anderson et al., *Autonomous Vehicle Technology: A Guide for Policymakers* (Santa Monica, CA: RAND Corporation, 2014), esp. 13–15; Daniel J. Fagnant and Kara Kockelman, "Preparing a Nation for Autonomous Vehicles: Opportunities, Barriers and Policy Recommendations," *Transportation Research Part A: Policy and Practice* 77 (2015): 167–81.

20. Tim Adams, "Job Hunting Is a Matter of Big Data, Not How You Perform at an Interview," *Guardian*, May 10, 2014.

21. For an extremely insightful discussion, see Cathy O'Neil, *Weapons of*

Math Destruction: How Big Data Increases Inequality and Threatens Democracy (New York: Crown, 2016). This is really an obligatory read for anyone interested in the potential effects of algorithms on society and politics.

22. Jean-François Bonnefon, Iyad Rahwan, and Azim Shariff, "The Social Dilemma of Autonomous Vehicles," *Science* 352, no. 6293 (2016): 1573–76.

23. Vincent C. Müller and Thomas W. Simpson, "Autonomous Killer Robots Are Probably Good News," University of Oxford, Blavatnik School of Government Policy Memo, November 2014; Ronald Arkin, "Governing Lethal Behavior: Embedding Ethics in a Hybrid Deliberative/Reactive Robot Architecture," Georgia Institute of Technology, Mobile Robot Lab, 2007, 1–13.

24. Bernd Greiner, *War Without Fronts: The USA in Vietnam*, trans. Anne Wyburd and Victoria Fern (Cambridge, MA: Harvard University Press, 2009), 16. For at least one reference for the emotional state of the soldiers, see Herbert Kelman and V. Lee Hamilton, "The My Lai Massacre: A Military Crime of Obedience," in *Sociology: Exploring the Architecture of Everyday Life Reading*, ed. Jodi O'Brien and David M. Newman (Los Angeles: Pine Forge Press, 2010), 13–25.

25. Robert J. Donia, *Radovan Karadzic: Architect of the Bosnian Genocide* (Cambridge: Cambridge University Press, 2015). See also Isabella Delpla, Xavier Bougarel, and Jean-Louis Fournel, *Investigating Srebrenica: Institutions, Facts, and Responsibilities* (New York: Berghahn Books, 2012).

26. Noel E. Sharkey, "The Evitability of Autonomous Robot Warfare," *International Review of the Red Cross* 94, no. 886 (2012): 787–99.

27. Ben Schiller, "Algorithms Control Our Lives: Are They Benevolent Rulers or Evil Dictators?," *Fast Company,* February 21, 2017.

28. Elia Zureik, David Lyon, and Yasmeen Abu-Laban, eds., *Surveillance and Control in Israel/Palestine: Population, Territory and Power* (London: Routledge, 2011); Elia Zureik, *Israel's Colonial Project in Palestine* (London: Routledge, 2015); Torin Monahan, ed., *Surveillance and Security: Technological Politics and Power in Everyday Life* (London: Routledge, 2006); Nadera Shalhoub-Kevorkian, "E-Resistance and Technological In/Security in Everyday Life: The Palestinian Case," *British Journal of Criminology* 52, no. 1 (2012): 55–72; Or Hirschauge and Hagar Sheizaf, "Targeted Prevention: Exposing the New System

for Dealing with Individual Terrorism," *Haaretz*, May 26, 2017; Amos Harel, "The IDF Accelerates the Crisscrossing of the West Bank with Cameras and Plans to Surveille All Junctions," *Haaretz*, June 18, 2017; Neta Alexander, "This Is How Israel Controls the Digital and Cellular Space in the Territories," *Haaretz*, March 31, 2016; Amos Harel, "Israel Arrested Hundreds of Palestinians as Suspected Terrorists Due to Publications on the Internet," *Haaretz*, April 16, 2017; Alex Fishman, "The Argaman Era," *Yediot Aharonot, Weekend Supplement*, April 28, 2017, 6.

29. Yotam Berger, "Police Arrested a Palestinian Based on an Erroneous Translation of 'Good Morning' in His Facebook Page," *Haaretz*, October 22, 2017.

30. William Beik, *Louis XIV and Absolutism: A Brief Study with Documents* (Boston: Bedford/St. Martin's, 2000).

31. O'Neil, *Weapons of Math Destruction*; Penny Crosman, "Can AI Be Programmed to Make Fair Lending Decisions?," *American Banker*, September 27, 2016.

32. Matt Reynolds, "Bias Test to Prevent Algorithms Discriminating Unfairly," *New Scientist*, May 29, 2017; Claire Cain Miller, "When Algorithms Discriminate," *New York Times*, July 9, 2015; Hannah Devlin, "Discrimination by Algorithm: Scientists Devise Test to Detect AI Bias," *Guardian*, December 19, 2016.

33. Snyder, *Road to Unfreedom*.

34. Anna Lisa Peterson, *Being Animal: Beasts and Boundaries in Nature Ethics* (New York: Columbia University Press, 2013), 100.

CHAPTER 4: EQUALITY

1. "Richest 1 Percent Bagged 82 Percent of Wealth Created Last Year—Poorest Half of Humanity Got Nothing," Oxfam press release, January 22, 2018; Josh Lowe, "The 1 Percent Now Have Half the World's Wealth," *Newsweek*, November 14, 2017; Adam Withnall, "All the World's Most Unequal Countries Revealed in One Chart," *Independent*, November 23, 2016.

2. Tim Wu, *The Attention Merchants* (New York: Alfred A. Knopf, 2016).

3. Cara McGoogan, "How to See All the Terrifying Things Google Knows About You," *Telegraph*, August 18, 2017; Caitlin Dewey, "Ev-

erything Google Knows About You (and How It Knows It)," *Washington Post*, November 19, 2014.

4. Dan Bates, "YouTube Is Losing Money Even Though It Has More than 1 Billion Viewers," *Daily Mail*, February 26, 2015; Olivia Solon, "Google's Bad Week: YouTube Loses Millions as Advertising Row Reaches US," *Guardian*, March 25, 2017; Seth Fiegerman, "Twitter Is Now Losing Users in the US," CNN, July 27, 2017.

CHAPTER 5: COMMUNITY

1. Mark Zuckerberg, "Building Global Community," Facebook, February 16, 2017, https://www.facebook.com/notes/mark-zuckerberg/building-global-community/10154544292806634.

2. John Shinal, "Mark Zuckerberg: Facebook Can Play a Role That Churches and Little League Once Filled," CNBC, June 26, 2017.

3. Shinal, "Mark Zuckerberg: Facebook Can Play a Role"; John Shinal, "Zuckerberg Says Facebook Has a New Mission as It Deals with Fake News and Hate Speech," CNBC, June 22, 2017.

4. Robin Dunbar, *Grooming, Gossip, and the Evolution of Language* (Cambridge, MA: Harvard University Press, 1998).

5. See, for example, Pankaj Mishra, *Age of Anger: A History of the Present* (London: Penguin, 2017).

6. For a general survey and critique, see Derek Y. Darves and Michael C. Dreiling, *Agents of Neoliberal Globalization: Corporate Networks, State Structures and Trade Policy* (Cambridge: Cambridge University Press, 2016).

7. Lisa Eadicicco, "Americans Check Their Phones 8 Billion Times a Day," *Time*, December 15, 2015; Julie Beck, "Ignoring People for Phones Is the New Normal," *Atlantic*, June 14, 2016.

8. Zuckerberg, "Building Global Community."

9. Time Well Spent, http://www.timewellspent.io, accessed September 3, 2017.

10. Zuckerberg, "Building Global Community."

11. Press Association, "Facebook UK Pays Just £5.1m in Corporation Tax Despite Jump in Profit," *Guardian*, October 4, 2017; Jennifer Rankin, "EU to Find Ways to Make Google, Facebook and Amazon Pay More Tax," *Guardian*, September 21, 2017; Liat Clark, "Loop-

holes and Luxuries: How Apple, Facebook and Google Stay Ahead of the Tax Man," *Wired UK,* May 4, 2017.

CHAPTER 6: CIVILIZATION

1. Samuel P. Huntington, *The Clash of Civilizations and the Remaking of World Order* (New York: Simon & Schuster, 1996); David Lauter and Brian Bennett, "Trump Frames Anti-Terrorism Fight as a Clash of Civilizations, Defending Western Culture Against Enemies," *Los Angeles Times,* July 6, 2017; Naomi O'Leary, "The Man Who Invented Trumpism: Geert Wilders' Radical Path to the Pinnacle of Dutch Politics," *Politico,* February 23, 2017.

2. Pankaj Mishra, *From the Ruins of Empire: The Revolt Against the West and the Remaking of Asia* (London: Penguin, 2013); Mishra, *Age of Anger;* Christopher de Bellaigue, *The Muslim Enlightenment: The Modern Struggle Between Faith and Reason* (London: Bodley Head, 2017).

3. "Treaty Establishing a Constitution for Europe," European Union, October 29, 2004.

4. Phoebe Greenwood, "Jerusalem Mayor Battles Ultra-Orthodox Groups over Women-Free Billboards," *Guardian,* November 15, 2011.

5. Bruce Golding, "Orthodox Publications Won't Show Hillary Clinton's Photo," *New York Post,* October 1, 2015.

6. Simon Schama, *The Story of the Jews: Finding the Words 1000 BC–1492 AD* (New York: Ecco, 2014), 190–97; Hannah Wortzman, "Jewish Women in Ancient Synagogues: Archeological Reality vs. Rabbinical Legislation," *Women in Judaism* 5, no. 2 (2008); Ross S. Kraemer, "Jewish Women in the Diaspora World of Late Antiquity," in *Jewish Women in Historical Perspective,* ed. Judith R. Baskin (Detroit: Wayne State University Press, 1991), esp. 49; Hachlili Rachel, *Ancient Synagogues—Archeology and Art: New Discoveries and Current Research* (Leiden: Brill, 2014), 578–81; Zeev Weiss, "The Sepphoris Synagogue Mosaic: Abraham, the Temple and the Sun God—They're All in There," *Biblical Archeology Society* 26, no. 5 (2000): 48–61; David Milson, *Art and Architecture of the Synagogue in Late Antique Palestine* (Leiden: Brill, 2007), 48.

7. Ivan Watson and Pamela Boykoff, "World's Largest Muslim Group Denounces Islamist Extremism," CNN, May 10, 2016; Lauren Mar-

koe, "Muslim Scholars Release Open Letter to Islamic State Meticulously Blasting Its Ideology," *Huffington Post,* September 25, 2014; for the letter, see "Open Letter to Al-Baghdadi," http://www.letterto baghdadi.com, accessed January 8, 2018.

8. Chris Perez, "Obama Defends the 'True Peaceful Nature of Islam,'" *New York Post,* February 18, 2015; Dave Boyer, "Obama Says Terrorists Not Motivated by True Islam," *Washington Times,* February 1, 2015.

9. De Bellaigue, *The Islamic Enlightenment.*

10. Christopher McIntosh, *The Swan King: Ludwig II of Bavaria* (London: I. B. Tauris, 2012), 100.

11. Robert Mitchell Stern, *Globalization and International Trade Policies* (Hackensack, NJ: World Scientific, 2009), 23.

12. John K. Thornton, *A Cultural History of the Atlantic World, 1250–1820* (Cambridge: Cambridge University Press, 2012), 110.

13. Susannah Cullinane, Hamdi Alkhshali, and Mohammed Tawfeeq, "Tracking a Trail of Historical Obliteration: ISIS Trumpets Destruction of Nimrud," CNN, April 14, 2015.

14. Kenneth Pomeranz, *The Great Divergence: China, Europe and the Making of the Modern World Economy* (Princeton, NJ: Princeton University Press, 2001), 36–38.

15. "ISIS Leader Calls for Muslims to Help Build Islamic State in Iraq," CBC News, July 1, 2014; Mark Townsend, "What Happened to the British Medics Who Went to Work for ISIS?," *Guardian,* July 12, 2015.

CHAPTER 7: NATIONALISM

1. Francis Fukuyama, *Political Order and Political Decay: From the Industrial Revolution to the Globalization of Democracy* (New York: Farrar, Straus and Giroux, 2014).

2. Ashley Killough, "Lyndon Johnson's 'Daisy' Ad, Which Changed the World of Politics, Turns 50," CNN, September 8, 2014.

3. "Cause-Specific Mortality: Estimates for 2000–2015," World Health Organization, http://www.who.int/healthinfo/global_burden _disease/estimates/en/index1.html, accessed October 19, 2017.

4. David E. Sanger and William J. Broad, "To Counter Russia, US Signals Nuclear Arms Are Back in a Big Way," *New York Times,* February

4, 2018; U.S. Department of Defense, "Nuclear Posture Review 2018," https://www.defense.gov/News/Special-Reports/0218_npr, accessed February 6, 2018; Jennifer Hansler, "Trump Says He Wants Nuclear Arsenal in 'Tip-Top Shape,' Denies Desire to Increase Stockpile," CNN, October 12, 2017; Jim Garamone, "DoD Official: National Defense Strategy Will Enhance Deterrence," press release, Department of Defense, January 19, 2018.

5. Michael Mandelbaum, *Mission Failure: America and the World in the Post–Cold War Era* (New York: Oxford University Press, 2016).

6. Elizabeth Kolbert, *Field Notes from a Catastrophe* (London: Bloomsbury, 2006); Elizabeth Kolbert, *The Sixth Extinction: An Unnatural History* (London: Bloomsbury, 2014); Will Steffen et al., "Planetary Boundaries: Guiding Human Development on a Changing Planet," *Science* 347, no. 6223, February 13, 2015.

7. John Cook et al., "Quantifying the Consensus on Anthropogenic Global Warming in the Scientific Literature," *Environmental Research Letters* 8, no. 2 (2013); John Cook et al., "Consensus on Consensus: A Synthesis of Consensus Estimates on Human-Caused Global Warming," *Environmental Research Letters* 11, no. 4 (2016); Andrew Griffin, "15,000 Scientists Give Catastrophic Warning About the Fate of the World in New 'Letter to Humanity,'" *Independent,* November 13, 2017; Justin Worland, "Climate Change Is Already Wreaking Havoc on Our Weather, Scientists Find," *Time,* December 15, 2017.

8. Richard J. Millar et al., "Emission Budgets and Pathways Consistent with Limiting Warming to 1.5 C," *Nature Geoscience* 10 (2017): 741–47; Joeri Rogelj et al., "Differences Between Carbon Budget Estimates Unraveled," *Nature Climate Change* 6 (2016): 245–52; Ashkat Rathi, "Did We Just Buy Decades More Time to Hit Climate Goals?," *Quartz,* September 21, 2017; Roz Pidcock, "Carbon Briefing: Making Sense of the IPCC's New Carbon Budget," Carbon Brief, October 23, 2013.

9. Jianping Huang et al., "Accelerated Dryland Expansion Under Climate Change," *Nature Climate Change* 6 (2016): 166–71; Thomas R. Knutson, "Tropical Cyclones and Climate Change," *Nature Geoscience* 3 (2010): 157–63; Edward Hanna et al., "Ice-Sheet Mass Balance and Climate Change," *Nature* 498 (2013): 51–59; Tim Wheeler and Joachim von Braun, "Climate Change Impacts on Global Food Security," *Science* 341, no. 6145 (2013): 508–13; A. J. Challinor et al., "A

Meta-Analysis of Crop Yield Under Climate Change and Adaptation," *Nature Climate Change* 4 (2014): 287–91; Elisabeth Lingren et al., "Monitoring EU Emerging Infectious Disease Risk Due to Climate Change," *Science* 336, no. 6080 (2012): 418–19; Frank Biermann and Ingrid Boas, "Preparing for a Warmer World: Toward a Global Governance System to Protect Climate Change," *Global Environmental Politics* 10, no. 1 (2010): 60–88; Jeff Goodell, *The Water Will Come: Rising Seas, Sinking Cities and the Remaking of the Civilized World* (New York: Little, Brown, 2017); Mark Lynas, *Six Degrees: Our Future on a Hotter Planet* (Washington, DC: National Geographic, 2008); Naomi Klein, *This Changes Everything: Capitalism vs. Climate* (New York: Simon & Schuster, 2014); Kolbert, *The Sixth Extinction*.

10. Johan Rockström et al., "A Roadmap for Rapid Decarbonization," *Science* 355, no. 6331 (March 23, 2017).

11. Institution of Mechanical Engineers, *Global Food: Waste Not, Want Not* (London: Institution of Mechanical Engineers, 2013), 12.

12. Paul Shapiro, *Clean Meat: How Growing Meat Without Animals Will Revolutionize Dinner and the World* (New York: Gallery Books, 2018).

13. "Russia's Putin Says Climate Change in Arctic Good for Economy," CBS News, March 30, 2017; Neela Banerjee, "Russia and the US Could Be Partners in Climate Change Inaction," *Inside Climate News,* February 7, 2017; Noah Smith, "Russia Wins in a Retreat on Climate Change," *Bloomberg View,* December 15, 2016; Gregg Easterbrook, "Global Warming: Who Loses—and Who Wins?," *Atlantic,* April 2007; Quentin Buckholz, "Russia and Climate Change: A Looming Threat," *Diplomat,* February 4, 2016.

14. Brian Eckhouse, Ari Natter, and Christopher Martin, "President Trump Slaps Tariffs on Solar Panels in Major Blow to Renewable Energy," *Time,* January 22, 2018.

15. Miranda Green and Rene Marsh, "Trump Administration Doesn't Want to Talk About Climate Change," CNN, September 13, 2017; Lydia Smith, "Trump Administration Deletes Mention of 'Climate Change' from Environmental Protection Agency's Website," *Independent,* October 22, 2017; Alana Abramson, "No, Trump Still Hasn't Changed His Mind About Climate Change After Hurricane Irma and Harvey," *Time,* September 11, 2017.

16. "Treaty Establishing a Constitution for Europe."

CHAPTER 8: RELIGION

1. Bernard S. Cohn, *Colonialism and Its Forms of Knowledge: The British in India* (Princeton, NJ: Princeton University Press, 1996), 148.
2. "Encyclical Letter Laudato Sí of the Holy Father Francis on Care for Our Common Home," Holy See, May 24, 2015.
3. First introduced by Sigmund Freud in his 1930 treatise *Civilization and Its Discontents*, trans. James Strachey (New York: W. W. Norton, 1961), 61.
4. Ian Buruma, *Inventing Japan, 1853–1964* (New York: Modern Library, 2003).
5. Robert Axell, *Kamikaze: Japan's Suicide Gods* (London: Longman, 2002).
6. Charles K. Armstrong, "Familism, Socialism and Political Religion in North Korea," *Totalitarian Movements and Political Religions* 6, no. 3 (2005): 383–94; Daniel Byman and Jennifer Lind, "Pyongyang's Survival Strategy: Tools of Authoritarian Control in North Korea," *International Security* 35, no. 1 (2010): 44–74; Paul French, *North Korea: The Paranoid Peninsula*, 2nd ed. (London: Zed Books, 2007); Andrei Lankov, *The Real North Korea: Life and Politics in the Failed Stalinist Utopia* (Oxford: Oxford University Press, 2015); Young Whan Kihl, "Staying Power of the Socialist 'Hermit Kingdom,'" in *North Korea: The Politics of Regime Survival*, ed. Hong Nack Kim and Young Whan Kihl (New York: Routledge, 2006), 3–36.

CHAPTER 9: IMMIGRATION

1. United Nations High Commissioner for Refugees, "Global Trends: Forced Displacement in 2016," http://www.unhcr.org/5943e8a34.pdf, accessed January 11, 2018.
2. Lauren Gambini, "Trump Pans Immigration Proposal as Bringing People from 'Shithole Countries,'" *Guardian*, January 12, 2018.
3. Tal Kopan, "What Donald Trump Has Said About Mexico and Vice Versa," CNN, August 31, 2016.

CHAPTER 10: TERRORISM

1. Ashley Kirk, "How Many People Are Killed by Terrorist Attacks in the UK?," *Telegraph*, October 17, 2017; National Consortium for the Study of Terrorism and Responses to Terrorism (START) (2016), Global Terrorism Database [data file], retrieved from https://www.start.umd.edu/gtd; Susan Jones, "11,774 Terror Attacks Worldwide in 2015; 28,328 Deaths Due to Terror Attacks," CNS News, June 3, 2016; "People Killed by Terrorism per Year in Western Europe," Datagraver, March 22, 2016; "Reports on International Terrorism: Statistics on Incidents of Terror Worldwide," Jewish Virtual Library, accessed April 11, 2018; Gary LaFree, Laura Dugan, and Erin Miller, *Putting Terrorism in Context: Lessons from the Global Terrorism Database* (London: Routledge, 2015); Gary LaFree, "Using Open Source Data to Counter Common Myths About Terrorism," in *Criminologists on Terrorism and Homeland Security*, ed. Brian Forst, Jack Greene, and Jim Lynch (Cambridge: Cambridge University Press, 2011), 411–42; Gary LaFree, "The Global Terrorism Database: Accomplishments and Challenges," *Perspectives on Terrorism* 4 (2010): 24–46; Gary LaFree and Laura Dugan, "Research on Terrorism and Countering Terrorism," in *Crime and Justice: A Review of Research*, ed. M. Tonry (Chicago: University of Chicago Press, 2009), 413–77; Gary LaFree and Laura Dugan, "Introducing the Global Terrorism Database," *Political Violence and Terrorism* 19 (2007): 181–204.

2. World Health Organization, "Deaths on the Roads: Based on the WHO Global Status Report on Road Safety 2015"; "About Multiple Cause of Death, 1999–2016," Centers for Disease Control and Prevention, https://wonder.cdc.gov/mcd-icd10.html, accessed April 11, 2018; World Health Organization, "Global Status Report on Road Safety 2013"; World Health Organization, "Road Safety: Estimated Number of Traffic Deaths, 2013," http://gamapserver.who.int/gho/interactive_charts/road_safety/road_traffic_deaths/atlas.html, accessed April 11, 2018; World Health Organization, "Global Status Report on Road Safety 2013"; Stav Ziv, "2015 Brought Biggest Percent Increase in U.S. Traffic Deaths in 50 Years," *Newsweek*, February 17, 2016.

3. World Health Organization, Regional Office for Europe, "The Challenge of Diabetes," http://www.euro.who.int/en/health-topics/noncommunicable-diseases/diabetes/data-and-statistics, accessed

April 11, 2018; World Health Organization, *Global Report on Diabetes* (Geneva: WHO, 2016); Adam Vaughan, "China Tops WHO List for Deadly Outdoor Air Pollution," *Guardian*, September 27, 2016.

4. For the battle, see Gary Sheffield, *Forgotten Victory: The First World War. Myths and Reality* (London: Headline, 2001), 137–64.

5. "Victims of Palestinian Violence and Terrorism Since September 2000," Israel Ministry of Foreign Affairs, http://mfa.gov.il/MFA/ForeignPolicy/Terrorism/Palestinian/Pages/Victims%20of%20Palestinian%20Violence%20and%20Terrorism%20sinc.aspx, accessed October 23, 2017.

6. "Car Accidents with Casualties, 2002," Central Bureau of Statistics [in Hebrew], http://www.cbs.gov.il/www/publications/acci02/acci02h.pdf, accessed October 23, 2017.

7. "Pan Am Flight 103 Fast Facts," CNN, December 16, 2016.

8. Tom Templeton and Tom Lumley, "9/11 in Numbers," *Guardian*, August 18, 2002.

9. Ian Westwell and Dennis Cove, eds., *History of World War I* (New York: Marshall Cavendish, 2002), 2:431. For Isonzo, see John R. Schindler, *Isonzo: The Forgotten Sacrifice of the Great War* (Westport, CT: Praeger, 2001), 217–18.

10. Sergio Catignani, *Israeli Counter-Insurgency and the Intifadas: Dilemmas of a Conventional Army* (London: Routledge, 2008).

11. "Reported Rapes in France Jump 18% in Five Years," France 24, August 11, 2015.

CHAPTER 11: WAR

1. Yuval Noah Harari, *Homo Deus: A Brief History of Tomorrow* (New York: HarperCollins, 2017), 14–19; "Global Health Observatory Data Repository, 2012," World Health Organization, http://apps.who.int/gho/data/node.main.RCODWORLD?lang=en, accessed August 16, 2015; United Nations Office of Drugs and Crime, *Global Study on Homicide, 2013* (Vienna: UNDOC, 2013); World Health Organization, "Disease Burden and Mortality Estimates: Cause-Specific Mortality, 2000–2015," http://www.who.int/healthinfo/global_burden_disease/estimates/en/index1.html, accessed April 11, 2018.

2. "World Military Spending: Increases in the USA and Europe, De-

creases in Oil-Exporting Countries," press release, Stockholm International Peace Research Institute, April 24, 2017.

3. "Report on the Battle of Tel-el-Kebir," 4, National Archives, http://www.nationalarchives.gov.uk/battles/egypt/popup/telel4.htm.

4. Spencer C. Tucker, ed., *The Encyclopedia of the Mexican-American War: A Political, Social and Military History* (Santa Barbara, CA: ABC-CLIO, 2013), 131.

5. Ivana Kottasova, "Putin Meets Xi: Two Economies, Only One to Envy," CNN, July 2, 2017.

6. GDP is according to the IMF's statistics, calculated on the basis of purchasing power parity: International Monetary Fund, "Report for Selected Countries and Subjects, 2017," https://www.imf.org/external/pubs/ft/weo/2017/02/weodata/index.aspx, accessed February 27, 2018.

7. Hamza Hendawi and Qassim Abdul-Zahra, "ISIS Is Making Up to $50 Million a Month from Oil Sales," Business Insider, October 23, 2015.

8. Ian Buruma, *Inventing Japan* (London: Weidenfeld & Nicolson, 2003); Eri Hotta, *Japan 1941: Countdown to Infamy* (London: Vintage, 2014).

CHAPTER 12: HUMILITY

1. "10 Remarkable Ancient Indian Sages Familiar with Advanced Technology and Science Long Before Modern Era," AncientPages.com, October 19, 2015; "Great Indian Hindu Sages Who Revolutionised the Field of Science," Hindu Janajagruti Samiti, 2014, https://www.hindujagruti.org/articles/31.html; "Shocking Secrets of the Vedic Science Revealed!," The Most Confidential Knowledge, http://mcknowledge.info/about-vedas/what-is-vedic-science, accessed April 11, 2018.

2. These numbers and the ratio can be clearly seen in the following graph: Conrad Hackett and David McClendon, "Christians Remain World's Largest Religious Group, but They Are Declining in Europe," Pew Research Center, April 5, 2017.

3. Jonathan Haidt, *The Righteous Mind: Why Good People Are Divided by Politics and Religion* (New York: Pantheon, 2012); Joshua Greene,

Moral Tribes: Emotion, Reason, and the Gap Between Us and Them (New York: Penguin Press, 2013).

4. Marc Bekoff and Jessica Pierce, "Wild Justice—Honor and Fairness Among Beasts at Play," *American Journal of Play* 1, no. 4 (2009): 451–75.

5. Frans de Waal, *Our Inner Ape* (London: Granta, 2005), ch. 5.

6. Frans de Waal, *Bonobo: The Forgotten Ape* (Berkeley: University of California Press, 1997), 157.

7. The story became the subject of a documentary titled *Chimpanzee*, released in 2010 by Disneynature.

8. M.E.J. Richardson, *Hammurabi's Laws* (London: T&T Clark International, 2000), 29–31.

9. Loren R. Fisher, *The Eloquent Peasant*, 2nd ed. (Eugene, OR: Wipf & Stock, 2015).

10. Some rabbis, by relying on typical Talmudic ingenuity, allowed desecrating the Sabbath in order to save a Gentile. They argued that if Jews refrain from saving Gentiles, this will anger the Gentiles and cause them to attack and kill Jews. So by saving the Gentile, you might indirectly save a Jew. Yet even this argument highlights the different value attributed to the lives of Gentiles and Jews.

11. Catherine Nixey, *The Darkening Age: The Christian Destruction of the Classical World* (London: Macmillan, 2017).

12. Charles Allen, *Ashoka: The Search for India's Lost Emperor* (London: Little, Brown, 2012), 412–13.

13. Clyde Pharr et al., eds., *The Theodosian Code and Novels, and the Sirmondian Constitutions* (Princeton, NJ: Princeton University Press, 1952), 440, 467–71.

14. Ibid., esp. 472–73.

15. Sofie Remijsen, *The End of Greek Athletics in Late Antiquity* (Cambridge: Cambridge University Press, 2015), 45–51.

16. Ruth Schuster, "Why Do Jews Win So Many Nobels?," *Haaretz*, October 9, 2013.

CHAPTER 13: GOD

1. Lillian Faderman, *The Gay Revolution: The Story of the Struggle* (New York: Simon & Schuster, 2015).

2. Elaine Scarry, *The Body in Pain: The Making and Unmaking of the World* (New York: Oxford University Press, 1985).

CHAPTER 14: SECULARISM

1. Jonathan H. Turner, *Incest: Origins of the Taboo* (Boulder, CO: Paradigm, 2005); Robert J. Kelly et al., "Effects of Mother-Son Incest and Positive Perceptions of Sexual Abuse Experiences on the Psychosocial Adjustment of Clinic-Referred Men," *Child Abuse and Neglect* 26, no. 4 (2002): 425–41; Mireille Cyr et al., "Intrafamilial Sexual Abuse: Brother-Sister Incest Does Not Differ from Father-Daughter and Stepfather-Stepdaughter Incest," *Child Abuse and Neglect* 26, no. 9 (2002): 957–73; Sandra S. Stroebel, "Father–Daughter Incest: Data from an Anonymous Computerized Survey," *Journal of Child Sexual Abuse* 21, no. 2 (2010): 176–99.

CHAPTER 15: IGNORANCE

1. Steven A. Sloman and Philip Fernbach, *The Knowledge Illusion: Why We Never Think Alone* (New York: Riverhead Books, 2017); Joshua Greene, *Moral Tribes: Emotion, Reason, and the Gap Between Us and Them* (New York: Penguin Press, 2013).
2. Sloman and Fernbach, *The Knowledge Illusion*, 20.
3. Eli Pariser, *The Filter Bubble* (London: Penguin Books, 2012); Greene, *Moral Tribes*.
4. Greene, *Moral Tribes*; Dan M. Kahan, "The Polarizing Impact of Science Literacy and Numeracy on Perceived Climate Change Risks," *Nature Climate Change* 2 (2012): 732–35. But for a contrary view, see Sophie Guy et al., "Investigating the Effects of Knowledge and Ideology on Climate Change Beliefs," *European Journal of Social Psychology* 44, no. 5 (2014): 421–29.
5. Arlie Russell Hochschild, *Strangers in Their Own Land: Anger and Mourning on the American Right* (New York: The New Press, 2016).

CHAPTER 16: JUSTICE

1. Joshua Greene, *Moral Tribes: Emotion, Reason, and the Gap Between Us and Them* (New York: Penguin Press, 2013); Robert Wright, *The Moral Animal* (New York: Pantheon, 1994).
2. Kelsey Timmerman, *Where Am I Wearing? A Global Tour of the Countries, Factories, and People That Make Our Clothes* (Hoboken, NJ: Wiley, 2012); Kelsey Timmerman, *Where Am I Eating? An Adventure Through the Global Food Economy* (Hoboken, NJ: Wiley, 2013).
3. Reni Eddo-Lodge, *Why I Am No Longer Talking to White People About Race* (London: Bloomsbury, 2017); Ta-Nehisi Coates, *Between the World and Me* (Melbourne: Text, 2015).
4. Josie Ensor, " 'Everyone in Syria Is Bad Now,' Says UN War Crimes Prosecutor as She Quits Post," *New York Times*, August 17, 2017.
5. For example, Helena Smith, "Shocking Images of Drowned Syrian Boy Show Tragic Plight of Refugees," *Guardian*, September 2, 2015.
6. T. Kogut and I. Ritov, "The Singularity Effect of Identified Victims in Separate and Joint Evaluations," *Organizational Behavior and Human Decision Processes* 97, no. 2 (2005): 106–16; D. A. Small and G. Loewenstein, "Helping a Victim or Helping the Victim: Altruism and Identifiability," *Journal of Risk and Uncertainty* 26, no. 1 (2003): 5–16; Greene, *Moral Tribes*, 264.
7. Russ Alan Prince, "Who Rules the World?," *Forbes*, July 22, 2013.

CHAPTER 17: POST-TRUTH

1. Julian Borger, "Putin Offers Ukraine Olive Branches Delivered by Russian Tanks," *Guardian*, March 4, 2014.
2. Serhii Plokhy, *Lost Kingdom: The Quest for Empire and the Making of the Russian Nation* (New York: Basic Books, 2017); Timothy Snyder, *The Road to Unfreedom: Russia, Europe, America* (New York: Tim Duggan Books, 2018).
3. Matthew Paris, *Matthew Paris' English History*, trans. J. A. Gyles, vol. 3 (London: Henry G. Bohn, 1854), 138–41; Patricia Healy Wasyliw, *Martyrdom, Murder and Magic: Child Saints and Their Cults in Medieval Europe* (New York: Peter Lang, 2008), 123–25.
4. Cecilia Kang and Adam Goldman, "In Washington Pizzeria Attack, Fake News Brought Real Guns," *New York Times*, December 5, 2016.

5. Leonard B. Glick, *Abraham's Heirs: Jews and Christians in Medieval Europe* (Syracuse, NY: Syracuse University Press, 1999), 228–29.

6. Anthony Bale, "Afterword: Violence, Memory and the Traumatic Middle Ages," in *Christians and Jews in Angevin England: The York Massacre of 1190, Narrative and Contexts*, ed. Sarah Rees Jones and Sethina Watson (York: York Medieval Press, 2013), 297.

7. Though the quote is often ascribed to Goebbels, it is only fitting that neither I nor my devoted research assistant could verify that Goebbels ever wrote or said it.

8. Hilmar Hoffman, *The Triumph of Propaganda: Film and National Socialism, 1933–1945* (Providence, RI: Berghahn Books, 1997), 140.

9. Lee Hockstader, "From Ruler's Embrace to a Life in Disgrace," *The Washington Post*, March 10, 1995.

10. Thomas Pakenham, *The Scramble for Africa* (London: Weidenfeld & Nicolson, 1991), 616–17.

CHAPTER 18: SCIENCE FICTION

1. Aldous Huxley, *Brave New World*, ch. 17.

CHAPTER 19: EDUCATION

1. Wayne A. Wiegand and Donald G. Davis, eds., *Encyclopedia of Library History* (New York: Garland, 1994), 432–33.

2. Verity Smith, ed., *Concise Encyclopedia of Latin American Literature* (London: Routledge, 2013), 142, 180.

3. Cathy N. Davidson, *The New Education: How to Revolutionize the University to Prepare Students for a World in Flux* (New York: Basic Books, 2017); Bernie Trilling, *21st Century Skills: Learning for Life in Our Times* (San Francisco: Jossey-Bass, 2009); Charles Kivunja, "Teaching Students to Learn and to Work Well with 21st Century Skills: Unpacking the Career and Life Skills Domain of the New Learning Paradigm," *International Journal of Higher Education* 4, no. 1 (2015). For the website of P21, see "P21 Partnership for 21st Century Learning," http://www.p21.org/our-work/4cs-research-series, accessed January 12, 2018. For an example of the implementation of new pedagogical methods, see National Education Association, *Preparing*

21st Century Students for a Global Society: An Educator's Guide to the "Four C's," http://www.nea.org/assets/docs/A-Guide-to-Four-Cs.pdf, accessed January 21, 2018.

4. Maddalaine Ansell, "Jobs for Life Are a Thing of the Past. Bring On Lifelong Learning," *Guardian,* May 31, 2016.

5. Erik B. Bloss et al., "Evidence for Reduced Experience-Dependent Dendritic Spine Plasticity in the Aging Prefrontal Cortex," *Journal of Neuroscience* 31, no. 21 (2011): 7831–39; Miriam Matamales et al., "Aging-Related Dysfunction of Striatal Cholinergic Interneurons Produces Conflict in Action Selection," *Neuron* 90, no. 2 (2016): 362–72; Mo Costandi, "Does Your Brain Produce New Cells? A Skeptical View of Human Adult Neurogenesis," *Guardian,* February 23, 2012; Gianluigi Mongillo, Simon Rumpel, and Yonatan Loewenstein, "Intrinsic Volatility of Synaptic Connections—A Challenge to the Synaptic Trace Theory of Memory," *Current Opinion in Neurobiology* 46 (2017): 7–13.

CHAPTER 20: MEANING

1. Karl Marx and Friedrich Engels, *The Communist Manifesto* (London: Verso, 2012), 34–35.

2. Marx and Engels, *The Communist Manifesto,* 35.

3. Raoul Wootlif, "Netanyahu Welcomes Envoy Friedman to 'Jerusalem, Our Eternal Capital,'" *Times of Israel,* May 16, 2017; Peter Beaumont, "Israeli Minister's Jerusalem Dress Proves Controversial in Cannes," *Guardian,* May 18, 2017; Lahav Harkov, "New 80-Majority Jerusalem Bill Has Loophole Enabling City to Be Divided," *Jerusalem Post,* January 2, 2018.

4. K. P. Schroder and Robert Connon Smith, "Distant Future of the Sun and Earth Revisited," *Monthly Notices of the Royal Astronomical Society* 386, no. 1 (2008): 155–63.

5. See especially Roy A. Rappaport, *Ritual and Religion in the Making of Humanity* (Cambridge: Cambridge University Press, 1999); Graham Harvey, *Ritual and Religious Belief: A Reader* (New York: Routledge, 2005).

6. This is the most common interpretation, although not the only one, of the combination hocus-pocus: Leslie K. Arnovick, *Written Reliquaries* (Amsterdam: John Benjamins, 2006), 250 n. 30.

7. Joseph Campbell, *The Hero with a Thousand Faces* (London: Fontana Press, 1993), 235.

8. Xinzhong Yao, *An Introduction to Confucianism* (Cambridge: Cambridge University Press, 2000), 190–99.

9. "Flag Code of India, 2002," Press Information Bureau, Government of India.

10. "Flag Code of India, 2002."

11. "Here's Why India's 'Tallest' Flag Cannot Be Hoisted at Pakistan Border," *The News International* (Pakistan), March 30, 2017.

12. Stephen C. Poulson, *Social Movements in Twentieth-Century Iran: Culture, Ideology and Mobilizing Frameworks* (Lanham, MD: Lexington Books, 2006), 44.

13. Houman Sarshar, ed., *The Jews of Iran: The History, Religion and Culture of a Community in the Islamic World* (New York: Palgrave Macmillan, 2014), 52–55; Houman M. Sarshar, *Jewish Communities of Iran* (New York: Encyclopedia Iranica Foundation, 2011), 158–60.

14. Gersion Appel, *The Concise Code of Jewish Law*, 2nd ed. (New York: KTAV, 1991), 191.

15. See especially Robert O. Paxton, *The Anatomy of Fascism* (New York: Vintage Books, 2005).

16. Richard Griffiths, *Fascism* (London: Continuum, 2005), 33.

17. Christian Goeschel, *Suicide in the Third Reich* (Oxford: Oxford University Press, 2009).

18. "Paris Attacks: What Happened on the Night," BBC, December 9, 2015; Anna Cara, "ISIS Expresses Fury over French Airstrikes in Syria; France Says They Will Continue," CTV News, November 14, 2015.

19. Jean de Joinville, "The Life of Saint Louis," in *Chronicles of the Crusades*, ed. M.R.B. Shaw (London: Penguin, 1963), 243; Jean de Joinville, *Vie de Saint Louis*, ed. Jacques Monfrin (Paris, 1995), 319, 157.

20. Ray Williams, "How Facebook Can Amplify Low Self-Esteem/Narcissism/Anxiety," *Psychology Today*, May 20, 2014.

21. *Mahasatipatthana Sutta*, ch. 2, sec. 1, ed. Vipassana Research Institute (Igatpuri: Vipassana Research Institute, 2006), 12–13.

22. *Mahasatipatthana Sutta*, ch. 2, sec. 1, 5.

23. G. E. Harvey, *History of Burma: From the Earliest Times to 10 March 1824* (London: Frank Cass, 1925), 252–60.

24. Brian Daizen Victoria, *Zen at War* (Lanham, MD: Rowman & Little-

field, 2006); Ian Buruma, *Inventing Japan, 1853–1964* (New York: Modern Library, 2003); Stephen S. Large, "Nationalist Extremism in Early Showa Japan: Inoue Nissho and the 'Blood-Pledge Corps Incident,' 1932," *Modern Asian Studies* 35, no. 3 (2001): 533–64; W. L. King, *Zen and the Way of the Sword: Arming the Samurai Psyche* (New York: Oxford University Press, 1993); Danny Orbach, "A Japanese Prophet: Eschatology and Epistemology in the Thought of Kita Ikki," *Japan Forum* 23, no. 3 (2011): 339–61.

25. "Facebook Removes Myanmar Monk's Page for 'Inflammatory Posts' About Muslims," Scroll.in, February 27, 2018; Marella Oppenheim, "'It Only Takes One Terrorist': The Buddhist Monk Who Reviles Myanmar's Muslims," *Guardian*, May 12, 2017.

26. Jerzy Lukowski and Hubert Zawadzki, *A Concise History of Poland* (Cambridge: Cambridge University Press, 2001), 163.

CHAPTER 21: MEDITATION

1. www.dhamma.org.

2. Britta K. Hölzel et al., "How Does Mindfulness Meditation Work? Proposing Mechanisms of Action from a Conceptual and Neural Perspective," *Perspectives on Psychological Science* 6, no. 6 (2011): 537–59; Adam Moore and Peter Malinowski, "Meditation, Mindfulness and Cognitive Flexibility," *Consciousness and Cognition* 18, no. 1 (2009): 176–86; Alberto Chiesa, Raffaella Calati, and Alessandro Serretti, "Does Mindfulness Training Improve Cognitive Abilities? A Systematic Review of Neuropsychological Findings," *Clinical Psychology Review* 31, no. 3 (2011): 449–64; Antoine Lutz et al., "Attention Regulation and Monitoring in Meditation," *Trends in Cognitive Sciences* 12, no. 4 (2008): 163–69; Richard J. Davidson et al., "Alterations in Brain and Immune Function Produced by Mindfulness Meditation," *Psychosomatic Medicine* 65, no. 4 (2003): 564–70; Fadel Zeidan et al., "Mindfulness Meditation Improves Cognition: Evidence of Brief Mental Training," *Consciousness and Cognition* 19, no. 2 (2010): 597–605.

INDEX

ABOUT THE AUTHOR

Yuval Noah Harari has a Ph.D. in history from the University of Oxford, and now lectures at the Hebrew University of Jerusalem, specializing in world history. His two books, *Sapiens: A Brief History of Humankind* and *Homo Deus: A Brief History of Tomorrow,* have become global bestsellers, with more than twelve million copies sold and translations in more than forty-five languages.

ynharari.com
Facebook.com/Prof.Yuval.Noah.Harari
Twitter: @harari_yuval
youtube.com/c/YuvalNoahHarari1

ABOUT THE TYPE

This book was set in Dante, a typeface designed by Giovanni Mardersteig (1892–1977). Conceived as a private type for the Officina Bodoni in Verona, Italy, Dante was originally cut only for hand composition by Charles Malin, the famous Parisian punch cutter, between 1946 and 1952. Its first use was in an edition of Boccaccio's *Trattatello in laude di Dante* that appeared in 1954. The Monotype Corporation's version of Dante followed in 1957. Though modeled on the Aldine type used for Pietro Cardinal Bembo's treatise *De Aetna* in 1495, Dante is a thoroughly modern interpretation of that venerable face.